W9-AAU-062

CONTRACT BARGAINING HANDBOOK

FOR LOCAL UNION LEADERS

CONTRACT BARGAINING HANDBOOK

FOR LOCAL UNION LEADERS

Maurice B. Better

The Bureau of National Affairs, Inc.
Washington, D.C.

Copyright © 1993
The Bureau of National Affairs, Inc.

Sixth Printing, May 1999

Library of Congress Cataloging-in-Publication Data

Better, Maurice B.
    Contract bargaining handbook for local union leaders / Maurice B.
Better.
        p.   cm.
    Includes index.
    ISBN 0-87179-803-4
    1. Collective bargaining—United States—Handbooks, manuals, etc.
I. Title.
HD6508.B42   1993
331.89'2   dc20   93-11496
                                                                    CIP

Authorization to photocopy items for internal or personal use, or the
internal or personal use of specific clients, is granted by BNA Books for
libraries and other users registered with the Copyright Clearance Center
(CCC) Transactional Reporting Service, provided that $1.00 per page is
paid directly to CCC, 222 Rosewood Dr., Danvers, MA 01923. 0-
87179-803-4/93/$0 + $1.00.

Published by BNA Books
1250 23rd St., N.W., Washington, D.C. 20037
International Standard Book Number: 0-87179-803-4
Printed in Canada

Preface

This handbook was prepared expressly for members of the local union bargaining committee. Emphasis is on the activities, tasks, tools, techniques, strategies, and tactics, the "nuts-and-bolts," of planning for and bargaining with the employer over pay, fringes, and other terms and conditions of employment. The focus is on the fundamentals of "what-to-do" and "how-to-do-it." The material is applicable to a variety of union–employer situations ranging from manufacturing to the retail and service sectors. Activities related to bargaining a first contract are given special attention.

While most of this handbook is devoted to traditional contract bargaining as it occurs in the private sector, some of the special tasks and tools employed in local government sector bargaining are presented as well. In addition, the relatively new interest-based (win-win) bargaining approach is examined.

Bargaining power, real and perceived, is an important factor in traditional bargaining outcomes. The relative strengths of the union and the employer can change from one bargaining period to another. Consequently, this handbook offers guidelines for determining if strike action is feasible and, if the answer is negative, guidelines for a no-strike strategy alternative. In the same vein, techniques for avoiding impasses and using third-party mediation are also covered.

Employers are now promoting employee-management cooperation which has produced new work arrangements, new forms of compensation, and the erosion of traditional work rules and practices. This handbook examines various employer policies and programs related to employee-management cooperation and offers a union response strategy designed to protect the interests of both employees and the union.

The tasks and tools described in this handbook are workable only when the employer is willing to share some decision-making authority with the union over pay rates and the other terms and conditions of employment. This does not mean that the employer is expected to give in to the union's position on every issue, but there must be some willingness to compromise.

This handbook is a product of the author's 17 years in the field of labor education. It is the outgrowth of teaching classes, institutes, and workshops in contract bargaining for both experienced and inexperienced union members, officers, and staff. While conceived as a reference work, this handbook could be used as a textbook for a course in contract bargaining.

Maurice B. Better
Madison, Wisconsin
August 1993

Acknowledgments

As is usually the case when developing a book of this type, the author is deeply indebted to many people. First, and foremost, are the many union leaders who attended my labor education classes over the years and freely shared their experiences and ideas about contract bargaining. They broadened my perspective on the art of contract bargaining and were the inspiration for many of the topics dealt with in this handbook.

Labor educators are a generous lot, always willing to share information, views, and insight. I, therefore, wish to acknowledge my debt to my colleagues in the field and in particular to my present and former co-educators at the School for Workers in Wisconsin and at the Center for Labor Education and Research in Alabama.

I acknowledge with gratitude the encouragement and editing help received from Harriet G. Berlin, now retired from BNA Books, and her successor, Camille D. Christie. Finally, I wish to thank my wife, Sybil, for providing additional help in editing the manuscript.

Contents

Part II: The Bargaining Process

Part III: Special Bargaining Situations

Part I

Preparation for Bargaining

Chapter 1

Organizational Activities

Preparations for contract bargaining begin months in advance of the first scheduled conference with the employer. Assembling the members of the bargaining committee is the first task. (See Appendix 1 for a checklist of bargaining tasks.) The role and activities of the committee prior to the start of actual negotiations are covered in the first part of this handbook. This chapter discusses how the bargaining committee is organized and examines some of its interunion, public relations, and administrative tasks.

THE BARGAINING COMMITTEE

The role of the bargaining committee is to help members, stewards, and officers identify weaknesses in the current agreement and then convert the findings into specific bargaining proposals. The committee helps establish priorities, develops arguments to support individual proposals, and tries to anticipate employer objections and prepare responses. Committee members are also responsible for collecting information about the employer's finances and operations, pay and fringe settlements bargained by other groups of employees, changes in the cost of living, and trends in the employer's industry, trade, or profession. In addition, the bargaining committee handles the procedural tasks of meeting the

3

notification requirements in the law, complying with all national or international union policies, scheduling bargaining sessions, arranging for lost time payments for committee members, mobilizing membership support, and conducting a public relations campaign aimed at other union groups and potential supporters in the larger community.

Once bargaining begins, committee members represent the union at the conference table. They present and defend the union's proposed employment terms and conditions, consider offers from the employer, and tailor compromises. Finally, the bargaining committee brings the final settlement back to the membership for ratification.

—*Task*—
Form the Bargaining Committee

The local union selects the members of the committee three to four months prior to the first bargaining session. Committee size, participant selection method, and duties are either determined by custom or spelled out in the local union's bylaws or the national or international union constitution. In general, the bargaining committee should be composed of people who know the needs of the local union membership, understand the problems of the workplace, and have bargaining skills and experience. It is not necessary, however, for every committee member to have all of these qualifications.

Representation on the Bargaining Committee

The duties of the bargaining committee suggest the kinds of qualities needed by the people who serve. All of the characteristics of good leadership are required including excellent communication skills, resourcefulness, willingness to delegate tasks, and the ability to make decisions. What is often overlooked in the selection process is the need to include representatives from all the varied interest groups within the local union.

A local union is composed of members with divergent needs and concerns related to the terms and conditions of employment.

Obviously, members have many common interests, otherwise the union would disintegrate. Higher compensation is an example of a bargaining objective with universal appeal. Conversely, some terms and conditions are of interest to small groups of members who may or may not perform the same job or work in the same department, office, or work area. For example, men and women who are 55 years of age or over with many years of service and younger, relatively newer employees have different employment-related interests even when performing the same type of job. Senior employees, already situated at the top end of the earnings scale, generally want longer vacations and other forms of paid leave. By contrast, junior employees just beginning their careers are usually more interested in such matters as promotional opportunities and an equal chance to earn extra money by working overtime.

Other groups of union members may have unique employment problems due to their sex, race, nationality, job assignment, work location, shift assignment, and even leisure-time interests. In one local union, a proposal to grant employees holding unpaid public office additional paid leave was not supported by most other members.

Committee members who identify with issues of importance to one or more segments of the rank and file will be more forceful in promoting them at the bargaining table. On the other hand, local union members who believe they are not being represented might be critical of the settlement package and could actively work against ratification. Consequently, the membership of the bargaining committee should be representative of as many of the important interest groups within the local union as possible. These groups include night shift employees, skilled trades, women, warehouse, junior, senior, and office employees, paint department employees, Native Americans, African-Americans, Hispanics, and so forth.

Selecting Members

Most local unions do not make a conscious effort to achieve the broadest representation of interest groups among the membership on the bargaining committee. Typically, the president and other officers become ex-officio members of the bargaining committee because of custom or the dictates of the union's bylaws. Other committee members may be appointed by the union president or elected by the membership. In some cases candidates are selected at large or by functional departments.

A bargaining committee composed of representatives of important interest groups is not guaranteed unless the union leadership makes a deliberate effort to achieve such an outcome. Groups of members with common employment-related problems and goals must be identified first. The president or executive board can then appoint bargaining committee members from these groups. Alternatively, each group could elect representatives from their own ranks. Elected union officers can still be part of the committee.

Committee Size

There is no one best size for the bargaining committee. The larger the committee, the broader the scope of membership representation, the greater the base of potential rank and file support for ratifying the final agreement. Conversely, large committees have more difficulty reaching agreement when it comes to selecting particular courses of action, such as whether to sacrifice a proposal. Maintaining control over the flow of information to the membership, the employer, and the general public also becomes more difficult with a large committee. Further, deadlocks between members on controversial issues are less likely if the committee is composed of an uneven number of people.

Principal Committee Functionaries

The officers of the bargaining committee include the chairperson, chief spokesperson, and secretary. They are either elected, appointed, or hold the job by virtue of their positions in the local union.

Committee Chairperson. The chairperson's role is to coordinate the activities of the committee and to report to the general membership (or direct some other committee member to do so) on bargaining progress. Although custom and bylaws vary, the local union president or business manager/representative is typically designated chairperson ex officio. For example, the Uniform Local

Union Constitution of the Laborer's International Union of North America states: "Unless otherwise provided, negotiations with employers shall be through a Negotiating Committee of the Local Union, of which the Business Manager shall be Chairman ex-officio."[1]

Chief Spokesperson. All members of the bargaining committee are present during meetings with the employer, but communications are channeled through the principal spokesperson. The chief spokesperson can be the chairperson or some other committee member. Frequently, a representative of the national or international union or an intermediary body, such as a joint council, conference, or district, joins the local bargaining committee and becomes the principal communicator by virtue of his or her expertise in bargaining or because of organizational policy. The role of a chief spokesperson is examined in Chapter 9, The Local Union Negotiator's Toolbox.

The Secretary. The secretary keeps written minutes of all bargaining committee meetings and sessions with the employer and maintains the bargaining book (see Chapter 3, Bargaining Proposals and Priorities). The position is filled by a volunteer or is rotated among committee members.

Role of Legal Counsel. Local unions unaffiliated with national or international unions often hire attorneys, mostly on retainer, to function as chief negotiators. To be effective, however, an attorney, as an outsider, must be willing to work closely with the local bargaining committee. The local leadership understands the nature of the problems facing employees and necessary solutions.

Attorneys are more commonly used to review contract language changes just prior to their acceptance by the union bargaining team. They are trained to identify the words and phrases that can be interpreted in ways that keep the union from realizing desired objectives.

Operating Procedures

Once the bargaining committee is formed, the members must establish operating procedures. These deal with such matters as

---

[1]Constitution of the Laborers' Int'l Union of N. Am. (AFL-CIO), 1986, p. 15.

the behavior of committee members at the bargaining table, processes for group decision making, and how the committee responds to the employer at the bargaining table.

As previously noted, there should be one major spokesperson for the union at the bargaining table. However, there may be times when other members of the bargaining committee disagree with what the spokesperson is saying and/or doing or want to express their views about tactics, settlement terms, or other matters. Consequently, some prearranged procedure is needed to call for a private group meeting or caucus. The best procedure is to permit any committee member to call for a caucus at any time by either writing a note or whispering the request to the chief spokesperson (see Chapter 9, The Local Union Negotiator's Toolbox).

In the absence of bylaw prohibition or general practice, the bargaining committee should assume it has the authority to drop or modify union proposals and to accept or reject employer offers during the course of bargaining without prior consultation with the membership. By the same token, the leadership has an obligation to report back to the membership on the progress, or lack thereof, being made at the bargaining table. The membership may also have the right to vote to accept or reject the employer's final offer of settlement terms.

Bargaining committee members must also agree on a procedure for group decision making. For example, committee acceptance of the employer's pay and fringe offer can be by consensus, where everyone must agree, or by majority vote. Consensus is far more difficult to achieve because every participant is required to either support the outcome or remain neutral.

A Tribute to Those Who Serve

Many unions have difficulty finding people to serve on the bargaining committee. The job is arduous and demanding with some risk and little tangible reward. People who are willing to perform this task deserve great respect.

Selecting the Bargaining Committee for the First Contract

Union activists differ over whether the in-house employee leaders of the organizing campaign should continue as the group responsible for bargaining the first contract. Some opponents of the idea believe organizing committees consist of too many people, most having little or no bargaining experience.

Supporters of combining the organizing and bargaining committees view it as the best way to keep supporters active during what is likely to be a lengthy process of achieving a first contract. In addition, members who are excluded may feel left out and lose interest. Some organizers even suggest the organizing cum bargaining committee be expanded to include one or two people who voted "no" in the representation election as a way of building support for the union.

INTERUNION AND COMMUNITY RELATIONS ACTIVITIES

A local union's position at the bargaining table is strengthened when its efforts to improve the terms and conditions of employment for its members are recognized and supported by other local unions, the general public, and the local news media. However, building good relations with these groups is an ongoing activity and not limited only to the period of bargaining. Further, starting a media campaign early in the process can serve to educate the public about collective bargaining and both the employees' and the community's stake in the outcome.

—*Task*—
Alert Other Labor Groups in the Community

What one local union achieves or fails to achieve in contract bargaining can affect the outcomes of other local unions in the same industry and/or community. For example, if one employer wins concessions, others will demand similar treatment.

Organized labor is strongest when individual unions are willing to support each other on the picket line and in other ways in times of crisis. For this to happen, however, unions must be in contact with each other. Ideally, this contact occurs on a year-round basis and not just during periods of contract bargaining.

One of the best ways for local unions to maintain ongoing communications with each other is to be active in the local AFL-CIO central labor council and/or building and construction trades council. This means sending delegates to regular meetings and generally participating in council activities. This contact can be supplemented during periods of bargaining by writing letters and/or making appearances at membership or executive board meetings of other local unions to keep them informed about the latest developments.

The community labor newspaper, often published by a central labor body or state federation, is another vehicle the union can use to keep labor activists and supporters in the local area apprised of progress in bargaining. The local union should prepare news releases expressly for these publications.

—Task—
Develop Contacts With Groups in the Community at Large

Community involvement and coalition building are long-term activities, but can pay off during times of crisis, such as during a contractual dispute with the employer.

Community Involvement

If union members are accepted as essential contributors to the welfare of the entire community, elected government officials and activists in other organizations may become more supportive of the union on workplace issues. Influencing public perception about the union takes time, perhaps years, to accomplish and has to be nurtured on a continuing basis thereafter. The potential benefit is great, particularly if union activists make friends with community leaders who have some influence over the employer and are willing to exercise it on behalf of the union. The following are forums for possible union activism:

1. Unions and their members work with religious, civic, and fraternal groups to establish drug and alcohol abuse programs, operate youth sports leagues, and care for the elderly, the disabled, and the homeless. Union members and

their families also benefit from many of these social services, which is an added incentive for participation. Information on how to get started is available from the AFL-CIO Community Services representative in the local community.

2. Members volunteer to serve on local government boards, councils, committees, and commissions as representatives of labor. This is one way of becoming known to the local political establishment who, as a consequence, may remain neutral during a strike rather than side with the employer. The president of the AFL-CIO central labor council in the community can assist union members interested in participating in local government.

Coalition Building

The union can broaden its reach even further by collaborating with other social and political action groups in the local community on a broad range of cases. This should not be difficult because members of labor organizations have many interests in common with activists supporting other causes such as fair employment, consumerism, the environment, war and peace, and the disadvantaged. Participation of this type helps the local union develop an image as an advocate for the needs of all working people and the broader public rather than as just another narrow interest group.

—Task—
Conduct a Media Campaign

Within 30 to 50 days prior to the first session with the employer, the union bargaining committee should begin using the local press, radio, and television to educate the public about the contract bargaining process in general and the union's position in particular. Friends can use the information to justify their support for the union. In addition, if the union can get its story out first, public opinion may not be as easily swayed when the employer later uses the news media to attack the union. The media are another way for the local union to reach its own members who also read the community newspaper, watch local television, and listen to local radio.

The union will be more successful in getting its message to the public when the proper procedures for dealing with the news media are observed. Consequently, the bargaining committee should establish a media relations subcommittee. The role of the subcommittee is to develop good relations with the local news media and, at the onset of bargaining, prepare one or more news releases.

Media Relations Subcommittee

The bargaining committee should form a subcommittee of two or three people to handle relations with the news media. Members of the subcommittee must have good writing and/or public speaking skills. They must also be well versed on what to emphasize and what to minimize when talking with media representatives. For example, the wage proposal, which reporters like to dwell upon, should be played down if the top priority issues are work rules.

The media relations and bargaining committees must work together to avoid embarrassing mistakes such as releasing the wrong information or the right information at the wrong time. One way of avoiding such mix ups is to have some overlap in membership between the two committees. Further, the union must speak with one voice; consequently, all officers and the general membership must be instructed to direct all inquiries from reporters to the media relations committee. At least one member of the committee must be accessible by telephone at all times, day and night, to the news media.

Working With the News Media

The first job for the media subcommittee is to compile a list of local newspapers, both daily and weekly, and radio and television stations. Each organization should be contacted by telephone or in person, the preferred way, to obtain information about publication or newscast times, deadlines for prepared news releases and breaking news stories, and the names of news editors, labor reporters, news directors, and newscasters. This information should be kept on permanent file and updated periodically.

Preparing a News Release

A news release is a brief written statement containing the information the union wants to publicize. The purpose of the initial press release is to attract the attention of the media in the period immediately preceding the start of the first bargaining session. The following are factors to consider when preparing a news release:

1. The text should be typewritten on an 8 ½ × 11 inch sheet of paper and double spaced. The release date is written at the top of the page, for example, "FOR IMMEDIATE RELEASE" or "FOR RELEASE ON MAY 18." Next, the union is identified by local number and name of parent organization. Finally, the heading should have the name and telephone number of a contact person in the union who is accessible and knowledgeable enough to supply additional information.

2. A news release should either be mailed or hand delivered, the preferred method, to news outlets. Again, the news organizations should be contacted in advance to determine the best time of day to deliver copy.

3. The first paragraph of a news release is called the "lead." The lead should answer the following five "W's" about upcoming contract bargaining: Who? What? Where? When? and Why? In other words, the opening paragraph should identify the union, the employer, and the number of employees involved. The three or four most important bargaining proposals (do not call them demands) should also be included along with justifications for requested improvements. The democratic procedures used to formulate the proposals should be mentioned as well. The following is an example of an opening paragraph for a news release:

> The 496 members of Local 414 of the United Fabrication Workers' Union met last night at the Labor Temple and voted unanimously to reopen the labor agreement with the Brandy Bay Corporation that expires on July 31 at midnight. Bargaining will begin May 21 and the union hopes to end a four-year freeze on wages. The company has earned record profits during the past two years.

The second and subsequent paragraphs of the news release should include information of declining importance since many news editors still follow the old journalistic practice of shortening news releases by "cutting from the bottom." The following is the continuation of the story begun in the preceding paragraph:

> The membership, by a show of hands, overwhelmingly voted to support a proposal calling for an eight percent hourly wage increase for each year of a new two-year agreement. Union members also instructed the bargaining committee to work toward the elimination of a merit pay plan which many referred to as being rife with favoritism. Proposals for improved vacation leave and higher pension benefits were also endorsed.

Opinions attributed to a source, and enclosed in quotation marks, can be included in the later paragraphs. The sample news release concludes with the following quotation from the union president:

> Speaking to the assembled workers, Local Union President Joe Hill stated, "the workers' standard of living is the backbone of the community. Most of our wages are spent here. We're the ones who buy Chevys, Fords, and Chryslers. We're the one's who buy the houses in this community. We're the people who shop at the local stores. When our standard of living falls the entire community suffers."

4. Radio and television stations may request an interview after receiving the news release. The interview itself will be short, perhaps no more than 10 seconds, so the union spokesperson must be prepared with brief and clear responses. Expressing one or two major ideas in several short sentences is the best approach. For example, the union issuing the above news release might stress the earlier wage freeze, the employer's high profits and, if there is time, the tie between the workers' standard of living and the welfare of the community.

Ongoing Media Campaign

The union may want to reinforce its own case as bargaining progresses by issuing additional news releases. The union could also be called upon by the media to respond to employer statements. Later, when bargaining is concluded, the settlement should be publicized. Every peaceful settlement should be reported if only to counter some of the negative press coverage generally received by unions.

OTHER ADMINISTRATIVE ACTIVITIES

A number of housekeeping tasks must be completed before the start of the first bargaining session. The membership may be required to vote on whether to renew the terminating contract. The employer and several public agencies must also be notified of the union's intent to bargain. A time and place for the first meeting must be arranged and the matter of who pays the lost time and other expenses of bargaining committee members may need to be resolved. Finally, it is usually necessary to comply with certain internal union policies affecting bargaining.

—Task—
Obtain Membership Approval to Renegotiate Contract

A local union is a democratic organization and all actions taken in its name must be authorized by the rank and file membership. As a consequence, a referendum authorizing the union leadership to renegotiate the existing contract is almost universally required. Most referendums are held during the course of a regular membership meeting, often the one just prior to the legal deadline for notifying the employer of the union's intent to bargain. Voting is by voice or by show of hands.

—Task—
Prepare and Deliver Legal Notices

A local union seeking to renegotiate the labor agreement has an obligation under the Labor Management Relations Act (LMRA)[2]

---

[2]Sections 8(d),(1) (3) (A) and (B) of the Labor Management Relations Act (LMRA), 1947, as amended. Throughout this text, references to the LMRA will be to the Taft-Hartley Act, as it is popularly known. Senator Taft and Congressman Hartley were the major authors of this 1947 law which amended the earlier

to notify the employer and the public of its intentions. The Taft-Hartley Act covers private sector collective bargaining and requires a 60-day notice to the employer (90 days in the health care industry). However, the existing labor agreement could specify a longer notice period, In addition, a 30-day notice to federal and state or territorial mediation agencies is required (60 days in health care).

All required notices can be issued at the same time using Form F-7, "Notice To Mediation Agencies," available from the nearest office of the Federal Mediation and Conciliation Service (FMCS). When the requested information is filled in, the original copy of the form is returned to FMCS at an address provided. The first carbon is sent to the state or territorial mediation agency, the second is delivered to the employer, and the third carbon is retained by the union. Public libraries have directories with the addresses for federal, state, and territorial government agencies.

The time frame for obtaining and distributing Form F-7 is specified in the law. The employer must receive the notice a full 60 days (90 days in the health care industry) in advance of the termination date of the current agreement or date of proposed modification or termination if the contract has no expiration date. If for some reason Form F-7 is unobtainable, the union can notify the employer by letter.

Strikes and lockouts during these 60/90 days, called the "cooling off" period, are prohibited and management cannot unilaterally change the existing terms and conditions of employment.[3] A strike would be legal during this period if the employer committed unfair labor practices (see Chapter 7, The Law of Contract Bargaining).

The local union might decide not to reopen the agreement fearing employer demands for concessions. Of course, management can take the initiative on renegotiating the contract and assume the burden of meeting the notification requirements. If this happens, the union is forewarned of a possible aggressive management posture at the bargaining table. If both sides fail to act, the language of the contract determines what happens next. Some agreements terminate, but others renew automatically, typically for a period of one year.

National Labor Relations Act (Wagner Act). The Taft-Hartley Act, as it relates to contract bargaining, is discussed in Chapter 7.

[3]LMRA §8(d) (4); NLRB v. Katz, 369 U.S. 736, 743, 50 LRRM 2001 (1962).

Notice Requirement for the First-Time Contract

Unions bargaining their first contract do not have to wait 60 or 90 days before holding the first bargaining session. The union should telephone the employer immediately after winning the election conducted by the National Labor Relations Board (NLRB) to arrange the date, time, and place for a first meeting. It does not matter if the union is not fully prepared, these early meetings are likely to amount to little more than getting acquainted sparring matches addressing few, if any, issues of substance.

Do not forget to notify the federal, state, or territorial mediation agencies that bargaining on a first contract is in progress. This can be done at any time—but certainly no later than 30 days, the health care industry included, before taking any overt action such as striking.

—Task—
Pick a Time and Place for Bargaining Sessions

Once the Form F-7 has been mailed, the chairperson of the bargaining committee must contact the appropriate representative of the employer to arrange a place and time for the first meeting of the bargaining sessions.

The Meeting Site

Bargaining sessions can be held on the employer's premises, at the union hall or office, in rented or rent-free space on neutral territory, or some combination of these locations. Many union and company negotiators refuse to meet on the other's turf believing there is a psychological disadvantage in doing so. One possible solution is to rotate the sessions between the employer's premises and the union's office.

If rented space is used, the cost is typically split between the parties. The union should search for free meeting sites in the community if it does not want to meet on the employer's property or incur financial expense. Examples of possible meeting sites include senior citizen centers, community centers, and social clubs.

The meeting room itself should be large enough to comfortably accommodate all parties. Additional private rooms should be available for individual group caucuses.

Scheduling Meetings

Meetings are commonly held during regular working hours unless the contract states otherwise. For example, the agreement between the City of Wausau, Wisconsin, and the Transit Workers' Union provides: "Negotiating sessions shall be conducted outside the normal work day, unless the parties mutually agree otherwise."[4]

Typically, at the end of one bargaining session, a date for the next one is set. The union must never refuse to set the date for another meeting. The risk of doing so is being accused of bad-faith bargaining (see Chapter 7, The Law of Contract Bargaining).

—Task—
Arrange Compensation for Members of the Bargaining Committee

Past practice or the labor agreement determines whether the union or the employer pays the wages/salaries of bargaining committee members when bargaining sessions are scheduled during regular working hours. For example, the agreement between the Social Service Paraprofessional Employees and Brown County, Wisconsin, provides: "the Union's Executive Committee shall be permitted to conduct certain Association business during working time without suffering any loss in wages. This Association business is limited to . . . contract negotiating sessions with management, including a brief presession and postsession caucus by the Executive Committee. . . . "[5]

Employers who pay lost time often place limits on their liability. The following is an example of a contract provision that caps management's cost:

---

[4]Agreement between the City of Wausau, WI, and the Amalgamated Transit Union, Local No. 1168, 1989–1991, p. 23.
[5]Agreement between Brown County, WI, and the Social Service Paraprofessionals, 1987–1988, p. 3.

Union representatives up to five (5) involved in contract negotiation sessions with the Company shall be paid for loss of wages attributed to these meetings up to a maximun of ten (10) sessions with a maximum of eight (8) hours per day. Such paid hours shall be credited toward weekly computation of overtime.[6]

The union pays the lost wages/salaries of bargaining committee members when the employer does not. The rate of reimbursement can be specified in the local's bylaws. For example, the bylaws of Local 2150, International Brotherhood of Electrical Workers states: "Any member required to lose time during regular working hours because of official duties for the Union shall be compensated for such time at his regular straight time hourly rate of pay."[7]

In the absence of contract language, it never hurts to ask the employer to pay all or part of the lost wages/salaries of bargaining committee members. If the employer agrees, the union has the beginnings of a past practice.

Bargaining committee members typically receive cash stipends from the union when bargaining occurs either after or extends beyond regular working hours. Again, the dollar amount may appear in the local union's bylaws. Further, the union is expected to reimburse bargaining committee members for meals and other out-of-pocket expenses incurred in the performance of their duties.

—*Task*—
Coordinate With Other Levels of the Union Organization

The local union must avoid intraunion conflicts by conforming to the policies and procedures of the national or international union or intermediary body where applicable. The nature and degree of regulation will vary by union, but most local affiliates are under the jurisdiction of the parent body when it comes to contract bargaining. For example, the constitution of one national union states: "Negotiations for collective bargaining agreements shall be subject

---

[6]Agreement between Appleton Paper, Inc., and the United Paperworkers Int'l Union, Local No. 469, 1989–1991, p. 48.

[7]Bylaws of Local No. 2150, Int'l Bhd. of Electrical Workers (AFL-CIO), 1987, p. 7.

to supervision by, and their terms, conditions and termination shall be subject to the approval of the International President."[8]

Local affiliates may also be required to obtain permission from the national or international president before calling a strike. The following is an example of this type of constitutional provision:

> No Local Union or affiliated body shall strike without previous notification to the International President in which the Local Union or affiliated body has stated that it has complied with all applicable notice requirements and has exhausted all possible means of achieving a negotiated settlement. If the Local Union or the affiliated body has not complied with the above mentioned requirements, the International President can veto the strike called by the Local Union or affiliated body. If the International president has vetoed any such strike, the Local Union or affiliated body may not call the strike thus vetoed.[9]

Some unions formulate compensation and protective language policies and programs at their national conventions and all local affiliates are expected to adopt them as contract goals. For example, the constitution of the Transport Workers' Union states: "Collective bargaining on behalf of any membership group shall be guided by the collective bargaining program and policy of the previous Convention."[10]

Sometimes opposition to a particular type of employment term or condition is so strong that it is included in the organization's constitution. The following provision is found in the constitution of the Boilermakers' union:

> The International Brotherhood reaffirms its opposition to all wage incentive, work measurement, job evaluation and merit wage systems in industry. It shall be the duty of the International Brotherhood and all of its subordinate bodies, where such wage incentive, work measurement, job evaluation and merit wage systems do exist, to seek their elimination through collective bargaining. Where such is not possible, every effort should be exerted to negotiate effective protective language in the collective bargaining agreement.[11]

---

[8]Constitution of the United Paperworkers Int'l Union (AFL-CIO), 1988, p. 44.

[9]Constitution of the Service Employees Int'l Union (AFL-CIO), 1988, p. 27.

[10]Constitution of the Transport Workers Union of Am. (AFL-CIO), 1985, p. 72.

[11]Constitution of the International Bhd. of Boilermakers (AFL-CIO), 1991, pp. 146–147.

Chapter 2

Developing Bargaining Proposals

The bargaining committee begins work on a bargaining agenda at the same time it is performing the activities described in Chapter 1. The bargaining agenda is the list of proposals for new and revised terms and conditions of employment for the new contract. Preparing an agenda also involves setting priorities on proposals and developing arguments to support each request.

Before the bargaining agenda can be created, the bargaining committee must identify members' work-related needs and concerns and review the strengths and weaknesses in the existing basic and all supplemental agreements. In addition, information needed to develop and support union claims is collected. Speculating about the employer's bargaining position is also part of the preparation process. These tasks are examined in the present chapter. Activities associated with producing the actual bargaining agenda, developing supporting arguments, and setting priorities on individual proposals are described in the next chapter. (See Appendix 1 for a checklist of bargaining tasks.)

IDENTIFYING MEMBERSHIP INTERESTS

Rank and file support for the union leadership is not necessarily automatic during the bargaining process. Employees who feel there is nothing worth "fighting for" among the union's proposals are not likely to get excited over the prospect of winning a new, or even a first, contract. On the other hand, members who normally show little interest in bargaining can become quite active if they disagree with the union's bargaining objectives.

The bargaining committee must permit, and, if necessary, encourage union members to express needs, raise problems, influence priorities, and in every other respect participate in setting the bargaining agenda. Structures to encourage rank and file involvement, such as the monthly membership meeting, are already in place.

—*Task*—
Determine Membership Interests Using the Membership Meeting

The membership meeting is the traditional forum for member participation in the affairs of the union and contract bargaining is no exception. One or more regular meetings can be devoted to a discussion of the bargaining agenda. Alternatively, special meetings can be called for the same purpose. Saturday and Sunday mornings are good times for special meetings when weekend work is not scheduled.

Accommodations

The meeting hall should be large enough to comfortably seat all participants. A good public address system is also required. Space should be rented if the regular meeting place is too small.

Conducting the Meeting

Bargaining committee members will have their own ideas about terms and conditions for the new contract and these can serve as a point of departure for a general discussion of contract proposals. A written copy of the committee's list of proposals could be given to union members as they enter the meeting hall.

The chairperson of the bargaining committee leads the audience through the list of proposals. He or she should explain why

the bargaining committee believes a recommended change or addition to the terms and conditions of employment is needed and how
the current situation would be improved as a result. Issues should
be dramatized by naming one or more employees who either have
been or could be hurt because of the shortcoming(s) in the existing
contract. For example, the chairperson might say the following:
"Joan Hill lost money last year because our agreement does not
allow a person to collect both holiday and vacation pay at the same
time."

Allow members sufficient time to respond to each of the committee's proposals. They are likely to have questions and comments
and may suggest additions, deletions, and other revisions. Members
who believe their needs and concerns are not being addressed must
be permitted to offer original proposals. Some good ideas can be
obtained this way, but be prepared for some "off the wall" proposals.
For example, on one occasion a motion was made and passed for
a $5 per hour across-the-board wage increase.

Smaller Group Meetings

Department or smaller group meetings provide another way of
reaching the membership, particularly where attendance at general
membership meetings is low. For example, stewards meet informally with members of their shop, office, or department during a
break or lunch period to solicit suggestions for the new contract. The
stewards, in turn, report their findings to the bargaining committee.

—Task—
Determine Membership Interests Using the
Bargaining Questionnaire

Another means of membership expression is the questionnaire.
Less direct than face-to-face meetings, questionnaires do give union
members an opportunity to communicate their views on changes
needed in the existing terms and conditions of employment. One
type of questionnaire asks employees to list their suggestions for
the new contract on a blank sheet of paper. Another requires members to respond to a set of written questions or statements prepared
in advance by the bargaining committee.

Questionnaire Design

Questionnaires should generally be brief, no larger than one side of an 8 1/2 by 11 inch sheet of paper. In most cases the focus is on fringe benefits. In one version, existing fringes, such as vacations, health care, and sick days, are listed on the page and respondents are instructed to check off the ones they believe are most in need of improvement. Respondents could also be asked to numerically rank the list of fringes on the basis of need. Space is often left at the bottom of the questionnaire for comments. Standardized questionnaires of this sort are relatively easy to tabulate. Generally, responses to open-ended questions tend to be wide ranging and it may be difficult to draw conclusions from the results. See Exhibit 2-1 for a sample questionnaire.

Questionnaire Distribution and Tabulation

The highest response rate is usually achieved when the stewards personally distribute questionnaires to union members at the workplace and later retrieve the completed forms. The bargaining committee tallies the responses and announces the results at the next regular membership meeting and/or in the local union newsletter. Even when questionnaires are used, members must still have an opportunity to vote on the final list of bargaining proposals either at a regular membership meeting or at a special meeting called for this purpose.

—Task—
Determine Membership Interests Using One-on-One Interviews

Another approach is to contact members individually, face to face, for a discussion about the new contract. This is a good way of reaching members who do not respond to questionnaires or attend union meetings.

Canvassing Committee

A special subcommittee should be formed to plan the face-to-face interviews, recruit and train canvassers (the people who make

---

Exhibit 2-1. Sample Membership Bargaining Interests Questionnaire

---

PLEASE HELP YOUR BARGAINING COMMITTEE DECIDE
WHAT TO INCLUDE IN THE 19XX BARGAINING AGENDA

Our current labor agreement terminates (month, day, year). We must
know what your needs are as we begin to prepare for bargaining. Please
take time now to complete this form and return it to your steward as soon
as possible, but no later than (month, day, year).

Listed below are a number of contract issues. Rank them by order of
importance by placing the number 1 in front of your first choice, the
number 2 in front of your second choice and so on. Make comments if
you feel it is necessary.

_____ Higher Wages (Salaries)
_____ Improved Grievance Procedure
_____ Less Overtime
_____ More Holidays
_____ More Vacations
_____ Pension Improvements
_____ Child Care Program
_____ Dental Plan
_____ Legal Plan
_____ Better Job Security Language (subcon-
tracting ban, advance notice of a factory
or office closing, severance pay, etc.)
_____ Other Items (please specify)_____
_____
_____

---

the actual one-on-one contacts), and generally coordinate the activity. Because this subcommittee must work closely with the bargaining committee, there should be some overlap in the membership of the two groups.

Planning the Canvass

The size of the union membership and the number of available
canvassers determines the nature of the one-on-one contact. Where

time and personnel are plentiful, members could be asked to converse at length about the kinds of changes desired in the new contract. If the reverse is true, the canvassing might be limited to evoking comments on two or three key issues certain to be raised by one side or the other during bargaining.

The leadership may want its position on the issues presented at some point during the interview. What the canvasser will say must be worked out in advance and a script prepared. In addition, some effort should be made to anticipate some of the questions members are likely to raise in response to the leadership's position and some answers readied. A leaflet with additional facts might also be prepared for a canvasser to hand out at the close of an interview.

Next, a schedule matching canvassers and members is prepared. The membership list can be broken down by work area, shift, or department. Canvassers are assigned to meet with employees individually or in small groups. The parties make their own arrangements concerning the exact time and place for the meeting. In most cases, the interviews are held at the workplace either before or after working hours or during breaks and lunch periods. Interviews are sometimes held in employees' homes. Finally, a time limit should be set for completion of all interviews.

Recruiting Canvassers

Local union officers, stewards, and active members form the pool of potential canvassers. The number of canvassers needed depends on the nature of the contacts. One canvasser can talk with 20 people if all he or she is doing is asking a few questions and distributing a flyer. More canvassers are needed when longer interviews are conducted.

Recruiting canvassers may not be easy. Few people are likely to volunteer given the nature of the task and the amount of time involved. Potential candidates should be contacted personally, given a description of what the work entails, informed about the importance of the membership canvass, and told how uniquely suited they are to do the job.

Training Canvassers

Canvassers must learn what to say during the interview. The interviewer could make an opening statement designed to get the member talking. Alternatively, the canvasser might ask a series of questions designed to evoke limited responses. Interviewers must also know the leadership's position on issues well enough to both explain them to the interviewees and to respond to questions and arguments.

People react more positively when someone they know takes time to talk to them directly. Canvassers should be instructed to enlist the support of those members who respond favorably to the personal contact by inviting them to participate in some activity such as attending a membership meeting where the bargaining agenda is discussed, showing up at a rally, or helping to collect information needed for bargaining.

REVIEWING THE CONTRACT

In addition to targeting membership needs and concerns, the bargaining committee must review the terminating agreement to identify areas in need of improvement. Old grievance and arbitration records are one source of information about shortcomings in the existing contract. Another is the stewards and grievance committee people who handle the day-to-day problems arising under the contract.

—Task—
Review Contract Using Grievance and Arbitration Records

Past grievances and arbitrations are studied to determine which ones were lost because contract language did not support the union's position. A review of this kind is possible only when grievance and arbitration documents are saved and filed in an orderly fashion. The filing system adopted need not be complex. One type consists of a set of manila folders, one for each article of the contract. Grievance and arbitration documents are filed in the appropriate folders. Problem areas are easily spotted because of the thickness of the individual file folders.

Assume the fattest manila folder holds grievances related to the employer's practice of filling vacant jobs from the outside rather than promoting from within. Further, most grievances are found to have been lost or withdrawn by the grievance committee because the language of the existing contract did not clearly prohibit the practice. The union can attempt to deal with this deficiency with a proposal to fill job vacancies with current employees.

—*Task*—
Review Contract Language and Other Problem Areas

The bargaining committee, stewards, and grievance committee members should hold one or more meetings to discuss both real and potential problems with the existing labor agreement. During these meetings, the contract is reviewed article by article and section by section in an effort to generate ideas for new language protecting individual employee rights and the security of the union. For example, a participant in one such proceeding was reminded by the article on wages of several employees who had been involuntarily transferred to lower paying jobs during the previous year due to the installation of new computer-aided machines. In response, several other parties expressed concern about similar transfers occurring in the future. Someone else mentioned having recently overheard members of management talking about plans to purchase more new machinery. The discussion ended with a recommendation for an amendment to permit workers who are involuntarily moved to lower paying jobs to retain their former wage rates, a practice known as "red circling."

The purpose of the review is to identify areas of the contract where improvements are needed and to recommend changes. In the previous example, the secretary of the bargaining committee simply made a note of the proposal made to red circle wage rates. The precise wording of the new language is developed later after the employer has had a chance to respond to the union's initiative (see Chapter 11, Bargaining Contract Language).

Committee members reading through the contract should also be on the alert for inconsistencies among various provisions. In addition, as new sections are added, deleted, and modified over the years, related subjects may appear in several different places in the agreement. The union can help the situation by proposing cross-reference language such as the following: "except as provided in Paragraph B(1) of Article III."

—*Task*—
Review Contract in Light of Changing Employer Policies

Another facet of the contract review process involves making an assessment of whether existing provisions have adequately protected employees from the effects of workplace changes involving new technologies, work processes, and employer practices. The bargaining committee should begin by examining whether employment has increased, declined, or remained the same during the preceding two or three contract periods. If there is a difference, particularly a drop in the number of employees, the causes should be identified. Perhaps the loss is attributable to a combination of factors including the introduction of new labor-saving technology, the introduction of teamwork, and a greater use of subcontracting. Next, the committee must determine how well the existing contract protected those employees who were displaced because of the conditions identified.

The committee's examination of the contract may reveal a need for new protective language. For example, there may be shortcomings in provisions dealing with bumping rights and job transfers, and no limitation on subcontracting. In addition, the leadership may recognize the need to lessen the pain for workers facing future permanent layoffs and propose new benefits such as severance pay and retraining programs funded by the employer.

INFORMATION REQUIREMENTS FOR BARGAINING

As part of its preparation activity, the bargaining committee must gather facts and figures about employees, the employer, the economy, contract settlements achieved by other unions, and any other information considered useful. The data assembled are used for a variety of purposes ranging from supporting union bargaining proposals and costing out fringe proposals and offers, to concession making. Knowledgeable bargaining committee members are also less likely to be deceived by employer arguments based either on faulty assumptions or designed purposely to mislead. Information requirements and sources are discussed below.

—*Task*—
Collect Information for Bargaining

In general, the bargaining committee should assemble the following facts about the bargaining unit:

- the number of employees;
- dates of birth;
- dates of hire;
- minimum, maximum, and average rates of pay by job class;
- average earnings;
- cost of living payments;
- total and average hours worked;
- overtime hours worked;
- descriptions of jobs performed; and
- vacation eligibility.

The committee cannot possibly bargain about the future of the work force without first knowing something about its current status.

Next, obtaining data on employee utilization of fringes is one way of determining whether existing benefits are meeting members' needs. For example, some benefits may have few users, perhaps owing to a lack of need or because the eligibility requirements are too restrictive. In the latter case, a loosening of the rules might be proposed.

In addition, statistics on the operation of the existing health care plan are needed because the benefit is both important to the membership and extremely costly. Copies of several yearly financial reports should be obtained from the plan's administrator and reviewed thoroughly. Evidence of waste and abuse should be gathered, such as over-used services, particularly in-hospital care and surgery, administrative costs that are rising faster than total program costs, and health care providers who habitually overcharge. Management, too, may be exaggerating the cost of health care by failing to account for dividends and/or retroactive rate credits received where plan usage has been low.

A description of health plan services should also be obtained (there should be an employee handbook) and studied to identify gaps or redundancies in coverage. For example, the plan may not provide the important alternatives to hospital care while, at the same time, promoting unneeded services. In addition, the bargaining committee should obtain copies of other plans to compare with its own in terms of benefits provided and costs incurred. Comparison data are available from both union sources and competing insurance companies, Health Maintenance Organizations (HMOs), and/or Preferred Provider Organizations (PPOs). Finally, it is also a good idea to review the language of the contract to determine whether the employer is living up to promises made concerning plan design and the rights of employees.

Information about retiree health benefits should be collected and examined in the same manner. Beginning in 1993, under a new accounting standard, employers' financial statements must report the cost of nonpension retiree benefits, such as health care and life insurance, as they are earned by employees during their working years, even though the benefits are not paid until after retirement. Previously, most employers did not prefund postretirement programs. Unfortunately, financial statements will show lower profits and higher liabilities with the implementation of the new standard. Employers are likely to respond by demanding modifications in existing retiree benefit programs, particularly health care, in an attempt to reduce costs.

Similarly, cost and operating data for other major benefit programs such as pensions, profit sharing, and 401k plans should be gathered. Plan descriptions provide information on gaps and redundancies in benefits. Annual financial statements contain data showing yearly changes in premium payments or employer contributions in self-insured plans, cost of claims, and administrative fees. Pension plan actuarial reports should also be reexamined periodically to determine whether the original projections on funding and disbursements are still correct. If the plan is overfunded, management should not be able to terminate the plan, pay off all liabilities, and divert the surplus to its own use. Another source of pension information, although more difficult to interpret, are the Form

5500s, which all pension plan administrators must submit to the Department of Labor, Office of Pension and Welfare Benefits. Employers must make copies of these reports available to the union on request.

Information acquired about the employer's operations can also be useful. Financial statements can shed light on the employer's ability to pay for higher wages/salaries and more generous fringe benefits (see Chapter 4, Presenting Financial Information in Bargaining). Management can also provide data on the dollar cost of individual fringes that the union can compare with its own calculations (see Chapter 10, Costing Out Contract Proposals).

Data on pay and fringe terms bargained by other employee groups in the employer's industry and in the local geographical area should also be collected. The union can use statistics showing the employer is lagging behind the pay rates and fringe levels earned by groups of employees in comparable employments to justify many of its own proposals on compensation (see Chapter 5, Presenting Pay and Fringe Benefit Comparisons). The bargaining committee can also justify proposals for new employee and union rights by citing other contracts where similar provisions already exist.

Information collected about conditions in the employer's industry may offer some insights into management's bargaining position. Similarly, data on consumer prices and productivity can sometimes be used to justify improvements in compensation (see Chapter 6, Presenting Economic Data in Bargaining).

Sources of Information

Most of the information needed by the bargaining committee is readily available. The more difficult problem is often one of finding union members willing to spend the time and energy required to retrieve the information needed. One possible approach is to assign specific areas of responsibility to individual committee members. For example, one person is given the job of keeping up with settlements reported in the national or international newspaper while another is assigned to visit the public library to read about conditions in the employer's industry or trade. Stewards and rank and filers could also be recruited for the information gathering task.

The National/International Union. One readily available source of information about the local employer and the industry is the national or international union. In some organizations, the function is carried out at the district, council, or conference level. The types of services offered local affiliates can vary depending on the size of the union. Some unions with research staffs prepare and distribute summaries of settlement terms bargained by local affiliates in covered industries or trades. Sometimes, financial and operational data for individual employers are also provided. The local union need only contact the research director to find out what information is available.

Most national and international unions publish monthly newspapers or magazines and almost all of them report on contract settlements and publish economic news. Coverage typically focuses on the industries and trades within the union's jurisdiction.

Finally, many national and international unions can provide the services of experts such as pension actuaries, accountants, lawyers, job evaluation and time study consultants, and other people with special knowledge who are on staff or on retainer. These outside experts are union representatives and have a right to enter the premises of the local employer to gather information and sit at the bargaining table. The local leadership should contact the national or international president when such expertise is needed.

Public and Institutional Libraries. Most publications dealing with business, the economy, individual industries and trades, and labor-management relations in general can be found in public, college, and university libraries. Many of these institutions house business publications in special departments often staffed by librarians who are specialists in the business field. Most of the journals, magazines, government documents, books, and newspapers referenced throughout this manual are available in large public, college, and university libraries.

The Employer. A considerable amount of the information needed by the union bargaining committee is in the employer's possession. This is not surprising since management maintains payroll and personnel records, prepares accounting and financial reports, and is the custodian of most documents concerned with personnel matters. Employers in manufacturing and service industries also typically administer all major employee benefit programs.

Union representatives have a legal right to information controlled by the employer provided it is "relevant" for contract bargaining.[1] Facts and statistics about the bargaining unit and the terms and conditions of employment are always relevant. The employer, however, is under no obligation to disclose anything unless and until a request is made by the union. Actually, the bargaining committee should never hesitate to ask for information on any subject. The relevancy test becomes an important consideration only after the employer fails to comply with the request.

The demand for information can be made verbally, but many unions prefer to do so in writing. A letter listing the types of information required, a statement of the relevancy of the request for contract bargaining, and a request for prompt attention is mailed, or hand delivered, to the employer, two or three months in advance of the first bargaining session. Exhibit 2-2 contains a sample letter requesting basic information needed for bargaining.

The courts give employers a period ranging from two and one-half weeks to two months to respond to demands for information. The union, therefore, must be persistent. If three or four requests for information have been made verbally and a reasonable period of time has elapsed without compliance, the demand should be restated in a letter. The specific items of information desired should be listed along with a brief explanation of why each one is essential for intelligent bargaining. Reference should also be made to the union's earlier, unsuccessful attempts to obtain the material. The letter must be dispatched by certified mail, return receipt requested, as proof of its posting. If the original petition was made in writing, one or two reminders should be prepared in the same manner.

Unfair labor practice (ULP) charges can be filed against the employer if all of the requests for information fail to draw a response within a reasonable period of time. The procedure for filing ULP charges with the National Labor Relations Board (NLRB) is discussed in Chapter 7, The Law of Contract Bargaining. Copies of all letters sent to the employer and the returned certified mail

---

[1]Truitt Mfg. Co. v. NLRB, 351 U.S. 149 (1956).

Exhibit 2-2. Sample Letter Requesting Basic Information for Bargaining

(NAME) _____
(RETURN ADDRESS) _____
(DATE) _____

(TO) _____
(ADDRESS) _____
(CITY, STATE, ZIP) _____

Dear Mr./Ms. _____

Due to the recent mutual agreement to begin contract bargaining, the local union is requesting the following information which is in your possession and is directly relevant to the issues to be discussed:

1. The name, address, classification, base rate of pay, date of birth, and date of hire of each employee on the payroll during the most recent social security quarter.

2. The straight-time average hourly (monthly) rate for all bargaining unit employees in the latest social security period, including cost of living and premium pay, but excluding shift and overtime premiums.

3. The starting, minimum, and maximum wage (salary) rates.

4. Information on incentive plan, bonuses, cost-of-living payments, and overtime worked during the four most recent social security quarters.

5. The total and average hours worked during the four most recent social security quarters.

6. The total number of employees who qualified for shift premium, holiday, funeral leave, report-in time, call-in time, sick leave, leaves of absence, jury duty, and other fringe benefits during the past full calendar year.

7. Total cost and cost per hour/month worked of each fringe benefit plan enumerated in #6 above.

8. A distribution of bargaining unit employees by hour (weeks) of vacation entitlement for the upcoming calendar year.

9. Up-to-date descriptions and copies of financial and other reports covering pension, medical, dental, life insurance, sickness and accident, profit sharing, productivity gainsharing, legal services, child care and any similar programs that cover current employees.

10. Copies of all current job descriptions.

11. Copies of all disciplinary notices issued during the latest calendar year (assuming the union does not already have this information on file).

I fully realize that this type of information takes time to compile, so I would suggest that you hand deliver it to me as it becomes available.

Please feel free to call me at (insert telephone number) if you have any questions.

Thanking you in advance.

Sincerely,

President, Local Union #

receipts serve as proof of the union's prior attempts to obtain this information.

The employer obligation to provide information could be made part of the labor contract. The relevancy test would no longer be a factor and the union's right to information becomes enforceable through the arbitration process rather than being subject to the vagaries of the legal system.

Sometimes information becomes relevant as a consequence of statements made by employer representatives at the bargaining table. For example, an employer might counter a union's request for higher wages/salaries by claiming financial hardship or by threatening layoffs. The bargaining committee has the legal right to verify the truthfulness of these poverty claims by examining the employer's financial records.

Alternatively, management might justify its denial of the aforementioned pay request by claiming that the company already pays the highest wages/salaries in the industry. This statement does not give the union the right to inspect the employer's financial data. However, the union would be entitled to examine all documents related to the wage and benefit survey relied on by the employer.

A caveat. A union can present a ton of information to justify the need to improve particular terms and conditions of employment only to have the employer say "No!" Rational support for proposals is only one consideration in bargaining. Power is another.

THE EMPLOYER'S BARGAINING POSITION

Part of the preparation for bargaining includes spending time trying to contemplate how management is likely to respond to the union's proposals and what it might demand in return. Viewing bargaining from the employer's perspective can help the union bargaining committee improve both its own preparations and its performance at the bargaining table. The task of predicting employer responses to individual union proposals is discussed in Chapter 3, Bargaining Proposals and Priorities, and Chapter 11, Bargaining Contract Language. The present discussion is a more general examination of factors the bargaining committee should consider when speculating about management's reactions to union proposals for higher compensation and more restrictive workplace rules and practices.

—*Task*—
Anticipate the Employer's Position on Wages/Salaries and Fringes

Employers adopt many of the same criteria as unions when developing positions on pay and benefits. They pay attention to the pattern of settlements bargained by other employers in their respective industries and/or local geographical areas. Considerations of enterprise profitability and competitive conditions in the marketplace also influence the size of the money package offered.

Some employers have broken with custom when it comes to bargaining pay and benefits by refusing to even consider external earnings data, economic factors, or the financial condition of the enterprise. They are primarily interested in holding down the rate of increase in payroll cost. As a consequence, unions have been confronted with demands for pay freezes or cuts, two-tiered wage/salary and/or fringe benefit structures, lump-sum bonuses in lieu of across-the-board wage/salary increases, fixed employer contributions on health and retirement programs, and/or deferred starting dates on pay and benefit improvements.

A bargaining committee able to anticipate management's tough stand on cost containment has more time to plan an appropriate response. The following are suggested union counterproposals to demands for pay and fringe benefit cuts and freezes:

1. *The parties should work together to find ways to reduce nonemployee costs.* Perhaps a joint union-management committee can be created to search for lower priced raw materials and energy. Even management efficiency should be opened to scrutiny.
2. *The parties should work together to find ways to control employee costs.* For example, a joint union-management effort could be made to contain health care costs by encouraging employees to consider both appropriateness and expense in the choice of medical care.

3. *The parties should share the "pain."* For example, redundant management personnel ought to be dismissed. Adjusting the dividend disbursements rate downward for corporate owners is another possibility.
4. *Employees should receive something in trade for pay and fringes sacrificed.* Perhaps new job security provisions can be included in the new contract. Other examples include a ban on subcontracting and/or a guarantee against layoffs. Further, employees who might be laid off in the future could be helped with contract language providing retraining benefits and extended health care coverage.

—Task—
Anticipate the Employer's Position on Contractual Rules

Since the contract places restrictions on management's freedom to manage the work force, the employer prepares for bargaining by reviewing its own experiences under the existing contract. Department supervisors and the employer's bargaining representatives meet to discuss what they perceive as problems with the existing contract including overly restrictive workplace rules and burdensome practices. Some of the practices may have resulted from unfavorable awards obtained in arbitration. As a consequence, unions can expect employer demands for relief from rules and past practices deemed overly restrictive.

The Multifacility Corporation

The bargaining position of the local employer can also be influenced by the ownership structure. Local management typically has less bargaining flexibility when it is only one factory, office, division, or branch of a larger corporation. In a multifacility corporation, decisions on compensation are typically made by executives at the corporate level and only after consideration of their corporatewide impact. Because fringes provided at one facility set a precedent for benefit requirements at all other locations, corporate management tends to keep fringes uniform throughout the organization. As a consequence, it is difficult for a local union at one location to break new ground on fringes.

Describing Management's Position to the Membership

The bargaining committee should prepare the membership for the employer's probable position on the various items in the union's bargaining agenda. Intelligent prediction softens the impact of management's statements and builds confidence in the leadership, particularly when their forecasts are correct.

DEVELOPING BARGAINING PROPOSALS FOR THE FIRST CONTRACT

In the case of a first contract, there is no existing agreement to review. However, the bargaining committee should study contracts of other local unions in the same industry and community to learn about prevailing wage/salary rates, standard fringe benefits, and common rules protecting employee and union rights. In addition, prototype contracts should be obtained from the national, international, or intermediary body. These model agreements contain well written clauses covering every conventional subject from recognition to termination.

Other sources of information are also available. Sample contract clauses for almost all topics are contained in the second binder of *Collective Bargaining Negotiations and Contracts.* This reporting service is offered by The Bureau of National Affairs, Inc., 9435 Key West Avenue, Rockville, MD 20850, (800) 372-1033. This publication is also available in many college and university libraries. National or international union staffers and even the employer may possess copies as well.

Chapter 3

Bargaining Proposals and Priorities

The bargaining committee must transform the many ideas, suggestions, requests, and information acquired, as a result of completing the tasks discussed in Chapter 2, into specific proposals for new and improved pay, fringe, and protective language terms. Before describing the procedure for developing proposals, however, a general discussion of the subject matter covered in contract bargaining is provided.

SUBJECT MATTER

In general, the terms of employment are direct wages and salaries, hours of work, premium pay, and fringes (sometimes called supplemental benefits), work rules and practices, procedural rules for contract administration, and union security. Pay and fringe items are often referred to as compensation or earnings while contractual rules are frequently identified as protective language. The sections below give a more detailed description of the compensation and protective language terms of employment.

Direct Wages and Salaries

Direct wages and salaries are paid to employees for time spent on the job, producing quantities of pieces (parts or products), or mastering numbers of skills. Related terms include hours of work and premium pay for various disagreeable features of employment such as overtime and shift work, and call-in and call-back requirements.

Special considerations for the union when bargaining pay and hours of work include: (1) Who prepares and approves job descriptions? (2) Will pay rates be determined by job evaluation or numbers of skills mastered? (3) How will inequities be dealt with? (4) Will there be single rates, job classes, piecework, and/or measured day-work? (5) Will employees progress through the pay structure on the bases of length of service and/or merit? (6) What will the pay level be? (7) What will the starting, minimum, and maximum pay rates be? (8) Will there be credit for education and/or prior experience? (9) What conditions merit premium pay? (10) What are the requirements to receive premium pay? (11) Will there be a bonus plan? (12) What is the definition of a workday, a workweek, and a work shift? and (13) What is the procedure for changing hours of work?

Employer-Paid Time Off

The purposes of paid time off from work are to furnish employees relief from job related stresses and strains and to provide time off to attend to personal, family, professional, and/or career matters. Specific benefits include holidays, vacations, sick days, work breaks, wash-up time, jury duty, military service, attendance at professional meetings, personal days, and family leave.

Special considerations for the union when bargaining paid leave include: (1) What are the numbers of days, hours, or minutes of benefit? (2) What are the eligibility requirements for benefits? (3) How will vacation and other paid leave time be calculated? (4) Will there be premium pay for work performed during leave time? and (5) How will leave time be scheduled?

Health and Welfare Benefits

The purposes of health and welfare benefits are to protect employees against the hazards of old age, sickness and injury, and unemployment. Specific provisions include pension, health and life insurance, sickness and accident, temporary disability, accidental death and dismemberment, dental, optical, prepaid legal, child care, and supplemental unemployment compensation.

Special considerations for the union when bargaining health and welfare include: (1) What are the eligibility requirements for benefits? (2) What is the duration of benefits? (3) What are the dollar benefits paid and types of services furnished? (4) What is the length of the waiting period for benefits? (5) Does the employee and/or the employer pay for the benefit? (6) Does the union and/or employer administer the program? and (7) Will a Taft-Hartley Act sanctioned joint union-management trust be established to fund benefits?[1]

Work Standards and Performance (Effort)

The purposes of the effort bargain are to define a "fair day's work" and establish a procedure for evaluating employee performance. Provisions deal with work standards and performance evaluations.

Special considerations for the union in the effort bargain include: (1) Who determines the workload limits? (2) Who determines the speed of the assembly line? (3) Who determines incentive standards? (4) What method and criteria will be used to evaluate performance? and (5) Will the employee have the opportunity to grieve if the evaluation is unsatisfactory?

Protective Language

One purpose of protective language is to establish the rights of individual employees in work. These are the rules governing

---

[1]See Section 302(c) of the Taft-Hartley Act. Taft-Hartley is the more popular title given to the Labor Management Relations Act (LMRA) of 1947 as amended.

promotion, transfer, layoff, recall, work assignments, discipline, discharge, safety, filing grievances, and career advancement.

Special considerations for the union bargaining employee rights include: (1) Will seniority be the determining factor for all personnel actions? (2) Will seniority be by classification, department, plant, office, or some other means? (3) Under what circumstances will seniority terminate? (4) What are the procedures for posting and filling job vacancies? (5) Will prior notice be required before layoff or recall? (6) Will there be bumping rights? (7) Will there be a health and safety committee? (8) Who pays for personal safety equipment? (9) Will there be protection against unfair discipline and discharge? (10) Will personnel files be periodically purged of old disciplinary records? (11) Will senior employees be protected against loss of employment? (12) How will bargaining unit work be preserved? and (13) What opportunities will there be for skill training and career advancement?

Union Security

Protective language also includes rules dealing with union security. The purpose of these provisions is to satisfy institutional needs such as protection from rival unions, ensure an ongoing source of money and new members, and protection for union leaders.

Special considerations when bargaining union security include: (1) Will there be exclusive recognition? (2) Will membership in the local union be a requirement of continued employment? (3) Will there be dues checkoff? (4) Will there be time off for union business? (5) Will there be a probationary period for new employees? (6) Will new facilities of the employer be covered under the contract? (7) Will national or international representatives have access to the employer's facilities? (8) Will employers pay lost time during bargaining? and (9) How many bulletin boards will there be for union use and where will they be placed?

Procedural Rules

Protective language also includes procedural rules. The purposes of these rules are to establish ways of dealing with disputes and changing the agreement. These are the rules governing grievance handling, arbitration, contract duration and renewal, and midterm reopening.

Special considerations for the union bargaining procedural rules include: (1) What are the steps of the grievance procedure? (2) Who will represent management at each step of the procedure? (3) What will the time limits be for completing each step of the procedure? (4) Will stewards be able to handle grievances during working hours without loss of pay? (5) How will the arbitrator be selected and paid? (6) Will the arbitrator have final and binding authority? (7) Will the union be notified before disciplinary action is taken? (8) Will suspension precede discharge or will the employee continue to work until the grievance procedure is exhausted? (9) Will union officials involved in contract enforcement have superseniority? (10) What will the term of the contract be? (11) Will the contract renew automatically? (12) Can the contract be reopened during its term and for what reason? and (13) What will the notification requirements be for reopening?

PREPARING THE BARGAINING AGENDA: COMPENSATION TERMS

While the range of potential subject matter is broad, fewer specific topics are considered during any single period of bargaining. The selection process began with the tasks described in Chapter 2. The bargaining committee must

- give rank and filers, stewards, and officers an opportunity to voice their needs and concerns;
- review the strengths and weaknesses in the existing contract;
- collect facts and statistics about company finances, pay and fringe terms bargained by employee groups in comparable employments, and the economy; and
- speculate about the employer's intentions.

Now, the bargaining committee must sort through the many ideas, suggestions, requests and pieces of information received and prepare proposals for new pay, fringe, and protective language terms. The total list of proposals constitutes the bargaining agenda.

Bargaining agenda preparations also include developing arguments to support individual proposals and anticipating employer responses and possible compromise positions. In addition, the individual agenda items must be ranked according to priority. Finally, a bargaining book is prepared.

The four tasks involved in preparing pay and fringe proposals are described below. A discussion of protective language proposals is deferred to Chapter 11, Bargaining Contract Language. (See also Appendix 1 for a checklist of bargaining tasks.)

—*Task 1*—
Select Pay and Fringe Proposals

As noted above, the preliminary activities of the bargaining committee has yielded a lengthy collection of ideas, suggestions, and requests for changes in compensation terms. Committee members must now sort through the end-product and develop a list of proposals. Screening is unpopular, and it is not uncommon for unions to have lengthy bargaining agendas. At a minimum, contradictory or silly ideas should be eliminated.

A long list of proposals gives the union plenty of items to concede when the time comes to do so. However, confronted with a lengthy and costly union agenda, management might have difficulty determining which items are important and, as a consequence, not take any of them seriously. Further, a large number of proposals can unrealistically raise membership expectations about what the union can achieve at the bargaining table. Consequently, the bargaining committee should consider whether to eliminate some pay and fringe items initially rather than later in the bargaining process. Possible set asides include proposals to liberalize benefits that have not been used much during the preceding three or four years.

Next, the bargaining committee may have to add substance to the many bare-boned suggestions made by the membership. For example, a request is made for a personal leave benefit of one kind or another and nothing more. The committee must fill in the missing details such as the number of leave days per year, whether days can be accumulated, whether personal days can be substituted for sick days, and whether employees are paid for unused leave days at retirement or when leaving employment.

Sometimes the union favors adding a benefit program like child care, but is either unsure how to proceed or the mechanics of setting it up are too complex to arrange within the short time frame available for bargaining. In such cases, the union should propose the creation of a joint union-management committee to perform whatever tasks are required to create the benefit. Some ground rules for committee operations must be established including a reasonable, specified time period for the committee to complete its work, the arbitration of all disputes, and mandatory employer acceptance of the final product.

Finally, the bylaws of the local union should be checked to determine whether the membership or the leadership has the final word on the contents of the bargaining agenda (including protective language proposals). Sometimes the rank and file must approve the individual proposals and the bargained settlement terms. The bylaws of a Paperworkers' local states: "All collective bargaining demands and results of all negotiations must be approved by a majority vote at a regular or special meeting of the local union."[2]

—Task 2—
Develop Supporting Arguments

If there is no reasonable way to corroborate the need for higher pay and improved fringes, the union will have a tough time getting anything. The union must develop arguments to support agenda items.

One commonly used union argument is equitable treatment. The bargaining committee cites pay and fringe gains bargained by employee groups in comparable employments in the same industry and local community to demonstrate how the bargaining unit has fallen behind (see Chapter 5, Presenting Pay and Fringe Benefit Comparisons). In the following example the union spokesperson is comparing the number of paid holidays provided by the employer

---

[2]Bylaws of Local 1319, United Paperworkers Int'l Union, 1989–1992, p. 67.

to the level of benefit existing elsewhere in the community: "We are two paid holidays behind A Company. We are behind the common practice in our area which is 10. B Company has 13. C Company has 10 or 11."

Improvements in compensation can also be justified on the basis of changes in other factors such as the cost of living, productivity, and economic conditions in the employer's industry or trade (see Chapter 6, Presenting Economic Data in Bargaining).

When the employer is profitable, the union can use that fact to argue for higher wages/salaries and improved fringes (see Chapter 4, Presenting Financial Information in Bargaining). Company financial statements are the proof of profitability. The cost of new fringes are also cited to demonstrate the reasonableness of the union's requests (see Chapter 10, Costing Out Contract Proposals).

The union can also argue the employer's own interests are served when compensation is raised. For example, the union might claim greater employee efficiency and morale will result from improved compensation. One union spokesperson held out the promise of mutual gain as follows: "Accepting our proposed jury duty pay benefit will help improve the image of the Company in the community."

Finally, if the union membership is strongly disposed toward a particular pay or fringe proposal, the bargaining committee should convey this fact to management. The argument is strengthened if there is actual membership poll or survey results to present. It also helps if members make their preferences known in the workplace, particularly at times when they can be overheard by their supervisors.

—*Task 3*—
Anticipate Employer's Counterarguments

In addition to preparing arguments in support of individual pay and fringe proposals, the union bargaining committee should consider potential management counterarguments. Predicting the possible nature of the employer's opposition before the start of bargaining gives the union leadership more time to review the degree of support for union proposals and plan alternative courses of action.

In general, the employer can be expected to challenge the union's arguments. For example, employee groups chosen by the union for pay and fringe comparisons might be attacked as biased or a poor match. In response, the union bargaining committee should advocate full disclosure of all information by all parties and, if necessary, the creation of a joint union-management committee to collect and analyze information from other mutually agreed-upon sources.

Management might give the need to control costs as the reason for opposing the union's pay and fringe proposals. In turn, the bargaining committee should declare its willingness to work with management to find ways to reduce all operating, not just labor costs (see Chapter 2, Developing Bargaining Proposals).

—*Task 4*—
Determine Potential for Compromise

With the completion of the second and third tasks, the union bargaining committee can assess what sacrifices they might be called upon to make in order to reach agreement on individual proposals. As noted in Chapter 2, management is not likely to agree to terms that exceeded those bargained by other, comparable employers in the same industry or local community. Further, where management is preoccupied with cost containment, the union may be forced to make major sacrifices in compensation proposals. If so, the bargaining committee should be prepared to request something in exchange, perhaps improvements in protective language.

RANKING PROPOSALS

While the union may start out with a long list of bargaining proposals, employer opposition eventually necessitates the revision and elimination of many proposals before bargaining is concluded.

Most union members do not consider it worthwhile to fight for every compensation and language proposal on the agenda. Consequently individual proposals should be ranked according to need. The following discussion of priorities is relevant for both compensation and protective language proposals.

—*Task*—
Establish Priorities

The bargaining committee may be reluctant to assign priorities at the outset of bargaining because every agenda item seems important. Nevertheless, preferences should be sorted out by the start of the concession-making phase of the bargaining process (see Chapter 8, Bargaining Activities). In the final, frenetic days and hours of scrambling to reach a settlement, bargaining committee members can avoid making mistakes if they are clear about the pay, fringe, and protective language items they must win and those they can sacrifice.

It is important to be sensitive to the needs and desires of the membership when setting priorities. In practice, however, the bargaining committee has a difficult time objectively determining the extent of member support for every one of a long list of proposals or the intensity of this support. As a consequence, bargaining committee members have to rely more on their own collective judgments than on the availability of hard facts.

The leadership must be careful not to favor one group of employees over another when setting priorities. The needs and concerns of all important interest groups within the local union, such as women, men, unskilled, skilled, young, and old, should be represented. Important interest groups who believe they have been ignored may not support the bargaining committee and could actively work to defeat what in every other respect are good settlement terms.

Meeting the special needs of employee groups is one important criterion for setting priorities; however, the bargaining committee should try and identify other employee and union interests as well. Asking questions similar to the following offers additional guidelines for ranking compensation proposals:

1. Do employees consider money or leisure time to be more important?
2. Does it make sense to spend a lot of time trying to liberalize benefits used by only a few employees?
3. Is the contract "deficient" with respect to certain benefits based on what is known about fringe benefit programs offered elsewhere in the industry and the local geographical area?

At times, the leadership may differ with the majority of rank and filers over what is in the latter's best interest. For example, in the late 1940s, the U.S. Supreme Court ruled retirement benefits were mandatory bargaining subjects, but many union leaders and their members disagreed over just how valuable the benefit was. Most members preferred immediate cash wages rather than deferred retirement benefits. Today, pensions are viewed as an important part of the benefit package, but in an earlier period some union officials were voted out of office for bargaining pensions in lieu of bigger wage increases.

Priorities of union negotiators can also change as the bargaining process unfolds. For example, a dental benefit viewed as critical at the outset of the proceedings might decline in importance once the employer has conceded on other health care related items.

Sometimes priorities are revised in the face of external pressures. As the settlement deadline nears or passes without agreement, members of the local union bargaining committee are encouraged to rethink their priorities by a representative of the national or international union and/or by federal and state mediators who have appeared on the scene.

A Simple Ranking System

The easiest way to prioritize compensation and protective language proposals is to rank them on a scale of one to three based on the assessment made of employee and union needs. The following is a description of each of the three rankings:

1. *Top priority status* is given to the "must win" or crucial pay, fringe, and protective language proposals. These are terms and conditions deemed urgent by the bargaining

committee and strongly endorsed by a large majority of members. The union is ready to take strike action if agreement cannot be reached on proposals designated as top priority. A similar response would occur if the employer demanded major concessions in these areas.

2. *Preferred status* is given to agenda items of serious concern to many bargaining committee members. Proposals given this ranking do not generate the sense of importance or have the kind of broad-based support within the membership as those in the top group. Nevertheless, they fall into this middle rank because committee and many rank and file members support them.

3. *Low priority status* is given to the expendables. These proposed improvements in compensation and protective language would be nice to have in the contract, but they are difficult to justify, perhaps they benefit only a few members. Low priority items are included in the bargaining agenda as filler, something to sacrifice when the time comes to make concessions.

Sometimes marginal proposals can be used, in the words of one union negotiator, "to help educate" the employer about the real issues of concern to the union. In one case, the bargaining committee kept insisting on limiting the term of the new agreement to one year even though it recognized the request was unrealistic given the high dollar cost of the union's proposals. Discussing the one-year term, however, gave union negotiators additional opportunities to complain about past pay freezes and to emphasize the importance attached to the real top priority issue, which was a "substantial" across-the-board pay increase. After the employer had improved its pay offer sufficiently, the union accepted a multiyear agreement.

PROPOSALS WITH SPECIAL CHALLENGES

Sometimes one or more agenda items pose special problems for the local union. One example is a proposal covering a unionwide rather than a local issue. Another is a proposal seeking to convert a past practice into a contractual right.

Unionwide Proposals

The unionwide proposal is prepared at the national, international, or intermediary union level for inclusion in the bargaining agendas of local affiliates. The subject is often a union security matter of concern to top level officials, but of no immediate local interest. For example, a number of years ago, some parent unions were being sued as a result of unauthorized walkouts by some local affiliates in violation of their contracts' "no strike" provisions. Many organizations responded by directing all affiliated locals to rewrite their no strike clauses to limit the parent union's liability.

Unionwide proposals are particularly difficult to sell because, in most cases, nobody at the local level has been affected by the problem. Consequently, most local union members give them low priority status. Employers are also likely to diminish their importance by considering them nothing more than national office rigmarole. Nevertheless, the bargaining committee must try and relate the unionwide agenda items to the local situation in an effort to gain support and lessen criticism.

Codifying Past Practices

Difficulties can also arise when an attempt is made to incorporate past practices into the basic agreement. Past practices are employee benefits and workplace procedures that do not appear in the written agreement, but are considered part of the terms and conditions of employment. An attempt is sometimes made to write them into the contract as a way of ensuring their continued existence.

There is a major risk involved in any attempt to codify a past practice. Failure usually leads to the loss of the past practice. The employer can be expected to discontinue the practice once bargaining is concluded, and if the union grieves, claim the bargaining committee traded it away for some other benefit. The union would be forced to prove otherwise in arbitration. This is difficult to do in the private sector because no official record of what transpired during bargaining sessions is kept. The union is forced to rely on its own notes of the proceedings which may not be viewed as credible.

FORMAL AGENDA

It is customary for the bargaining committee to provide employer representatives with a written copy of the union's pay, fringe, and protective language proposals shortly before or during the opening bargaining session. In addition, the union should prepare a bargaining book for its own use and convenience in keeping track of progress on individual proposals.

—*Task*—
Prepare Copy of Proposals for Employer

The copy of the union's proposals presented to the employer should be typewritten or prepared on a word processor and printed on one side of 8 1/2 × 11 inch sheets of paper. Each request must be labeled with the appropriate article and section of the contract for identification purposes. The following is a sample entry:

Article V. Paid Holidays

Section 1. Add: The employee's birthday
and the day after Thanks-
giving.

—*Task*—
Prepare a Bargaining Book

The secretary of the bargaining committee is responsible for maintaining the bargaining book. The bargaining book contains a copy of the union's bargaining agenda together with other relevant documents. This plus the minutes taken of each bargaining session provides the union with a complete day-to-day record of what transpired at the conference table.

A three-ring, loose-leaf notebook is typically used for the bargaining book. The following items are usually included:

1. Copies of all union proposals and counterproposals made to the employer with time and date tendered written on them.
2. Copies of all demands, offers, and counteroffers received from the employer with date and time received noted.
3. Data supporting the union position such as cost of fringes, employer finances, compensation survey results, and references to former grievances.
4. Copies of all important handouts, letters, records, and telephone messages received from the employer or initiated by the union.
5. Copies of tentative agreements reached, initialed, or signed and dated by both sides (see Chapter 9, The Local Union Negotiator's Toolbox).
6. Statements about how the parties intend new and revised terms and conditions of employment to work in practice.

This last item is a way of avoiding future disputes involving contract interpretation.

The bargaining committee may find it helpful to record the status of agenda items in the bargaining book at the close of each bargaining session. One possible format is to list the union's proposals, using one or two descriptive words as opposed to complete sentences, on an 8 1/2 × 11 inch sheet of paper, leaving space to record meeting dates and bargaining outcomes. The secretary records the standing of each proposal using terms such as "agreed," "held," and "withdrawn." A sample form is shown in Exhibit 3-1.

Exhibit 3-1. Status of Union Proposals

Item	*Date 1*	*Date 2*	*Date 3*
Wages	Held	Held	Agreed
Skill Premium	Held	Held	Agreed
Holidays	Held	Held	Agreed
Jury Duty	Held	Withdrawn	

Chapter 4

Presenting Financial Information in Bargaining

Financial data are used to demonstrate the employer's ability to pay for wage/salary and fringe improvements. Gathering, evaluating, and presenting financial data are the tasks discussed in this chapter. (See Appendix 1 for a checklist of bargaining tasks.)

THE ABILITY TO PAY ARGUMENT

It is not unreasonable for employees to expect advances in wages/salaries and fringes to go hand-in-hand with improvements in the general financial condition of the business. In other words, if the employer has made profits in the past, the union is justified in requesting additional compensation.

Management may dispute the ability to pay argument and give more weight to other factors such as labor cost. The usual claim is high labor cost is putting the employer at a competitive disadvantage in the marketplace. Nevertheless, just knowing the employer is profitable can give the bargaining committee a psychological boost.

SOURCES OF FINANCIAL DATA

Under normal circumstances, the bargaining committee can learn everything it needs to know about company finances from the employer's annual income statement and balance sheet. Conversely, whenever management pleads financial distress and demands major concessions from employees, the union should have a professional accountant examine all of the underlying general accounting journals and ledger sheets.

The income statement provides information about the employer's sales income, expenditures, and profit or loss during the year. Data on assets, liabilities, and net worth/stockholder's equity for the same period is reported on the balance sheet. For bargaining purposes, two or three consecutive end of fiscal year income statements and balance sheets are required, beginning with the most current. Examining the yearly changes in the data is informative.

—*Task*—
Collect Financial Information

Local management is the immediate source for both income statements and balance sheets. A copy of the outside auditor's report attesting to the accuracy of the data in these reports should also be requested. See Chapter 2 for a discussion of the union's right to information held by the employer.

If local management is unwilling to provide copies of income statements and balance sheets, alternative sources are available, particularly when ownership is in the form of shares of stock held by the general public.

Publicly Owned Corporations

A corporation whose stock is bought and sold in the marketplace must disclose data on income, expenditures, profits, assets, liabilities, and equity. It does so in an annual report and in other documents prepared for stockholders and the federal Securities and Exchange Commission (SEC). This is all public information and unions should take advantage of its availability. Published sources of financial information are discussed below.

Stockholders' Reports. The stockholders' report is mailed annually to every owner and is made available to other interested parties upon request. Contents include income statement and balance sheet data for a number of consecutive years. Most of the dollar values reported are totals for all factories, offices, divisions, and/or subsidiaries operated by the employer. These consolidated statements may appear useless to a local union bargaining committee interested in the finances of a single factory, office, division, or subsidiary. Nevertheless, they can be used as leverage to obtain the local information required. The employer is likely to complain about the use of consolidated statements claiming they do not accurately report financial conditions at the local facility. The local operation may even be described as losing money. When that happens, the union is entitled to copies of income statements and balance sheets for the local operation in order to verify these assertions.

The bargaining committee should obtain a copy of the corporation's latest annual report even when financial information is provided by management. The document often provides useful insights into the employer's bargaining position. At least one local union was able to accurately predict management's plan after reading the Chairman of the Board's letter printed in the preceding year's annual report. In the letter, the Chairman informed stockholders of the acquisition of two plants and the expenditure of $17.4 million for modernization of existing facilities and the purchase of new equipment during the year. He then stated, "The Company had planned to fund a major portion of its capital expenditures with long-term debt but deferred any significant long-term financing when interest rates escalated rapidly; consequently, expenditures were largely financed from internal cash flows and short term bank borrowing. As a result, the Company's working capital declined during the year for the first time in five years."

The union correctly interpreted the Chairman's statement to mean the employer would be hard pressed for cash to pay off its short-term debts during the upcoming year and would resist taking on any additional burden of a wage increase. In fact, management approached the union at the outset of bargaining with demands to "hold the line" on wages and cap future cost of living adjustments. In a separate news release, the employer warned of future investment cutbacks at the local plant should the union fail to agree to its demands.

A copy of the most recent stockholders' report may be available from local management. If they are unwilling or unable to comply, a copy can be obtained by writing directly to the corporation secretary at the headquarters address of the parent corporation. For best results, the member making the request should do so as a potential investor interested in purchasing the stock of the company rather than as a representative of the union. If the parent corporation is unknown, consult *America's Corporate Families* and *America's Corporate Families and International Affiliates*, published annually by Dun & Bradstreet, Inc., available at most public, college, and university libraries. Many libraries also collect annual reports for companies located in their respective geographical regions.

Announcement of the Annual Meeting of Stockholders. Information about executive compensation and corporate investment policies can be found in the annual meeting notice to stockholders. The stockholders of a corporation meet once a year to elect the members of the board of directors and to transact other business. The salaries and other financial perquisites paid to top executives are reported in the meeting notice. In addition, board directors seeking reelection use the meeting announcement to discuss their plans for the future of the company. This is must reading for union officials at any time and particularly when preparing to negotiate a labor contract. Request a copy of the most recent meeting notice when writing to the corporation secretary for a copy of the annual report.

Securities and Exchange Commission (SEC) Form 10-K. Financial data not usually included in corporate annual reports can be found in Form 10-K. This is a third item to request when writing to the corporation secretary. Form 10-Ks can also be obtained by writing directly to the SEC, Public Reference Room, 450 Fifth Street N.W., Washington, DC 20549, (202) 272-7420, or to one of its regional offices. A modest fee is charged for reproducing copies of reports.

Commercial Publishers of Corporate Financial Data. A number of private publishers report income statement, balance sheet, and related operating data for publicly held corporations. The following are the best known publications:

1. Moody's *Manuals* categorize employers alphabetically in one of seven manuals with the following titles: Industrial, OTC Industrials, Small OTC Industrials, Public Utilities, Transportation, Banks and Financial Institutions, and International Companies. Bound volumes of these manuals are issued annually. Periodic updates are provided throughout the year.
2. Standard & Poor's *Standard Corporate Descriptions* list employers alphabetically in six binders. Information is updated throughout the year.

Most public, college, and university libraries carry one or both of these publications. Ask the librarian in the business section for help.

Closely Held Enterprises

The union has a tougher time obtaining financial information from outside sources when the employer is a partnership, a single owner company, or a corporation whose stock is not distributed to the general public. These forms of ownership are not subject to the same disclosure rules as corporations whose stock is traded. Financial reports for tax purposes are all that is normally required and these are not made available to the general public. Fortunately, even closely held enterprises are occasionally forced to reveal information of a financial nature. They might be part of federal or state government regulated industries with disclosure requirements, or parties to actions of one sort or another in a court of law. Obtaining information from these sources may prove difficult but not impossible.

Federal Government Sources. Employers in industries regulated by the federal government must file annual reports, often including income statement and balance sheet data. Federal regulators include the Federal Communications Commission (radio and television stations), Federal Energy Regulatory Commission (electric and natural gas utilities, and oil pipelines), Interstate Commerce Commission (railroads and intercity bus lines), Federal Deposit Insurance Corporation (insured banks), the Federal Reserve Board (national banks, member state banks), and the Environmental Protection Agency (any employer with a project affecting the environment). Most of the information collected by these agencies is available to the public under the Freedom of Information Act.

The *Federal Regulatory Directory*, published by Congressional Quarterly, describes jurisdiction and reporting requirements for 103 regulatory agencies. It also contains lists of telephone contacts and mailing addresses for each agency, including regional offices, and its Freedom of Information officer. A copy of this directory is available at local public, college, and university libraries.

State Government Sources. State governments also collect information from many of the businesses that operate within their borders. Insurance companies and locally chartered banks file financial reports with insurance and banking commissions. Private corporations doing business in some states must file annual reports, often including financial data, with the Secretary of State's office. In Wisconsin, a group of railroad workers obtained copies of their employer's income statement and balance sheet from the State's Department of Transportation. Most states also require businesses to divulge operating data in connection with the enforcement of environmental laws. The *National Directory of State Agencies* classifies state agencies by function and lists telephone contacts and mailing addresses. A copy of this directory is available at most public, college, and university libraries or contact Cambridge Information Group Directories, Inc., (800) 227-3052.

Court Records. Occasionally an employer is a plaintiff or defendant in a law suit where financial and other operating data are revealed. This information is included in the transcript of the trial, which is a public document. Investigating this source requires searching through defendant and plaintiff case indices available at the civil section of the circuit, district, or superior court branch where the case was heard.

Nonprofit Corporations and Foundations

Some hospitals, nursing homes, and universities are organized as nonprofit corporations and foundations. As private, tax-exempt organizations, they must file a Form 990 with the Internal Revenue Service. This annual report includes information on revenues, expenditures, and net worth or equity. Under the federal Tax Reform Act of 1986, most nonprofit organizations are required to provide copies of their last three annual Form 990 filings immediately to anyone asking to see them during normal business hours (private foundations need only provide access during a 180 day window each year). This information is also available directly from the Internal Revenue Service, but requests take weeks to process. In addition, some state's require similar financial reporting.

READING FINANCIAL STATEMENTS

As noted earlier, the best source of data about the financial condition of the employer is the income statement and balance sheet. In this section, the organization of these basic financial reports is examined and the important terms defined.

The Income Statement

The income statement summarizes revenues earned from sales of products or services, expenses incurred in acquiring these revenues, and the resulting profit or loss during a specified period of time. Exhibit 4-1 shows the format of an income statement and presents the terminology. The major categories of the income statement are net revenues, cost of goods/services sold, selling and administrative expenses, interest, taxes, and retained earnings.

The Balance Sheet

The balance sheet shows the values for assets, liabilities, and the owner's stake in the business at a particular point in time, typically the ending date on the accompanying income statement.

Exhibit 4-1. Income Statement for Year Ending December 31, 1992 (in thousands of dollars)[a]

Net Revenues[b]	$115,000
Cost of Goods/Services Sold[c]	−90,000
Depreciation[d]	−5,000
Selling and Administrative Expenses[e]	−10,000
Operating Profit (Loss)[f]	10,000
Net of Other Income/Expenses[g]	+10,000
Interest owed[h]	−5,000
Pretax Profit[i]	15,000
Income Tax[j]	−5,000
Net Profit (Loss)[k]	10,000
Dividends Paid[l]	−6,700
Retained Earnings[m]	$ 3,300

a. "In thousands of dollars," means the last three zeros have been omitted from all dollar figures in order to save space.

b. Net revenues are the total value of products or services sold less any refunds to customers or clients.

c. Cost of goods/services sold includes all of the direct costs of producing a product or providing a service, such as payroll, raw materials, general supplies, electric and other utilities, property and other taxes, rents on buildings, and interest payments on money borrowed for operating capital.

d. Depreciation is the decline in useful value of purchased buildings, machinery, and equipment.

e. Selling and administrative expenses include salaries and benefits paid to managerial, professional, and technical personnel; salaries, commissions, and benefits paid to the sales force; advertising; publicity; and other expenses not directly related to producing a product or providing a service.

f. Operating profit or loss is the difference between net revenues and all categories of operating costs.

g. Net of other income and expenses is the difference between rents, dividends and/or interest earned from rental property and holdings of marketable securities and expenses related to activities not related to the main purpose of the business.

h. Interest owed is the cost of borrowing money, either through the sale of bonds or by mortgaging property.

i. Pretax profit or loss is the amount of profit or loss subject to an income tax.

j. Income tax is the amount of federal and state income taxes due.

k. Net profit or loss is the excess or short fall in revenues remaining after all costs of doing business have been met.

l. Dividends are cash payments made to the owners of incorporated businesses. The equivalent in noncorporate forms of ownership are bonuses paid to owners out of profits.

m. Retained earnings are the amount of profits remaining after dividends or bonuses have been paid. Retained earnings are added to the owners' equity account on the balance sheet. The retained earnings are the source for higher wages/salaries and fringe benefit improvements in a new contract.

The format of a balance sheet and its terminology are presented in Exhibit 4-2.

Exhibit 4-2. Balance Sheet
December 31, 1992
(in thousands of dollars)

CURRENT ASSETS	
Cash, Marketable Securities, Accounts Receivables, and Inventories[a]	$100,000
FIXED ASSETS	
Real Estate, Buildings, Machinery, and Equipment[b]	900,000
Less Accumulated Depreciation[c]	370,000
Net Fixed Assets[d]	530,000
TOTAL ASSETS[e]	$630,000
CURRENT LIABILITIES	
Accounts Payable, Notes Payable, and Accrued Expenses[f]	$116,700
Long-Term Debt[g]	200,000
STOCKHOLDERS' EQUITY/NET WORTH[h]	
Preferred Stock[i]	80,000
Common Stock[j]	180,000
Capital Surplus[k]	20,000
Retained Earnings[l]	33,300
TOTAL LIABILITIES & EQUITY	$630,000

a. Cash, marketable securities, accounts receivables or money owed by customers, inventories in the warehouse, and prepaid expenses or money paid for unused services, such as insurance, are current assets because they are either cash or assets easily converted to cash within one year.

b. Real estate, buildings, machinery, and equipment are fixed assets because they are durable and not easily disposed of.

c. Accumulated depreciation is the estimated reduction in the value of fixed assets due to wear and tear from use and the passage of time. The number of years used to depreciate assets, mostly a matter of judgment and the tax laws, can influence profitability.

d. Net fixed assets refers to the value of durable assets less depreciation.

e. Total assets is the sum of current and fixed assets.

f. Accounts payable or money owed to regular business creditors, notes payable or bank debt, and accrued expenses or money owed for services rendered are current liabilities because they must be paid within one year. The excess of current assets over current liabilities is called net working capital. The cash needed to pay higher wages/salaries comes from working capital.

g. Long-term debt refers to money borrowed that does not have to be paid
(continued on next page)

Exhibit 4-2.—*Continued*

---

back for many years. Mortgages and bonds are examples of long-term liabilities. The cost of borrowing this money is called interest and is recorded on the income statement.

h. Stockholders' equity or net worth is what remains after total liabilities are subtracted from total assets and represents what ownership in the business is worth at "book value." On a corporate balance sheet, net worth or stockholders' equity includes preferred and common stock, capital surplus, and retained earnings.

i. Preferred stock represents the amount of money invested in the business by one class of owners. Preferred owners receive dividends before payments are made to common stockholders.

j. Common stock represents the amount of money invested in the business by a second class of owners. Management determines the size of the common dividend or whether a dividend is paid at all.

k. Capital surplus is the total dollar amount received from the original sales of preferred and common stock that was in excess of the dollar figure printed on the stock certificates.

l. Retained earnings are the accumulated reinvestment of the net profits earned by the business since it began operations. The amount includes the $3.3 million of retained earnings shown on the income statement.

FINANCIAL ANALYSIS

Is the employer making a profit? Is business growing or stagnating? What other groups besides employees might claim a share of company profits? Can the employer afford the union's proposals for higher pay and enhanced fringes? Analyzing the income statement and the balance sheet provides the answers to these and similar questions relevant to contract bargaining.

—*Task*—
Evaluate the Financial Performance of the Employer

Two methods for appraising the financial performance of the employer are described in this section. The first examines the direction of changes, or trends, in the values of key income statement and balance sheet items over a period of years. The second approach is called ratio analysis. Relationships between income statement and balance sheet items are computed and the results compared with existing standards. Again, the direction of trends are examined.

Identifying Long-Term Financial Trends

Copies of income statements for the most recent three or more consecutive years are placed side by side. Next, the direction of yearly changes in numerical values of key items is noted. For example, revenues have either risen, declined, or stayed the same over the period. It is a very good sign if revenues have been growing by increasingly larger amounts each year.

Similarly, the trend for net profit should be determined. Has it been increasing each year? Remember, the employer's ability to increase wages/salaries and enhance fringes is dependent on the growth of profits. If profits have been increasing steadily, in the absence of contrary information, the union can assume the trend will continue.

Balance sheet data are examined in the same way. What is happening to debt from year to year? If it is rising, it could reduce the share of profits available for future increases in employee compensation. In addition, the stockholders' equity account should not be overlooked. If it is growing, the presumed dollar value of the owner's investment in the business is increasing. This is a sign the owners are getting richer.

It is also important to read the footnotes to the financial statements. They explain why changes have occurred in revenues, profits, debt and equity, and whether the underlying causes are temporary or permanent. Additional information may be gleaned from reading an annual report to stockholders if one is produced.

Using Financial Ratios

The sample income statement in Exhibit 4-1 reports a net profit for the year of $10 million. Is this good? The answer might be "yes" because the employer earned the amount of revenues of $115 million, a profit margin of almost 9 percent. On the other hand, the same profit on sales of $1 billion is a meager, disappointing

1 percent return. Calculating ratios, such as profit to sales, reveals the strengths and weaknesses of the employer's financial position.

The bargaining committee is interested in finding out whether the employer has made money and, if so, what portion of it can be used to raise wages/salaries and enhance fringes. The emphasis, therefore, is on ratios of profitability, dividend payout, cash position, and long-term indebtedness.

Profitability. There are three profitability ratios. Return on equity measures the dollar amount of net profit the employer earns in a year on each dollar invested by the owners. The remaining two ratios relate year-end profit to purchases of fixed assets and the sales of goods or services respectively. These ratios give different results, so the union should use whichever one best supports its position. The employer can be expected to do the same. These ratios are calculated and interpreted as follows:

1. The return on equity for the year is found by dividing pre- or posttax profit by stockholders' equity or net worth. Using values for pretax profit and stockholders' equity taken from the sample statements presented in Exhibits 4-1 and 4-2, the return on equity is:

Pretax Profit $ 15,000,000
Stockholders' Equity   313,300,000   or .0478 or 4.78 percent[1]

The rate of return on the monies which the owners have invested in the business was almost 5 percent. In other words, each dollar of investment earned 4.78 cents.

The business made money, but there remains the question of whether a 4.78 percent return on equity is good. This 4.78 percent figure must be compared to earnings obtained from other forms of investment such as risk free certificates of deposits sold by commercial savings banks. If banks are paying more than 4.78 percent, the employer will be looking for ways to reduce, not raise, wage/salary payments.

The 4.78 percent return on equity figure can also be compared with a generally accepted standard representing "normal" performance in the employer's own industry. Data on industry norms

---

[1]Sometimes the average stockholder's equity or net worth over two consecutive years is used. This provides a more conservative measure of equity. Further, net profit could be substituted for pretax profit in the formula.

for most financial ratios are found in two publications: *Quarterly Financial Reports*, published by the Federal Trade Commission, is available by subscription from the Superintendent of Documents, U.S. Government Printing Office, Washington, DC 20402, and *Annual Statement Studies*, is published by Robert Morris Associates, Philadelphia National Bank Building, Philadelphia, PA 19107. These publications are also found in the business sections of public, college, and university libraries.

Finally, the return on equity ratio should be computed for each year in which information is available. The yearly changes can then be compared. Ideally, the ratio should be getting larger each year.

2. Return on fixed assets is found by dividing pretax profit for the year by durable assets. Again, using data from the exhibits, the return is:

Pretax Profit $\underline{\$\ 15{,}000{,}000}$
Net Fixed Assets $530{,}000{,}000 = .0283$ or 2.83 percent

The rate of return on fixed assets is 2.83 percent, or each dollar of assets earned 2.83 cents. The return on assets is lower than the return on equity. Next, the 2.83 percent figure is compared with the industry standard to determine if the rate of return is good or bad. The ratio for each fiscal year should be computed and the annual changes compared. Ideally, the rate of return should be increasing.

The value for net fixed assets used in the above example was the original purchase price less depreciation for years of use. This is the customary way, but some employers claim their existing plant, machinery, and equipment should be worth what it would cost to replace them at current market prices. The affect of using the current replacement value is to drastically reduce profitability. The union should question the validity of this uncommon approach, but must avoid being drawn into a debate about accounting methods. The latter is a complex subject and such quarrelling serves only to distract from the more important discussion about the need to improve wages/salaries and fringes.

3. Return on revenues is pretax profit divided by net revenues. In some industries, notably retail and service, the return on revenues can be low relative to the other measures of profitability.

However, two or three cents earned on every dollar of revenues adds up to big profits when the business is selling many hundreds of millions of dollars worth of products or services.

Again, both intraindustry and annual comparisons must be made. The employer may be making money, but the rate of return on revenues over time is also important. For example, a relatively flat annual growth rate for revenues usually means the employer's share of the product or service market is rigid. The potential for future profit growth is limited for employers in highly competitive industries.

Owners' Claim to Profit. Another important ratio is the size of the dividend payout or bonuses to owners. Dividends and bonuses reduce the amount of net profit available to fund improvements in employee pay and benefits. The payout ratio for the year, using data from the sample income statement, is:

Dividends Paid $ 6,700,000

Net Profit   10,000,000 = .67 or 67 percent

Dividends consume a hefty two-thirds of the profit earned during the year. This leaves a maximum one-third of profit available for higher pay and improved fringes. Again, the ratios for two or three previous years should be calculated to discover how the stockholders have fared over time. The dividend rate should also be compared with an industry standard.

The union committee should question both the size and trend of the dividend or bonus payout percentage, particularly when employees are being asked to make sacrifices in compensation to contain costs. The union is being perfectly reasonable when it asks owners and management to absorb some of the "pain" brought on by stiffer competition and stagnate or declining profits.

Liquidity. The focus of liquidity ratios is on working capital. Working capital is the difference between current assets and liabilities. The employer may be profitable but still be short of cash as a result of having many short-term financial obligations. Under such circumstances, management can be expected to oppose wage/salary increases that require new and immediate cash outlays.

Two measures of liquidity are the current ratio and the quick ratio. These relationships are calculated and interpreted as follows:

1. The current ratio determines whether the dollar value of current assets exceeds current liabilities and by how much. Using data from the balance sheet in Exhibit 4-2, the current ratio is:

Total Current Assets $\underline{\$100,000,000}$

Account & Notes Payable, etc. $116,700,000$ = 0.85

The current ratio is 0.85 to 1 or 85 cents in cash and liquid assets are on hand to cover each dollar of current debt. A "normal" current ratio is 2 to 1 but industry standards do vary.

2. The quick ratio, sometimes called the acid-test ratio, is similar to the current ratio. The quick ratio excludes inventory from the asset side of the equation because it is difficult to liquidate merchandise on short notice. A "normal" quick ratio is 1 to 1, but many businesses have lower ones.

Ratios for two or three consecutive years should be calculated and compared. Examine whether short-term debts are accumulating at a faster rate than the current assets used to pay for them. If so, expect the employer to be more interested in finding ways to improve its cash position than in paying higher wages/salaries and improving fringes.

Next, the individual categories of current assets and current liabilities should be studied to discover where the cash has gone. For example, activity in the notes payable category over several years suggests cash is being used to repay short-term loans. These loans could have been invested in company expansion or used for other less productive purposes. Likewise, a stable inventory account could mean cash is tied up in warehousing products because of a shortage of customers. Further, surplus and marketable securities accounts should be examined for hidden cash. In noncorporate enterprises, owners use surplus cash to pay themselves higher salaries and bonuses. Some employers hide cash in surplus accounts to avoid paying it out to employees in the form of higher wages/ salaries.

Long-Term Debt. A measure of whether the employer will be able to afford higher wages/salaries and improved fringes in the future is the relationship between permanent debt and the funds invested by owners. The long-term debt to equity ratio is:

Long-Term Liabilities $\underline{\$200,000,000}$
Stockholders' Equity   313,300,000 = .638 or 63.8 percent

Fixed debt is equal to 63.8 percent of equity. In general, the lower the percentage the better, but industry standards do vary.

Examine the debt to equity ratios for several consecutive years. A high and rising ratio means the employer is borrowing a lot of money to stimulate growth. This is good so long as sales are also increasing and there is enough cash on hand to cover the added interest liability. An employer doing well on borrowed money can earn big profits and, consequently, afford to pay more to employees. Should revenues decline, however, the employer will seek to reduce payroll costs through pay cuts and layoffs in order to meet debt obligations and remain solvent.

PRESENTING FINANCIAL INFORMATION

The bargaining committee should prepare a chart showing trends and ratios to see what general patterns emerge. Statistics are easier to understand when presented pictorially such as in a chart or graph. The union can also use the table(s) or graph(s) of trends and ratios at the bargaining table to underscore its argument that the employer has the ability to pay for wage/salary and fringe improvements. Although a picture is worth a thousand words, the bargaining committee must also be prepared to explain its choice of trends and financial ratios, how the calculations were done, and the meaning of the findings with regard to the employer's financial condition.

—Task—
Chart Trends

A table showing changes in selected financial indicators over time is illustrated in Exhibit 4-3. Values for the financial indicators

Exhibit 4-3. Trends in Key Financial Indicators[a]

Financial Indicator	1992	1991	Amount of Increase or (Decrease)[b]	Percent Increase or (Decrease)[b]
Net Revenues	$115,000	$110,400	$4,600	4.2
Net Profit	10,000	9,600	400	4.2
Stockholders' Equity	313,300	310,000	3,300	1.1
Long-Term Debt	200,000	200,000	0	0.0

[a]*Source*: Employer's income statements and balance sheets.
[b]In thousands of dollars.

are given in the horizontal rows of the table. The second and third columns contain the dollar values for the two comparison years. The remaining columns show the magnitude of the year-to-year changes in both absolute (dollar) and relative (percentage) terms. The table has a title at the top and the primary sources of information are noted at the bottom.

The table in Exhibit 4-3 makes it easy to visualize what has happened to sales, profits, owner's equity, and debt during the period. Absent contrary information, growth in sales, profits, and equity can be expected to continue while debt remains stable. Clearly, this data shows the employer can afford to improve pay and benefits.

—Task—
Chart Financial Ratios

Exhibit 4-4 contains a table showing financial ratios along with generally accepted industry norms. The ratios for three years are placed in the horizontal rows of the table. The standards are located in the last column.

Again, the table in Exhibit 4-4 makes it easy to see the pattern in the data. The company is profitable but growing slowly as indicated by the flat rates of return on equity, assets, and sales over

Exhibit 4-4. Comparison of Financial Ratios and Industry Standards Over a Three-Year Period

Ratios	1992[a]	1991[a]	1990[a]	Industry Average (R.M.A.)[b]
Return on Stockholders' Equity	0.0478	0.0478	0.0465	0.0465
Return on Assets	0.0283	0.025	0.025	0.02
Return on Revenues	0.13	0.13	0.13	0.13
Dividend Payout	0.67	0.67	0.67	N/A
Current Ratio	0.85	0.85	1.00	1.50
Debt to Equity Ratio	0.638	0.645	0.60	2.00

[a]*Source*: Employer's income statements and balance sheets.
[b]*Source*: Robert Morris Associates, 1990–1992.

the three-year period. In addition, the long-term debt to equity ratio rose and the cash position worsened. The business is also in step with industry norms except with regard to the current and debt/equity ratios. However, after viewing this data, the union can expect the employer to be very reluctant to offer more than modest improvements in wages/salaries and benefits at the bargaining table.

Chapter 5

Presenting Pay and Fringe Benefit Comparisons

Another way of supporting proposals for improved pay and benefits is to demonstrate how the bargaining unit has lost ground relative to other groups of workers in similar employments elsewhere in the employer's industry and/or the same geographical area. The present chapter discusses the comparables argument and describes the tasks associated with making pay and fringe comparisons and presenting the findings to management. The use of comparables in public sector bargaining is discussed in Chapter 14.

DEVELOPING THE COMPARABLES ARGUMENT

The comparables argument is based on equity. Groups of employees who perform jobs that are similar in content, have the same level of skill, or produce essentially the same product or service should receive equivalent rates of compensation. It should not matter who the employer is or where the business is located.

Further, in some industries, trades, and professions, individual employers have emerged over time as "leaders" or "pattern setters" on pay levels and fringes. There are also historical rivalries among groups of employees, such as the constant attempt of fire fighters to maintain parity with police officers with whom they share many similar occupational characteristics. Such longstanding relationships, particularly where they are the outgrowth of collective bargaining, should be preserved unless fundamental changes in underlying conditions occur.

DEVELOPING WAGE AND FRINGE COMPARISONS

In practice, it is not always easy to find suitable comparisons. The products and services produced and the conditions of work can be very dissimilar even among factories and offices operated by the same employer. The differences can be even greater when comparing employers within the same industry and/or geographical area. Further, even when matching groups of employees are found, the union cannot expect every benefit won in one place of employment to be accepted by another employer.

A number of tasks are involved in making wage/salary and fringe comparisons. First, target groups of employees must be located. Next, the employment characteristics of targeted groups must be compared. Finally, the pay and benefit data of selected employee groups must be gathered.

—*Task*—
Identify Potential Targets for Comparisons

The bargaining committee must resist the temptation to seek out only groups of employees with pay structures and settlement terms that support its bargaining position. The choice of targets should be made with care and concern for credibility.

In the search for comparable employee groups, the bargaining committee should look where the potential of finding them is greatest. The following sources should be investigated:

1. Other factories, offices, hotels, restaurants, and hospitals operated by the same employer, especially when organized by the same union.

2. Other facilities of the same employer when organized by other unions.
3. Unionized employers in the same industry or trade. This is a particularly good choice where the employer competes directly with other identifiable enterprises.
4. Unorganized employers in the same industry or trade. This may be necessary in industries and geographical areas where there are few unionized employers.
5. Unionized employers in the same community. The geographical area could be a town, city, or larger region.
6. Other employee groups in the same community where comparability has been established. Again, police officers and fire fighters in the same community compare with each other.

—*Task*—
Choose Comparable Employments

Good comparisons are those that are acceptable to the employer. Management is likely to object strongly where the union chooses new or atypical target groups of employees in an attempt to move the standing of the bargaining unit up to a level of pay and fringes not previously enjoyed. On the other hand, where the selections are used simply to show the progress being made by other groups and the union's goal is limited to recovering lost ground, the question of comparability becomes less important to the employer. Not unimportant, but less important.

In general, the more employment characteristics employee groups have in common the better the match. The following are potential features of compatibility:

1. *Product or service markets are equivalent.* Matching on the basis of product or service mixes is not always easy to do. Even a product such as insurance is not homogeneous. Different types of insurance, such as health, fire, casualty and life, are sold in dissimilar markets. Markets for some types of insurance are more profitable than others.
2. *Jobs or occupations are similar in content.* Typically, it is the key jobs or occupations that are compared. Key jobs

are usually the most common ones or those considered to be pivotal in the job classification system. Further, the functions performed, not job titles, must match. For example, the duties of a claims adjuster in some insurance companies includes all aspects of processing claims including opening the mail, reviewing information, keying data into a computer, and writing benefit checks. Other employers divide these tasks up among a number of different people, but all have the title of claims adjuster.

3. *Labor market conditions are similar.* Employers do not accept labor markets located in other geographical regions. For example, employers in Madison, Wisconsin, pay a premium to attract computer programmers from the higher paying Chicago job market, approximately 300 miles away. These same employers, however, resist efforts by Madison office workers with programming skills to use the Chicago market for comparison purposes in local bargaining.

4. *Collective bargaining relationships are similar.* Many unions resist making comparisons with groups of employees who are unorganized even if they are in the same industry. In the service sector, on the other hand, union organization is still in its infancy and in many cases it is difficult to make meaningful pay and benefit comparisons without including nonunion employers.

5. *The periods of contract coverage are similar.* A union should avoid comparisons with employers whose labor agreements will expire either shortly before or after its own new contract is bargained. Contracts with similar beginning and ending dates are preferable.

6. *Base wage/salary rates match.* The base rate is free of all premium enhancements, such as overtime, that tend to distort other types of earnings figures. Likewise, when comparing wage/salary classes, the actual figures and not averages should be used. The average represents an entire pay class as a single statistic or number which is not as descriptive as comparing the base rate for each job separately. Base rates are printed as an appendix in most contract booklets.

7. *Key fringes match.* Long and complicated lists of fringe benefit comparisons should be avoided. For example, in the case of health insurance it may simply be enough to know whether other employers provide this benefit. If additional information is required, such as the existence of co-payments and deductibles, the inquiry should be limited to just these questions. Trying to compare every provision in two or more health insurance programs only leads to unnecessary confusion.

—*Task*—
Collect Data for Comparison Purposes

Once the comparables have been identified, the bargaining committee is ready to collect the required earnings data. Vast quantities of statistics are available, but not all of them are useful or make sense in the context of local union bargaining. The data source selected will depend on whether the union is seeking information for an entire industry, trade, or profession, or a single group of employees or occupation. The most common sources include collective agreements from other local unions, national or international unions, pay and benefit surveys, and government and commercial publishers.

Collective Agreements

Labor agreements of targeted employee groups are the best source of information about prevailing wage/salary rates and fringe benefit levels. Details of pension and medical benefits are usually contained in separate printed handbooks.

Every local union should maintain a file of contracts, particularly those of other local unions within the same industry and local community. Union activists should make it a practice to exchange copies of contracts when they meet other union officials at central labor council meetings, conventions, conferences, and training programs. Most union leaders are willing to reveal their terms of employment, particularly if reciprocity is observed. In addition, local AFL-CIO central bodies could perform a service by becoming depositories for labor contracts of unions in their service area.

An exchange of contracts helped the leadership of one local union confirm suspicions they had about their employer's wage policy. The private employer was the food service contractor for a number of campuses in the same statewide university system. Food service employees at one campus became convinced they were being paid a lower hourly wage than their counterparts working on other campuses where the employer had concessions. To prove their suspicions, the local leadership wrote to the different unions representing food service workers at the other locations with an offer to trade contract books. All organizations contacted agreed to the exchange, and, as a result, suspicions were confirmed. Employees on the other campuses were earning between $1.00 and $1.50 more per hour on all jobs.

National/International Union

Another source of pay and fringe data is the national or international union and, in some cases, an intermediate body. Most union constitutions require local affiliates to provide the national office or other designated representative with copies of their basic and all supplemental agreements. Organizations with staffs available to process this material can provide local affiliates with a wealth of information. For example, twice each year, the Service Employees' Union publishes information on bargained settlements by industry sector. Included in the report are wage rates and general wage rate changes for key jobs. In addition, there are brief descriptions of newly negotiated changes in contract provisions dealing with such terms and conditions as union security, premium pay, reporting and recall pay, shift differentials, leave time, holidays, vacations, pensions, and health insurance.

Pay and Benefit Surveys

In the absence of suitable published material, a local union can conduct its own wage/salary and fringe survey. The inquiry can be simple or elaborate in style and formal or informal in implementation. The following are examples of survey design:

1. A local union representing employees of a large health insurer located in a Midwestern city surveyed a dozen or more insurance establishments headquartered in the community as part of its bargaining preparations. There was no attempt to distinguish between employers by type of insurance sold. In addition, a large majority of employers were also nonunion and all organized employees were affiliated with different organizations.

The amount of information sought was modest. Wage coverage was limited to the job of claims adjuster, a common job title in the insurance industry. The union was also interested in learning whether dental insurance, sick leave, and a flexible summer work schedule were provided. No attempt was made to obtain details of any existing benefits.

Targeted unions were surveyed by telephone. A representative of each union was contacted and asked the survey questions. Nonunion employers were visited by union members posing as prospective job applicants. The job interview was used as the pretext for gathering information.

2. A local union of nurses commissioned a faculty member of a university-based labor education program to conduct a more formal statewide survey of hospital employment practices involving nurses. The information sought included: (1) starting and maximum wage rates, (2) years required to reach the maximum rate, (3) night shift differentials, (4) premiums for working in intensive care units, (5) weekend work premiums, (6) extra pay for extra work or responsibility, (7) employer contributions toward health care, (8) amount of deductibles on fee-for-service health care, (9) existence of college tuition reimbursement programs, (10) number of vacation days, (11) number of paid legal holidays, and (12) pay provisions for holidays worked. The following nonmonetary work practices were also examined: (1) uses of innovative work scheduling such as 12-hour shifts and weekender programs and (2) ways of coping with shortages of nurses, such as mandatory overtime, use of agency nurses, closing beds, and closing admissions.

A questionnaire containing 16 items was prepared and mailed to 153 hospitals. The documents were coded so respondents could be identified by number of beds and type of operating authority, such as government, private/nonprofit, and private/for profit. Completed questionnaires were returned directly to the university for tabulation. An 82 percent return was achieved which gave the union a significant amount of information to work with.

The questions were printed on both sides of one 8 1/2 by 11 inch sheet of paper. The union paid for paper, postage, and the cost of reproducing the questionnaire. There was no charge for the services of the university staff member who compiled the questionnaire and tallied the results.

Government Sources

Another source of pay and benefit statistics is the Bureau of Labor Statistics (BLS), an agency of the U.S. Department of Labor. Periodic publications include: *Area Wage Surveys* (covering office, professional, technical, maintenance, custodial, and material handling jobs in major metropolitan areas), *Area Wage Summaries* (offering the same coverage as the surveys but in less detail), and *Industry Wage Surveys* (providing wage, benefit, and detailed occupational data).

The monthly *Compensation and Working Conditions* offers details of wage and benefit settlements. Most issues contain articles about major collective bargaining settlements in the private and public sectors. Another monthly publication, *Employment and Earnings*, provides state and area employment and earnings statistics. Finally, BLS collects and publishes earnings and hours worked statistics for 82 service industries and conducts an annual employee benefit survey that is reported in the *Monthly Labor Review* and in various bulletins.

All of the aforementioned publications are available for purchase, some on a subscription basis from the Superintendent of Documents, U.S. Government Printing Office, Washington, DC 20402. BLS offers a free quarterly catalog of publications called *BLS Update* which can be obtained by writing to Publications, Bureau of Labor Statistics, 442 G Street N.W., Washington, DC 20212. Copies of these publications are available in many public, college, and university libraries, particularly those designated as depositories for government documents. Ask a librarian for help.

State governments frequently reproduce portions of BLS statistics pertaining to their respective jurisdictions. In addition, some states periodically survey private and public sector employers on a range of employment and earnings related issues. A state's department of labor or equivalent agency would be the source for this type of information.

There are difficulties in using government data for contract bargaining. Part of the problem is timeliness. Publication of government statistics often lags far behind the date of collection so the information is old and not always relevant. In addition, some statistics are not collected on a regular basis. Finally, data collection typically cover the entire nation or a large geographical region, firms with 1,000 or more employees, and broad industry categories. Consequently, the findings are not always useful in local contract bargaining where the typical employer employs relatively small numbers of workers and operates in only a narrow segment of an industry.

Commercial Publications

At the community level, Chambers of Commerce regularly survey pay and benefits provided by local employers. Typically, these studies include a cross section of all industries represented in the community, including government, and both union and nonunion establishments. Employers who participate in these studies usually receive a copy of the results. If the employer will not share its Chamber of Commerce survey, the union may find a copy at a local public, college, or university library.

Industry and trade associations often study trends in compensation. The results are published in the organization's journal or newsletter. Copies of these publications can often be found in the employer's front office or at the local library.

Finally, reporting services such as *Union Labor Report* and *Collective Bargaining Negotiations and Contracts* reprint BLS statistics. They also report pay and fringe settlements and other terms of employment obtained from nongovernmental sources. These publications are available on a subscription basis from The Bureau of National Affairs, Inc., 9435 Key West Avenue, Rockville, MD 20850 (800) 372-1033. These BNA publications are also available in public, college, and university libraries.

PRESENTING THE PAY
AND BENEFIT COMPARISONS

The bargaining committee's verbal explanation of the wage and fringe comparisons will be easier to understand if accompanied

Exhibit 5-1. Wage and Fringe Comparisons[a]
June, 1993

COMPANY	Our Employer	Employer A	Employer B
LOCATION	Midwest	Northeast	Southeast
UNION	Our Union	Union A	Union B
REOPENING DATE	October 1993	March 1993	May 1993
BASE WAGE RATES FOR KEY JOBS:			
Maintenance Mechanic	$10.64	$11.17	$10.92
Fabricator I	$9.97	$10.56	$10.35
Janitor	$6.60	$6.93	$ 6.90
Negotiated Settlement			
First Yr	(In Negotiation)	4%	4%
VACATIONS	1yr-1wk	1-4yr-1wk	1-4yr-1wk
	2-19yr-2wk	5-14yr-2wk	5-14yr-2wk
	20yr-3wk	15-24yr-3wk	15-19yr-3wk
		25yr-4wk	20yr-4wk
HOLIDAYS	6	7	7
MEDICAL INS	yes	yes	yes
PD BY EMPL'ER	100%	100%	88%
YR DEDUCTIBLE	$150/Person	$250/Single	$100/Single
	$375/Family	$750/Family	$200/Family
PENSION	yes	yes	no
BASIC BENEFIT (Mo			
Per Yr Service)	$12.00	$14.00	
401(k) PLAN	no	no	yes
PD BY EMPL'R			Matching
PROFIT SHARING	no	no	yes
CHILD CARE	no	yes	no

[a]*Source*: Collective Agreements between Our Employer and Our Union, 1991–1993; Employer A and Union A, 1991–1993; Employer B and Union B, 1991–1993.

by a pictorial presentation such as a table. The table should be presented to the employer during one of the early bargaining sessions when compensation issues are being discussed. Union negotiators must also be prepared to explain the choice of comparables and to interpret the data shown in the table.

—*Task*—
Chart the Comparables

Displaying data on the comparables using a tabular format is shown in Exhibit 5-1. The names of the target employers are printed across the horizontal plane and the labels for the wage and fringe data are listed down the vertical axis. The table has a title and is dated with the month, day, and year when the information was collected. The data source is noted at the bottom of the table.

Chapter 6

Presenting Economic Data in Bargaining

The cost of living, productivity, and economic conditions in the employer's industry or trade are topics raised any time the merits of the union's proposals or the employer's offers of pay and fringe improvements are discussed at the bargaining table. The present chapter discusses the importance of this type of information for union negotiators and examines the tasks involved in collecting and presenting economic data.

IMPORTANCE OF ECONOMIC INFORMATION

The cost of living, productivity, and competitive conditions in the marketplace affect both the profitability of the employer and the standard of living of employees. Information about these economic indicators at the time bargaining takes place can be used by the union to document bargaining proposals. For example, when the employer's trade or industry is prospering and growing, and the employer is an important competitor, the bargaining committee cites these facts when arguing for pay and fringe improvements. Similarly, if the cost of living has risen during the life of the terminating contract, the union seeks to restore employees' purchasing power by raising pay levels. A rise in productivity is also used to support pay increases. Conversely, a decline in productivity may cause management to demand a pay freeze or reduction.

The union must also consider the economics of the employer's industry and the local community when deciding whether to take strike action. Walking off the job at a time when the industry and the employer are in recession is unlikely to bring about the desired concessions from management. In fact, the employer saves on labor costs while employees remain off the job. Conversely, the employer is eager to keep employees working in periods of business growth. A strike would be more costly to the employer in terms of lost business and profits.

Economic conditions in the local community are also important in strike planning. An employer seeking to operate the business during a strike would have little trouble finding replacement workers in a community experiencing high unemployment. Strikes are more successful in periods of general labor shortages.

Finally, the union bargaining committee must have economic information on hand in order to refute employer statements about economic conditions. For example, management may claim consumer product and service prices have stabilized and then question the need to continue the Cost of Living Adjustment (COLA) clause. In order to respond intelligently, members of the union bargaining committee must know what actually happened to the cost of living during the life of the old agreement. It would also help to have information on the predicted future movement of consumer prices.

HOW TO USE ECONOMIC INFORMATION

All economic data have limitations and should not be accepted on trust. All facts and figures presented, particularly from nongovernmental sources, should be questioned. Both outdated and biased information must be discarded. However, information should not be discarded solely because it does not support the union's position.

Unfavorable economic data should not be ignored. At the very least, the bargaining committee will gain some insight into the employer's probable position at the bargaining table. However, whether the news is good or bad, the union should resist being drawn into a debate over economics that causes it to stray far away from the merits of the proposals.

EMPLOYER'S INDUSTRY OR TRADE

There are two parts to any investigation of the employer's industry or trade. The first involves gathering information. The second part involves putting the data collected into a form suitable for presentation to company negotiators.

—Task—
Collect Economic Data About the Employer's Industry or Trade

Most of the sources used by business researchers and investors are available to union members interested in learning about economic conditions in the employer's industry or trade. Some information sources can even be accessed by computer. However, the place to begin the data search is in the journal or newsletter published by the employer's industry or trade association.

Trade and Industry Publications

Most industries and trades have employer associations. These organizations routinely report on economic conditions in their respective industries or trades in a journal or newsletter. Reading current and back issues of these publications, the bargaining committee will quickly discover whether the industry or trade is prospering, stagnating, or declining. These publications also discuss current financial and operating problems, the new technologies being introduced, the effects of government policies, and the current status of labor-management relations from a management perspective. Sometimes the focus of an article or report is on one specific company or a particular segment of the industry. In addition, January issues frequently contain annual projections for a host of economic indicators.

Examples of industry and trade publications include *American Machinist, Pulp & Paper, Defense News, Dairyfoods, Agribusiness Worldwide, Commercial Carrier Journal, CommunicationsWeek,* and *Super Marketing.* A reference guide to newsletters in print is the *Oxbridge Directory of Newsletters,* available from Oxbridge Communications, 150 Fifth Avenue, New York, NY 10011. This publication is available in the reference department of many public, college, and university libraries.

Copies of trade and industry publications should not be difficult to locate. Some employers keep back issues in the main office area for use by visitors. The employer might even be willing to circulate copies to a union officer on a regular basis. Alternatively, the union could subscribe on its own, the cost is usually modest. Again, public, college, and university libraries often subscribe to the journals and newsletters of industries and trades operating in their territory.

Additional Sources of Industry and Trade Data

Commercial publishers offer a steady stream of economic information about individual industries and trades. The following is a sampling of publications available in most large public, college, and university libraries:

1. *Industry Surveys* offers continuous economic and investment analysis of 33 industry groupings, covering a total of 65 individual industries. The publisher is Standard & Poor's Corp., 25 Broadway, New York, NY 10004.

2. *The Value Line Investment Survey* provides information about the stocks of individual corporations. The entries, however, are grouped by industry and each grouping is preceded by a one- or two-page summary of the latest industry developments and trends. Performance data on the national economy are also reported. The publisher is Value Line, Inc., 711 Third Avenue, New York, NY 10017.

3. The *New York Times* and *USA Today,* newspapers with national circulations, report on industry and national economic trends. The same is true of publications devoted exclusively to business news such as *Business Week,* the *Wall Street Journal, Forbes,* and the *Journal of Commerce.* All of these publications are available by subscription.

4. The *Business Periodicals Index* can be used to find recently published articles about individual industries, trades, employers, and business executives. The index, updated monthly, references hundreds of newspaper, magazine, and journal articles about business and economic affairs alphabetically by topic. The listing gives the title of the article, the name of the publication it appears in, and the month, date, and page number.

5. The *Daily Labor Report, Labor Relations Week,* and *Construction Labor Report* cover developments in their respective industries and trades on a continuing basis. All are published by The Bureau of National Affairs, Inc., 9435 Key West Avenue, Rockville, MD 20850, (800) 372-1033.

Computer Databases

The local union with a desktop or portable computer and a modem can access electronic libraries. These libraries store databases or collections of data on all sorts of subjects. Some databases contain performance data for industries, trades, and publicly owned corporations. There is usually a fee associated with using electronic libraries. The following are examples of what is available:

1. *News On Line* provides industry and company news prepared by Standard & Poor's. This database is File 132 from Dialog Information Services, 3460 Hillview Avenue, Palo Alto, CA 94304, (800) 334-2564.

2. *Industry Data Sources* offers economic growth forecasts for individual industries. This database is File 189 from Dialog Information Services.

Union Sources

Most national and international unions and some of the larger districts, councils, and other intermediate bodies have staff members responsible for research activities. Some of this research involves collecting and analyzing economic data for the industries and trades within the union's jurisdiction(s).

In addition, trade and industrial departments of the national AFL-CIO publish information about economic and other developments in covered trades and industries. Finally, the AFL-CIO Department of Economic Research is a source of information about the national economy. Address correspondence to the appropriate department at AFL-CIO Building, 815 16th Street, N.W., Washington, DC 20006.

—*Task*—
Chart Data About the Employer's Industry or Trade

Most of the previously cited information sources present information in tabular or graphic form. The bargaining committee need only reproduce what it needs in sufficient quantities for distribution to management and the union membership. In addition, the union leadership can create its own tables or graphics using the data from these same sources. Verbal explanations are easier to understand when accompanied by a pictorial representation. Exhibit 6-1 contains an example of a table comparing firm and industry growth figures.

The bargaining committee must be able to explain the meaning of the numbers on any pictorial exhibit it prepares. The table in Exhibit 6-1 shows the firm and the industry moving in lock step with regard to the percentage growth in sales and profits over the three-year period. However, the employer's profit margin is lower.

Exhibit 6-1. Comparison of Sales and Profits for the Employer and the Industry for Years 1990–1992

| YEAR | EMPLOYER[a] | | INDUSTRY[b] | |
	SALES	PROFIT	SALES	PROFIT
1990	$5,434,000	$1,811,000	$54,340,000	$21,736,000
1991	5,720,000	1,907,000	57,200,000	22,880,000
1992	6,006,000	2,002,000	60,060,000	24,024,000
1990–1992	10.52%	10.54%	10.52%	10.53%
Profit Margin[c]		33.33%		40.00%

[a]*Source*: Employer's Financial Statement.
[b]*Source*: Industry Trade Journal.
[c]The ratio of sales to profit.

Management may put the blame for this on high labor cost, but its own inefficiencies could also be a contributing factor. The union should demand to see other operating data such as workers' compensation cost, frequency of equipment breakdowns, and numbers of scheduling foul-ups.

THE COST OF LIVING

Changes in the cost of living over the life of the existing contract are a measure of how well employees' earnings have kept pace with increases in prices charged for food, clothing, shelter, health care, and other purchases of products and services. When the prices of these items have risen faster than employee take-home pay, the effect is the same as a reduction in pay because each dollar buys less than before. In other words, employees are poorer at the end of the contract period then they were at the start, clearly grounds for a wage/salary increase. The tasks associated with collecting and presenting data on changes in the cost of living are examined below.

—*Task*—
Collect Data on the Cost of Living

Changes in the cost of living are reported as index numbers. The most commonly used index is the Consumer Price Index (CPI), prepared and published by the Bureau of Labor Statistics (BLS). The American Chamber of Commerce Research Association (AC-CRA) also produces an index of consumer prices. The nature of indexing and how one is used to measure changes in consumer prices are discussed below.

BLS Index of Consumer Prices

The BLS index compares the current average price of a fixed market basket of consumer products and services to their average prices in a base period, currently 1982 through 1984 (indexes using 1967 and other base periods are also published). Current prices are reported as a percent of the base, the latter being equal to 100.

If, for example, the index is at 141.0, the overall cost of living has increased 41 percent above the base period.

Actually, BLS publishes two monthly indexes, CPI-U, the All Urban Consumers Index, and CPI-W, the Urban Wage Earners and Clerical Workers Index. The CPI-W is more useful for local union bargaining because the market basket of products and services used in the measurement is more representative of daily purchases by union members. There is an all-city average CPI-W and separate indexes for a number of large cities. CPI-W's are also calculated for geographical regions, both urban and nonurban.

Changes in the CPI-W are reported monthly. News releases summarizing the latest CPI-W statistics are mailed free of charge upon request to any of the BLS's regional offices. The most recent information is available by telephone in some major cities (see listing in telephone directory under "Government").

CPI information is also available via the Department of Labor's Electronic, "Labor News" Bulleting Board System. The data are accessible for downloading free of charge at virtually any time to persons with computers, modems, and communications software. The telephone number for the bulletin board is (202) 219-4784. The "library" containing CPI data is called CPIINFO. Information about the bulletin board can be obtained by telephone at (202) 219-7343.

A comprehensive report of CPI changes is prepared each month and can be purchased from Publications, Bureau of Labor Statistics, 442 G Street, N.W., Washington, DC 20212, (212) 523-1913. The statistical tables and charts are also published in the Current Labor Statistics section of the *Monthly Labor Review*. This publication is available in most public, college, and university libraries or by annual subscription from the Superintendent of Documents, U.S. Government Printing Office, Washington, DC 20402. Another source is the *Union Labor Report*, a weekly reference service published by the Bureau of National Affairs, Inc., 9435 Key West Avenue, Rockville, MD 20850, (800) 372-1033.

Chamber of Commerce Price Index

The American Chamber of Commerce Research Association (ACCRA) publishes *The All-City Cost of Living Index*. Each quarter, the index compares the average prices of 59 consumer goods and services in separate cities around the country with the combined average prices in 268 cities. The data are collected by staff members of local chambers of commerce. The index usually shows a smaller rise in consumer prices than the CPI-W.

The ACCRA index is not used by labor unions because very little is known about the consistency of the measurements. In addition, the sample of goods and services priced is small and may not be representative. Finally, the Chamber of Commerce does not have the same impeccable reputation as the Bureau of Labor Statistics.

—Task—
Chart Data on Consumer Prices

Data showing the change in employees' purchasing power during the life of the terminating agreement can be put in tabular form. A sample format is presented in Exhibit 6-2. Average earnings of employees (wages/salaries plus fringes) in current dollars in each contract year are recorded in the first column of the table. The second column contains the corresponding CPI-W index numbers. Real earnings for each year, the amount needed to preserve purchasing power, are presented in the third column. Real earnings are determined by multiplying average current dollar earnings by the percentage change in the CPI-W.

Exhibit 6-2. Actual Earnings and Earnings Needed to Preserve Purchasing Power Contract Period March 1990 Through March 1992

Year	EARNINGS[a] (Current $)	CPI-W[b] (1982–84 = 100)	EARNINGS (Real $)
1990	$12.64	127.1	$12.64
1991	13.20	133.0	13.28
1992	13.46	137.0	13.625

[a]*Source*: Employer's payroll records.
[b]*Source*: Bureau of Labor Statistics.

Again, the union must explain what the numbers in the table mean. The data in Exhibit 6-2 show average take-home earnings in column one increasing by 6.48 percent over the life of the contract ($13.46–$12.64 / $12.64 = 0.0648 or 6.48 percent). Consumer prices, on the other hand, increased by 7.79 percent, so employees lost buying power. If take-home earnings had kept pace with changes in the CPI, earnings in real dollars would have increased by 7.79 percent as well ($13.625–$12.64 / $12.64 = 0.0779 or 7.79 percent). Thus, a proposal in 1992 to increase earnings by 1.2 percent would only restore employees' purchasing power to 1990 levels.

Management may claim the union's findings are misleading because many employees have paid-up home mortgages and grown families and, as a consequence, are not greatly affected by increases in the cost of living. The union, in turn, should remind management about the younger employees who are just starting their families and spending most of their earnings for food, clothing, and shelter. Moreover, health care cost, one of the fastest growing components of the CPI-W, places a heavy burden on all age groups.

—Task—
Bargain a Cost of Living Adjustment (COLA) Clause

What can the union do to protect its members if consumer prices are expected to rise during the term of the new agreement? An across-the-board pay increase in an amount equal to the anticipated rise in the CPI-W would result in the greatest gain. An alternative is a COLA clause. Total earnings rise less with a COLA clause because pay adjustments are made only after consumer prices have increased. By contrast, regular pay increases take effect immediately upon contract ratification.

The components of the COLA clause must be clearly stated in the labor agreement. The following are key bargaining issues:

1. What index is used to measure price changes? The selection should be clearly written in the agreement; for example, "CPI-W, U.S. City Averages, All Items, as reported by the BLS, 1982–1984 = 100."

2. How frequently will the changes in consumer prices relative to wages/salaries be measured? The shorter the period, the

more frequent the adjustments and the more money received. Typically, measurements are taken on either an annual, semiannual, or quarterly basis. The exact dates when measurements will be made are written in the contract.

3. What is the adjustment factor, or how much must the CPI-W rise before employees receive the pay supplement? It is customary for wages to rise in single penny-per-hour increments, and salaries by increments of one dollar-per-week, for each point or multiple point rise in the index. Ideally, the percentage wage/salary increase should equal the percentage increase in the CPI-W.

4. Will pay increases resulting from changes in the CPI be folded into the base wage/salary rate? The ideal answer is in the affirmative.

5. Will there be a floor under wages/salaries in the event the CPI falls? Again, the preferred outcome is the establishment of a floor.

6. Will there be an upper limit or cap on the amount of automatic pay increases allowable in response to increases in the CPI? A negative answer is desirable.

7. Will there be gaps or corridors during which COLA adjustments are not made? This provision works as follows: COLA wage adjustments occur until a certain level is reached; they are discontinued in the gap or corridor, but resume once the CPI rises above the top limit of the corridor.

8. Will COLA increases be included in the wage/salary rates used to determine holiday pay, vacation pay, overtime pay, and other similar pay-related benefits? Ideally, the answer will be in the affirmative.

PRODUCTIVITY

The terms "productivity" and "production" are sometimes confused. Production is the total quantity of goods or services produced. By contrast, productivity refers to the efficient utilization of the work force. Productivity measures the amount of labor required to produce a given quantity of product or provide a specific service. The more products produced or services performed and sold using the same or less labor, the greater the employer's profits. In general, work force productivity is affected by factors such as the amount of labor-saving technology in use, management's ability to organize production, and the skill level of the work force. The quality of the products manufactured or services delivered is closely related to the productivity factor.

Collecting information about productivity is important for several reasons. If the quantity of products or services sold has increased with no change in the number of employees used, the union can claim a share of the added profit in the form of higher pay and better fringes. If this increase in earnings exceeds the rise in consumer prices, employees have gained purchasing power and can afford to buy more products and services such as boats or additional trips to Las Vegas. In other words, the standard of living of employees and their families has improved.

In recent years, productivity has become a management issue at the bargaining table. Many employers, seeking to reverse a trend of declining productivity, have introduced new work methods, employment rules and practices, and forms of employee compensation. In some workplaces, bonuses tied directly to improvements in productivity have become part of the pay package (see Chapter 15, Employee-Management Cooperation).

—*Task*—
Collect Productivity Data

Data on productivity trends for the national economy and individual industries are readily available from government sources. Individual employer productivity must be calculated directly.

Published Sources of Data

The Bureau of Labor Statistics (BLS) measures productivity changes for the U.S., economy and for selected industries on a quarterly basis. They are published in report form and in the *Monthly Labor Review*. The industries surveyed are selective and the statistics are not always current, but a telephone call to the nearest BLS regional office can sometimes produce the required data (see listing in telephone directory under "Government"). The *Union Labor Report* publishes productivity data as part of its reference service. As noted earlier, it is available on subscription from the Bureau of National Affairs, Inc.

Productivity data are much harder to obtain in the public sector because measurement is so difficult. Market forces that set prices in the private sector do not operate in the public sector, so it is difficult to assign values to many governmental services. For example, the general public hopes the police, fire, and medical emergency services are never used, but they want them available in the event they are needed. Again, the BLS is the source for data on government productivity.

Presenting Productivity Data from Published Sources. Exhibit 6-3 illustrates one way of presenting productivity data found in published sources. The table presents productivity indexes for two industries. These productivity indexes, published by BLS, are constructed in the same manner as the Consumer Price Index.

If the bargaining committee uses a table similar to the one in Exhibit 6-3, it must be prepared to explain the numbers to management. In the example, productivity in the paper industry increased 1 percent between 1989 and 1991 (128.3–127.0 / 127.0 = 0.010 or 1.0 percent). On the other hand, grocery store productivity declined by over 1 percent during the same period. When both

---

**Exhibit 6-3. Productivity Indexes for Two Industries[a]
for the Period 1989 Through 1991**

Year	Paper, Paperboard & Pulp Mills (1982 = 100)	Grocery Stores (1982 = 100)
1989	127.0	90.6
1990	127.9	89.5
1991	128.3	89.6

[a]*Source*: Bureau of Labor Statistics.

firm and industry data are available, the yearly percentage changes in both sets of data can also be compared.

Sources of Data on Employer Productivity

The Bureau of Labor Statistics does not measure productivity changes at the local factory or office level. The union bargaining committee must do this on its own. It can either work with the employer to develop a procedure for measuring productivity or select one of a number of ready-made productivity gainsharing plans available commercially. All of these prepackaged plans measure productivity by dividing employer outputs of products and services by the input of labor used in production. Some measures are in dollar terms while others are in physical terms. All provide a formula for distributing some of the gain among employees in the form of bonuses (the rest remains with management). The better known plans go by such names as Scanlon, Rucker, Improshare, and Multifactor. The national or international union should be contacted for more detailed information about productivity gainsharing plans (see also Chapter 15, Employee-Management Cooperation).

COMPUTING ENTERPRISE PRODUCTIVITY

A local union bargaining with a local employer is most interested in measuring and displaying the rate and direction of productivity changes in the immediate workplace during the life of the terminating agreement. One simple method for calculating changes in yearly productivity is demonstrated below. In addition to the written explanation, the data are put in tabular form. The union bargaining committee should consider using similar pictorial aids when discussing productivity at the bargaining table.

—Task—
Measure and Chart Changes in Employer Productivity

The method used to calculate annual changes in productivity in the following example relies on the dollar values of sales (output) and payroll (input). However, when comparing the change in sales dollars between two years, it is hard to know whether the increase or decrease is due to productivity or inflation. Therefore, the annual sales figures must be adjusted for inflation.

Assume the employer's actual sales in 1991 and 1992 were $5,720,000 and $6,006,000 respectively. These figures can be converted to constant 1982–1984 dollars by using the CPI-W as a deflator. The annual CPI-W, U.S. City Average, was 134.3 in 1991 and 138.2 in 1992. Each year's sales figure is then divided by the appropriate index number: 1991 = $4,259,121 ($5,720,000 / 134.3 × 100 = $4,259,121); 1992 = $4,345,875. A table showing these results is presented in Exhibit 6-4.

With the sales figures adjusted for inflation, the change in productivity can be measured. Assuming a payroll cost of $1,716,000 in each year, the sales per dollar of payroll in 1992 was $2.53 ($4,345,875 / $1,716,000 = $2.53) compared with $2.48 in 1991. Consequently, productivity increased by 2 percent between the two years ($2.53–$2.48 / $2.48 = 0.02 or 2 percent). In other words, the quantity of goods and services produced increased while labor cost remained constant. If all other business expenses remained the same, the employer's profit increased by 2 percent. A table showing the growth in productivity is presented in Exhibit 6-5.

Wage/salary increases tied to productivity have the added virtue of being noninflationary. If, in the preceding example, the union had bargained a 2 percent wage increase in 1992 and payroll dollars grew to $1,750,320, the output per dollar of payroll would remain at $2.48. This means the employer does not have to raise product or service prices to offset the higher labor cost and maintain its profit margin.

Exhibit 6-4. Sales Adjusted for Inflation
Years 1991 and 1992

YEAR	SALES[a] (Actual $)	CPI-W [b] (1982–84 = 100)	SALES (Constant $)
1991	$5,720,000	134.3	$4,259,121
1992	$6,006,000	138.2	$4,345,875

[a]*Source*: Company Financial Statement.
[b]*Source*: Bureau of Labor Statistics.

Exhibit 6-5. Change in Productivity
Years 1991 and 1992

YEAR	SALES (Constant $)	PAYROLL	OUTPUT PER $ OF PAYROLL	PRODUCTIVITY (Percent)
1991	$4,259,121	$1,716,000	$2.48	
1992	$4,345,875	$1,716,000	$2.53	+2.0

Part II

The Bargaining Process

Chapter 7

The Law of
Contract Bargaining

The practice of contract bargaining in the United States is governed by both law and custom. The law prescribes the rules of fair play for unions and employers when dealing with each other at the bargaining table. Examples of bargaining procedures include face-to-face meetings, inflated proposals, secrecy, deadlines, caucuses, and the exercise of power. Bargaining behavior is considered in Chapters 9 through 13.

The present chapter examines the Taft-Hartley Act[1] obligation of private sector employers and unions to bargain in good faith. The Act's requirements for notifying the employer and the public of the union's intent to renegotiate the contract are explained in Chapter 1, Organizational Activities. The Taft-Hartley rules governing strikes and picketing are examined in Chapter 13, Strikes and the Strike Alternative. In addition, local public sector bargaining and the law is covered in Chapter 14.

The purpose of the legal information provided in this chapter is to acquaint members of the bargaining committee with their

---

[1]The Taft-Hartley Act is the popular title for the Labor Management Relations Act of 1947 as Amended (LMRA). For a more comprehensive review of the Taft-Hartley Act requirements, see Bruce Feldacker, *Labor Guide to Labor Law*, 3rd ed. (Englewood Cliffs, N.J.: Prentice-Hall, 1990).

105

rights and responsibilities as participants in the bargaining process. The discussion is not exhaustive and union negotiators with questions about their duty to bargain or that of the employer are advised to consult with a competent attorney before taking action.

OBLIGATION TO BARGAIN

Sections 8(a) and (b) of the Taft-Hartley Act describe employer and union behaviors that are unfair labor practices (ULPs). A refusal by an employer to bargain in good faith with the certified bargaining agent of its employees (the union) is a Section 8(a)(5) violation. Refusal by a union to bargain with the employer is an 8(b)(3) violation.

The requirements for good faith bargaining are stated in Section 8(d) of the Act. In addition, there is a body of interpretive rulings of Section 8(d) made by the National Labor Relations Board (NLRB) and the federal courts.

Rules of Conduct for Bargaining

Good-faith bargaining is defined in Section 8(d) of the Act as the obligation of the employer and the union to (1) meet at reasonable times; (2) confer in good faith with respect to wages, hours, and other terms and conditions of employment; and (3) execute a written contract incorporating the terms of agreement, if requested by one of the parties. The duty to bargain does not require either the employer or the union to "agree to a proposal" or "make a concession." A more detailed description of each of these requirements follows.

Meet at Reasonable Times

Section 8(d) does not explain what "reasonable times" are, but the intent of the law is to encourage peaceful resolution of disputes. Unions and employers cannot reach agreement if they do not meet and bargain. Consequently, a union bargaining committee should never refuse an employer request for a bargaining session even when the prospects for accomplishing meaningful results appear bleak.

Similarly, premature breakdowns in bargaining activities are contrary to the Act's objectives. Bargaining committee members must never walk out in the middle of a session no matter how unreasonable the employer's position appears to be at the moment. Leaving the conference table in this manner is also difficult to explain to the membership, particularly if bargaining breaks down as a consequence. The employer, of course, will deny having said or done anything to cause the union representatives to leave the meeting room.

Confer in Good Faith

The term "confer good faith" is not defined in Section 8(d) of the Taft-Hartley Act either. The NLRB and the courts decide questions of good and bad faith on a case-by-case basis by examining the behavior pattern of the charged party. For example, an employer's reluctance to counter union proposals may be viewed as evidence of "hard" as opposed to "unfair" bargaining if it is unaccompanied by delaying tactics or other attempts to stall efforts to reach agreement.

In general, the employer and the union are bargaining in good faith when they make an honest effort to reach agreement by carefully considering each other's proposals and advancing counterproposals of their own. One reason the union comes to the conference table with a long list of inflated proposals is to have something to concede in this atmosphere of give and take. The following are examples of bad faith bargaining by employers, but unions engaging in similar sorts of practices would also be at risk:

1. Management engages in surface bargaining, that is, doing little more than going through the motions. Examples of surface bargaining behavior include (1) refusing to justify position with facts and proofs, (2) refusing to make counteroffers in an attempt to reconcile differences with union proposals, (3) declining to bargain exclusively with the union committee while appealing directly to employees for support of the employer's position, (4) refusing to budge

e status quo by putting forth only the old contract,
ing contract terms on a take it or leave it basis, and
cting the union's total position out of hand without
some alternative.

2. Management refuses to provide information relevant for bargaining when requested to do so by the union. See Chapter 2, Developing Bargaining Proposals, for a discussion of the union's right to information in the possession of the employer.

3. Management's demands foreclose future bargaining. Examples of predictably unacceptable demands include (1) an excessively long or short contract term, and (2) management prerogatives so broad that the union is left with no rights at all.

4. Management engages in delaying tactics. Examples of such tactics include (1) showing a lack of diligence in scheduling or attending bargaining sessions, (2) taking excessively long periods of time (three and one-half months in one case) to respond to a union's request for written counterproposals, (3) submitting new proposals after several months of bargaining, and (4) raising new issues after agreement has been reached.

5. Management's actions threaten the continuation of the bargaining process itself. Examples of disruptive behavior include (1) employer representatives acting as if they are sovereigns graciously coming to hear the petition of their subjects rather than dealing with the union bargaining committee as equals, and (2) making unilateral changes in employment terms and conditions while bargaining is in progress.

6. Management commits unfair labor practices that are per se violations of Section 8(a) of the Taft-Hartley Act. Examples of such practices include (1) threats to close the business or discharge strikers, and (2) discriminatory layoffs made in response to the union's bargaining position.

Subject Matter

Section 8(d) requires good faith bargaining with regard to wages, hours, and terms and conditions of employment. The NLRB divides the subject matter of bargaining into three categories: mandatory, permissive, and nonbargainable. These distinctions are important for determining whether deadlock or total impasse in bargaining exists and if any subsequent strike or lockout is legal.

Mandatory Subjects

Mandatory subjects can be bargained to impasse, the union can strike, and the employer can engage in an offensive lockout. Compensation in all forms is a mandatory subject of bargaining. Compensation includes wages/salaries, pensions, stock purchase plans, productivity and profit sharing plans, insurance, signing bonuses, and employee discounts. Other examples of mandatory subjects are pay classifications and progression, hours of work, overtime, seniority, promotion, transfer, union shop, a no-strike clause, discipline, a mandatory drug testing program, and the effects of a plant closure or removal of work. The decision to close or remove work can itself be subject to bargaining if it is based on labor cost.

Permissive Subjects

Permissive subjects are considered too remote from the employment relationship to be a right of either the employer or the union. These voluntary topics can be discussed at the bargaining table, but cannot be carried to impasse. Consequently, strikes and lockouts resulting from deadlocks over permissive subjects are illegal. Some examples of voluntary topics are benefits for retirees, the employer's decision to close a plant for reasons other than labor cost, contents of a strike settlement agreement, preemployment drug testing, choice of union bargaining representatives, and procedures for employee ratification of the settlement.

Nonbargainable Subjects

Some subjects are nonbargainable because they are either included or excluded from the contract by federal labor law. For example, a provision recognizing the union as the exclusive bargaining agent must be included in a contract when requested by the union. However, a recognition clause is binding for only three years even if the agreement itself runs for a longer period. A procedure for handling grievances is also obligatory.

Some topics are considered inappropriate for bargaining. Examples of prohibited topics include (1) pay, hours, and conditions of employment for nonbargaining unit employees including supervisors, (2) pay for work not performed, (3) the closed shop and most other forms of union security when prohibited by state law, (4) the right to discharge for union activity, (5) a "hot cargo" clause prohibiting the employer from handling goods of other businesses with which the union has a dispute, and (6) a provision requiring employees to violate any existing employment laws.

Written Agreement

Section 8(d) also requires that agreements reached at the bargaining table be put in writing if requested by either party. Agreements must also have fixed terms. In addition, pay and other contract provisions can be written to permit reopenings to adjust wages/salaries and other terms during the lifetime of the collective agreement, usually by mutual consent of the parties.

Obligation to Compromise or Reach Agreement

Employers do not have to make concessions or agree to any union proposals. Congress, in passing the Taft-Hartley legislation, believed unions and employers would eventually reach agreement on the terms and conditions of employment if they acted in good faith, and were encouraged to work out their differences by exchanging proposals and offers. In practice, however, employers with no interest in reaching agreement can take advantage of these features of the law to drag out the proceedings until either the union feels compelled to strike or employees choose to work without a contract.

Duration of the Duty to Bargain

The existence of a signed agreement does not necessarily end the employer's duty to bargain. The obligation may continue even after a business is sold or the employer files for bankruptcy.

Continuing Duty to Bargain

The duty of the employer to bargain over a mandal continues during the life of the labor agreement. However, the current contract must be silent on the topic and the matter must not have been discussed during the previous period of bargaining. Mandatory subjects meeting these tests must be bargained to impasse. At impasse, the employer can act and the union is free to strike unless the contract contains a "no-strike" clause.

Successor Employers

An employer who purchases the business of another must also recognize and bargain with the existing union. A successor employer is not bound by the previous owner's labor contract, but must bargain with the union over a new one. In general, a successorship is established if the new employer has taken over the business of another employer, retained a majority of the former employer's work force, and continued operations in the same industry.

Bankruptcy

An employer's duty to bargain may not end even during bankruptcy. The Bankruptcy Act Amendments of 1984 limit the employer's right to unilaterally cancel a labor agreement after declaring bankruptcy. Approval of the bankruptcy court is needed and can be granted only if (1) the parties have bargained to impasse over any changes in the existing agreement demanded by the employer, (2) the union has rejected "necessary" contract modification without good cause, and (3) other affected parties in the bankruptcy, such as creditors, have also made sacrifices. The existing contract remains in force while these conditions are being met.

ENFORCING THE DUTY TO BARGAIN

The local union bargaining committee has three courses of action to follow when it believes the employer has broken its bargaining obligation. First, the employer may be asked to voluntarily comply with the requirements of Sections 8(a)(5) and 8(d) of the Taft-Hartley Act. Second, formal ULP charges may be filed against the employer. Finally, a ULP strike can be instituted. These actions can be implemented separately or undertaken simultaneously.

Achieving Voluntary Compliance

Sometimes threatening to complain to the NLRB is enough to dissuade an employer from continuing to violate the law. Responsible employers do not relish the prospect of litigation nor the accompanying bad publicity. Even employers who are consciously embarked on a course of bad-faith bargaining want to be scrupulous in compliance with the letter of the law, particularly where there is little or no advantage to be gained from not doing so.

Filing Unfair Labor Practice Charges

The union choosing to file ULP charges should write or telephone the nearest regional or subregional office of the NLRB (see listing in telephone directory under "Government") to request a copy of Form 501, the standard form for filing ULP charges. Filling out the form gives the union the opportunity to record those facts about the employer's conduct it believes violates the duty to bargain. NLRB personnel will help the union complete the form upon request.

The union should return the original and four copies of the complaint form to the NLRB office in the region where the unfair labor practice occurred within six months of the date of the alleged violation(s). The union must also mail a copy of the complaint to the employer within 10 days of submitting the original to the NLRB.

The regional NLRB office investigates the charges and if they are valid, schedules a hearing. Each ULP complaint is judged on its merits after consideration of all the circumstances surrounding the employer's behavior, including whether other violations of the Taft-Hartley Act have occurred. Individual actions appearing harmless when considered separately could, when taken together, constitute a breach of the bargaining duty. The outcome of the hearing at the regional level can be appealed by the losing party to the full

NLRB sitting in the District of Columbia and from there through the federal courts of appeals and the U.S. Supreme Court.

Seeking redress from the NLRB and the courts can be a time-consuming process, taking years, and the remedy provided is generally meager. For example, an employer found guilty of bad-faith bargaining is simply ordered back to the conference table to try again. There are no provisions for fines or punitive money damages. Tougher penalties are needed and unions have been working to change the law. In the meantime, local unions should continue to file charges since the publicity surrounding the action can sometimes turn the local community against a recalcitrant employer.

The Unfair Labor Practice Strike

The ULP strike is another form of response to bad-faith bargaining by the employer. A ULP strike is a protected activity under Taft-Hartley, which means strikers are entitled to reinstatement to their former jobs once the dispute is resolved.

A ULP strike is risky because the union cannot be sure the charge(s) will stick. The NLRB and the courts make the final determination on whether an unfair labor practice was committed, but this does not usually occur until after the strike is underway. If the ruling goes against the union, the strike is illegal. Employees face discharge for participating in illegal strikes.

BARGAINING THE FIRST CONTRACT

The Taft-Hartley Act confers a number of rights and responsibilities on a union after it has won a representation election. These rights include:

1. Upon certification, the union must notify the employer of its interest in bargaining over a first contract (see Chapter 1, Organizational Activities, for an explanation of the notification procedure). The employer is then obligated to meet with the union bargaining committee and bargain in good

faith over mandatory subjects in accordance with Section 8(d) of the Act.

The union has one year from the date of certification to negotiate an agreement. Afterwards, the employer may cease to bargain if it has a good faith doubt, based on proof, of the union's continued majority status among employees in the bargaining unit. If, however, the employer is charged with committing an unfair labor practice during the year, and the NLRB upholds the charge, the year requirement for bargaining begins again from the date of the infraction.

2. Once the union has won the representation election, the employer cannot unilaterally change the mandatory terms of employment without bargaining with the union. This is the case even when objections to the election are pending and the union has not yet been certified.[2]

3. The union has a right to handle grievances for employees even in the absence of a collective agreement. The right to grieve is a "concerted activity" under Section 7 of the Act. The union can grieve employer personnel policies at the same time it is trying to change them at the bargaining table. Grievances must also be filed on behalf of employees who have been disciplined, discharged, or discriminated against for their union activities. These sorts of grievances should also be brought directly to the bargaining table for resolution.

---

[2]See David A. Rosenfeld, *Offensive Bargaining* (Silver Spring, Md.: George Meany Center for Labor Studies, 1992) 22–23.

Chapter 8

Bargaining Activities

The legal framework for contract bargaining was presented in Chapter 7. The rules, activities, tasks, and communications involved in the process of reaching agreement are considered in this chapter. Actually, two different bargaining approaches are discussed. The first is the traditional model featuring exchanges of proposals, arguments, offers, deadlines, and tests of strength leading to compromise settlements. The second method relies on union-management cooperation and group problem solving techniques to advance both the separate and mutual interests of the parties. Advocates refer to this latter approach as interest-based bargaining, win-win negotiations, and *Getting To Yes*[1] among other labels.

Traditional bargaining is discussed first. Procedures for reviewing and ratifying settlement terms are also provided. Next, the interest-based or win-win approach is presented. Tools, tactics, and techniques associated with the two bargaining methods are provided in Chapter 9, The Local Union Negotiator's Toolbox.

TRADITIONAL BARGAINING

Traditional bargaining has "rules of play" and evolves through a series of phases, each with its own unique set of tasks. The type

---

[1] A pioneering work in the field is Roger Fisher and William Ury, *Getting To Yes: Negotiating Agreements Without Giving In* (New York: Penguin Books, 1983).

115

of information communicated also changes at each stage of the process.

The Rules of Play

Practitioners of traditional bargaining must follow certain customs. While not "rules" in any formal sense, breaches by either the employer or the union can complicate the process of reaching agreement. These rules of play are presented below.

Rule: Positions announced at the outset of bargaining are not what the parties expect on settlement.

The employer and the union adopt extreme but not fixed positions at the outset of bargaining. Typically, the union asks for a lot more than it expects to receive. Similarly, the employer demands preservation of the status quo, or worse, concessions. Both parties know their initial positions are bargainable and will be modified.

The author was privy to a local bargaining situation where management's failure to follow the "initial position" rule complicated the settlement process. The employer announced its maximum wage and fringe offer three and one-half months prior to the termination date of the existing contract. It was a generous package and would become effective immediately, but it was rejected by the union bargaining committee after management refused to consider proposed changes in work rules and practices.

Bargaining resumed and agreement was eventually reached on most of the union's protective language proposals, but management refused to improve upon its original offer of compensation. At first, the union bargaining committee assumed management would behave as it always had and increase the money offer at the very last moment. When this did not happen, the committee feared accepting the same money offer it had rejected months earlier would be viewed as a defeat by the membership. A strike ensued while the parties searched for a way out of their dilemma. The impasse lasted 13 weeks. It ended only after intervention by state and federal mediators and the international union. The international representative engaged in hard bargaining with both the employer and the local union leadership to end the dispute. The settlement extended the term of the new contract by one year and added several fringe improvements that were scheduled to begin in the final period.

Rule: True bargaining positions and priorities are kept concealed from the opposition.

The employer conceals information about its true bargaining priorities, limits, and deadlines because it fears that such knowledge would give the union some unspecified advantage. The union feels compelled to be secretive too for purposes of self-defense. Consequently, the parties spend much of their time at the conference table trying to learn something about each other's true objectives and priorities.

Rule: Arrival of a deadline motivates the parties to settle.

The deadline is the expiration date and hour of the terminating labor agreement. The employer does not usually deal with the union's top priority proposals, typically pay and fringes, until the deadline. Management believes that doing otherwise gives the appearance of being eager for a settlement and makes the union even more intransigent. Consequently, the union committee should also avoid making major concessions until the arrival of the deadline.

Rule: Outcomes are determined by the relative power positions of the parties.

The union "wins" if it is, or is perceived by management to be, able to impose a penalty or cost on the employer for failing to reach agreement. Further, this penalty must be greater than the cost to the employer of reaching agreement. An impotent union is forced to accept the dictates of the employer. When both the union and the employer are powerful, bargaining ends in compromise.

The union's principal means of inflicting real costs on an employer is the strike. In recent years, some unions have tried other forms of sanctions such as corporate campaigns and workplace actions. The relative bargaining positions of the union and employer are influenced by economic conditions, membership solidarity, community, and political factors (see Chapter 13, Strikes and the Strike Alternative).

Sequence of Bargaining Table Activities and Communications

In addition to the procedural rules, there are a series of activities characteristic of traditional bargaining. While tasks overlap, some are more important during the early sessions, others take over in the middle period, and still others dominate in the closing rounds. Further, the nature of the communications between the opposing sides changes along with the tasks being performed.

Early Sessions

Union and employer representatives typically meet for the first time within one to two weeks following delivery of the required reopening notice (see Chapter 1, Organizational Activities, for a discussion of notice requirements). Starting earlier does not pay because the deadline is too far away to create the sense of urgency needed to stimulate serious discussion. Sometimes the employer requests an earlier than normal starting date. When this occurs, the union should propose setting an artificial deadline, perhaps a maximum of four or five weeks away, after which the early round of talks ends.

The parties may meet only once a week during this early period. Each meeting is also fairly short, often no more than three or four hours in length.

The adversarial nature of traditional bargaining is reflected in the seating arrangement. From the first session onward, management and union representatives sit facing each other across what is usually an oblong-shaped conference table.

Both parties present brief opening statements at the first session. For example, the union might speak generally of the income and security concerns of its members and pledge to work with management to achieve a settlement that is fair to all parties. Management, in turn, can be expected to make a speech about the difficulties the employer is facing because of the competitiveness of the industry, the union's restrictive work rules, and excessively high labor costs. They may also request confidentiality on all matters discussed at the conference table. The union should remind management of its own past noncompliance in this area.

The union committee introduces its list of proposals and offers arguments in support of each one. All requests are described as top priority, "must have," items. However, the employer is unlikely to be overly impressed because, as noted above, a certain amount of misrepresentation of the union's true position is expected.

The employer may have its own list of demands to announce. These represent management's needs and are not necessarily direct responses to union proposals even though there may be some overlap. Management's agenda can run the gambit from making only a small number of work rule modifications to demands for major give-backs or concessions on employee pay, fringes, and rights.

—*Task*—
Argue the Union's Case

The bargaining committee uses these early meetings to justify the need for each and every change being sought in the terms of employment. The employer can always be expected to question the need for change with deprecating comments such as, "We're not aware of any problem" and "Your proposal doesn't enhance our agreement." The union, of course, should respond similarly to management's demands.

The arguments presented are the ones developed at the time the bargaining agenda was being prepared. Included as well are all of the supporting statistics and facts collected, analyzed, and charted during the preparations period. These data could be financial, industry, productivity, cost of living, and wage and benefit comparisons. Reference may also be made to old grievance and arbitration cases, workplace policies that have had detrimental effects on the work force, and provisions in other contracts viewed as precedent setting for the bargaining unit. For more discussion see Chapter 2, Developing Bargaining Proposals, Chapter 3, Bargaining Proposals and Priorities, and Chapter 11, Bargaining Contract Language. Other tools used to sell the union position are discussed in the next chapter.

—*Task*—
Clarify the Union's Position

The employer listens to the union's arguments and explanations and generally responds with questions in an attempt to gain additional insights. This gives the union an opportunity to further explain its position on individual agenda items. The following is an example of this type of exchange:

> U: "The clause now reads: 'Whenever practicable, scheduled overtime will be assigned to the employee who has worked on the job during the week in which the overtime is scheduled.' We want to substitute 'whenever overtime is scheduled' for 'whenever practicable.'"
>
> E: "Aren't there cases when it would not be practicable?"
>
> U: "Yes."
>
> E: "That's what the language is for."
>
> U: "When the person doesn't come, then you can do what you want."
>
> E: "This is what we want."
>
> U: "Say it."

Middle Sessions

With four to five weeks remaining until the contact expiration deadline, union and company representatives begin to actively search for areas of compromise. The union typically waits for management to make the first move, but could initiate the action on its own. The risks are minimal because true bargaining positions are not exposed nor are commitments made to any actual settlement terms.

The number of weekly meetings doubles and may even triple. Sessions also last longer and provision should be made for lunch and supper breaks of reasonable length. In addition, rest periods are scheduled during each session and, if feasible, coffee or other refreshments could be available.

—*Task*—
Investigate the Potential for Compromise

The dialogue of exploration takes the form of suggestions, questions, thinking out loud, making analogies, and hinting at possible concessions. The following are samples of employer statements indicating where movement is possible:

1. "We can do something on wages and the vacation schedule, but we are very negative on continuing COLA. Setting up anything outside of our control is distasteful to us."
2. "We are not inflexible on items #1 and #2 (on the union's list of proposals). You raise some good points. Your language would hurt us, but we need to work something out."

The employer also prepares the union for possible disappointment through exchanges similar to the following:

U: "What about our sick leave pay proposal?"
E: "Absolutely not! We can't do it!"

The bargaining committee must prepare in advance for the task of identifying potential settlement terms. This means setting priorities and giving early thought to where concessions on union proposals might be made in order to gain acceptance from the employer (see Chapters 3 and 11). For example, having anticipated the employer's sentiments about uncertainties surrounding COLA clauses, the union is ready with sympathy and a possible solution: "We could cap COLA. You cannot get much closer to knowing your costs."

—Task—
Communicate Needs and Priorities

The various arguments made in behalf of the union's proposals during the earlier sessions are repeated. In addition, the union may now threaten to strike in connection with some proposals. Nonverbal communications also become important in this period. Threats and nonverbal communications are examined in Chapter 9.

Closing Rounds

In the final week or two before the contact expiration deadline, union and employer negotiators commit to particular outcomes. Typically, the employer opens the round by announcing its first comprehensive offer of mainly protective language terms. Relatively lower priority protective language items are dealt with first in order to avoid an impasse before the arrival of the deadline. The most controversial pay and fringe issues are settled last. While all of this is going on, the union has the additional task of keeping track of its original proposals and the employer's changing responses.

The parties meet almost continuously during this period, holding both day and night sessions. Breaks are taken periodically for meals and sleep.

—*Task*—
Structure Settlement Terms

The union can expect the employer to proceed cautiously. Management will respond to the union's proposals in a series of offers and counteroffers. Each offer will contain a mix of outright rejection of most union proposals, potential agreement on other proposed items if changes can be made, and specific terms on other proposals. Over time, the quality and quantity of terms offered improves. For example, previously rejected proposals are accepted. By the arrival of the deadline, the employer's total offer is disclosed.

The union bargaining committee responds to the employer's offers by encouraging management to do even more. This is accomplished by asking questions, making suggestions, and repeating many of the same persuasive arguments and threats advanced in the earlier sessions.

Concession making becomes a necessity for the union in this period as well. The bargaining committee caucuses frequently to reexamine its position and to decide what concessions to make and when and how to make them (see Chapter 9).

The union responds to management offers with counterproposals. The union may simply restate its original proposal. Alternatively, the union might try to package proposals in new ways designed to increase their appeal. A counterproposal can also contain a concession.

The offers, proposals, counteroffers, and counterproposals continue until the deadline hour. At 11:59 P.M., with midnight as the deadline, the parties make a last ditch effort to package enough of the pay, fringe, and protective language items remaining to produce a comprehensive agreement (see Chapter 9).

—*Task*—
Keep Track of Original Proposals

The union must not lose track of its top priority proposals during the rush to reach agreement by the contract expiration deadline. Sacrifices should be made consciously and not as the result of oversights. To maintain control, bargaining committee members should make it a practice to inventory both settled and unsettled agenda items when they caucus during this period. The secretary's notes of the bargaining sessions can help with this task (see Chapter 9). A well maintained bargaining book also makes it easier to review the status of individual proposals. See Chapter 3 for a description of the bargaining book.

Communicating With the Membership During Bargaining

The bargaining committee must maintain communications with the membership during the time it is meeting with management. Members have a right to know what is going on at the bargaining table. Moreover, an informed membership can respond in a more positive way if questioned by the employer, their neighbors, or friends. Secrecy breeds suspicion and distrust and can work to the disadvantage of the union leadership.

—*Task*—
Keep the Membership Informed

The bargaining committee should report on the bargaining position and conduct of the employer at regular monthly or special membership meetings and in the local newsletter. Information should be forthcoming even when bargaining is proceeding smoothly. There is no point in having angry members if a satisfactory settlement is close at hand.

The membership should also know when bargaining is tough. They have cause for anger and should be encouraged to express it. Sometimes progress at the bargaining table is influenced by the employer's assessment of employee support for the union's bargaining agenda. Further, after being kept in the dark for months about a difficult bargaining situation, rank and filers are going to be upset when suddenly confronted with the need to strike.

Keeping the membership informed does not mean the bargaining committee has to be specific when reporting to the membership about possible outcomes and tentative agreements. The membership often takes what it hears from the leadership as a commitment even though the latter may view what it is saying as mere speculation. Suppose the leadership mentions a dental plan as a possible benefit. If the final settlement does not include this benefit, some members may use the fact as an excuse to defeat what in every other respect is a good settlement. Rather than risk such an outcome, the leadership should report only in broad generalities. In the example, it would be sufficient to describe the discussion with the employer as having covered "health care" issues.

Members with questions should have quick access to knowledgeable leaders. One approach is to have members of the bargaining committee on duty at the local union hall or office on a regular schedule. Another is a telephone call-back arrangement. Local union members are provided with a telephone number to use if they have questions. Messages are recorded on an answering machine and are answered as promptly as possible, again by telephone.

Displaying Employee Solidarity During Bargaining

If bargaining with the employer is expected to be tough or is proving particularly difficult, a showing of rank and file support for union proposals can enhance the credibility of the bargaining committee. The leadership must organize these expressions of rank and file solidarity.

—*Task*—
Demonstrate Rank and File Support During Bargaining

Weekly before-and-after work and, where possible, lunchtime rallies and demonstrations can be held even before the first bargaining session begins. These events need not last more than 10 or 15 minutes. Prominent union and other community leaders could speak in support of the union's major proposals.

In the workplace, stewards should encourage employees to voice their feelings on important proposals, particularly when they are likely to be overheard by supervisors. Certain days of the week can also be set aside for wearing buttons or badges to express support for a particular benefit. Members should also be encouraged to express their support for the union's position in the local union newsletter and in the "letters to the editor" column of the community newspaper.

Countering Employer Publicity During Bargaining

At some point during the bargaining process, the employer might decide to use the news media to publicize its position on the issues. The union should respond in a manner that enhances both media and public understanding and knowledge of contract bargaining in general and the union's proposals in particular.

—*Task*—
Respond to Employer Publicity During Bargaining

The local union might decide to issue a press release (see Chapter 1, Organizational Activities) or hold a news conference to respond to the employer. The news conference can be held at the union hall or office provided the facility is sufficiently large, well lighted, and easily accessible. It is also important to have enough electrical outlets scattered about for use by television camera crews.

Representatives of the news media should be notified as far in advance of the news conference as possible. In the case of radio and television, the person to contact is the assignment editor in the news department. For newspapers, the managing editor at the city desk is the relevant party. When time is of the essence, these people can be contacted by telephone. Knowing media people personally can be helpful when trying to schedule a news conference at the last moment.

The best time for a news conference, from the media's perspective, is late morning, between 10 A.M. and noon. Reporters also like to have a fact sheet summarizing the major themes in the union's message. This fact sheet should be a one page, 8 1/2 × 11 inch, typed, and double spaced sheet of paper.

There should be one union spokesperson. Other union officials are present to help answer questions when necessary. In terms of presentation, the spokesperson makes a brief statement relaying the union's message and then asks for questions. The opening statement and answers to questions should be short and to the point. Brevity is required for television and radio news stories which are short, 30 seconds or less in most cases.

The designated spokesperson must avoid being too specific on bargaining table issues when talking with the news media. The employer might feel compelled to answer back and before long public speechmaking becomes a substitute for true bargaining.

Public statements that could be interpreted as bad faith name calling should also be avoided. The employer will only become indignant and the bargaining process could slow down as a result.

The union can also counter employer publicity by purchasing time and space in the electronic and print media. Most local unions cannot compete financially with the employer when it comes to advertising; therefore, the nature of the union response and the timing of its release to get maximum exposure becomes important. The local union should obtain expert advice before beginning such an enterprise. Assistance may be available from the national, international, or intermediate level union staff.

Ratifying Settlement Terms

Membership approval of all additions and changes to the basic and all supplemental agreements is required by the bylaws of most local unions. Before this approval is sought, however, the text of every document must be checked for accuracy. Once ratified by the membership and signed by the union leadership, a contract, including all errors contained therein, is binding on all parties.

—*Task*—
Proofread the Agreement

The employer typically performs the clerical function of preparing the new agreement. The local union could just as easily do the job if it had copies of all the original agreements stored in a desktop or portable computer with word processing software. Whatever the source, the final written version of the new agreement must be checked for errors.

A minimum of two people are needed to proofread an entire contract, but all members of the bargaining committee should be involved. Each proofreader is given a copy of the agreement. While one person reads the text out loud, the others compare what they are hearing and reading against their notes and recollections of the settlement terms originally agreed upon. The secretary's minutes and the bargaining book, if kept up-to-date, can aid the collective memory.

All sorts of mistakes are possible when the final draft of an agreement is prepared. The following are some of the more common types of errors:

1. Wording of the new clause does not reflect what the union thought it had agreed to.
2. Language agreed to has been left out.
3. Language not agreed to has been put in.
4. Typographical errors have changed the meaning of words and phrases.

Following the review, the bargaining committee requests a meeting with the employer for the purpose of correcting the mistakes uncovered. Management should be told the union is not interested in resuming bargaining, but does want the written agreement to reflect what the parties believe they agreed to.

Employer representatives may dispute some or all of the errors declared by the union. At such times, the union can support its claims with a well maintained bargaining book and carefully prepared notes of the bargaining sessions.

—*Task*—
Ratify the Agreement

Once the contract has been proofread and all mistakes corrected, the bargaining committee convenes the membership for a ratification vote. An explanation of the proposed settlement terms is followed by the referendum. If the vote is negative, the leadership must return to the bargaining table for another try. If there has been a strike, the back-to-work agreement must also be approved in the same manner.

Meeting Arrangements

A large turnout of members can be expected at the ratification meeting. The meeting place must be large enough to seat everyone and have a good public address system. The employer or the union should also prepare a written summary of the settlement terms for distribution at the meeting. This handout can be used as a discussion guide.

Divulging the terms of the settlement in advance of the ratification meeting has risks. Experienced negotiators know that it is hard to please every member. Some warn that if the membership is given too much time to study the negotiated agreement, someone will find fault. It often takes only one person to "bad mouth" a proposed settlement and everyone else jumps on the bandwagon to defeat it.

The Bargaining Committee's Report

All members of the bargaining committee must be present for the ratification meeting even though the chairperson is the sole presenter. The spokesperson begins by reminding the rank and file of their right to discuss, amend, accept, or reject any and all advice given. After a brief description of the character of bargaining, the terms of the settlement are explained. The presentation must be frank and honest, both on principle and to avoid future trouble. Specific examples could be cited to show how the new or changed provisions would work in practice.

The chairperson concludes the report with a recommendation either for or against acceptance. The bargaining committee should not hesitate to call for approval when it believes the employer's terms are reasonable. On the other hand, advising rejection is proper when the employer's settlement terms are considered to be impossible.

The employer may try to pressure members of the bargaining committee to do more than make a positive recommendation on settlement terms. However, efforts to sell the agreement could end in embarrassment should the membership subsequently vote to reject.

The bargaining committee is perfectly within its rights to mobilize membership support on behalf of its recommendation. Members can be recruited to speak out during the meeting in favor of or in opposition to some or all proposed settlement terms. Supporters, strategically placed around the meeting hall, can also respond vigorously to any opposing views expressed during the discussion period.

Voting Procedure

The national or international constitution or local union bylaws describe voting procedures. Voting is typically by secret ballot. A majority of the votes cast is normally required for acceptance or rejection.

Reproducing the New Labor Agreement

Every member is entitled to a personal copy of the new labor agreement. In most cases, the employer pays the cost of printing the required number of new contract booklets. Preparation of a contract booklet is discussed in Chapter 11, Bargaining Contract Language.

INTEREST-BASED (WIN-WIN) BARGAINING

The second method of bargaining is relatively new and the impetus for it has come mainly from employers and government officials. Interest-based (win-win) bargaining uses assumptions, tasks, and tools originally developed by behavioral experts to train members of organizations, such as corporations, to function more effectively. Key features include group problem solving, open communications, cooperation, trust, and emphasis on the mutual interests of participants. Advocates believe settlements achieved through interest-based bargaining are fundamentally superior in content to those resulting from traditional bargaining practices.

The appeal of interest-based bargaining is greatest among unions and employers who have some history of working together to solve work-related problems such as cost reduction or productivity enhancement. Satisfied with the results, the parties decide to try and sustain their cooperative relationship when the time comes to renegotiate the labor contract. Other practitioners have turned to interest-based bargaining because of dissatisfaction with the adversarial nature of the traditional process.

Switching to interest-based bargaining means learning new rules. However, the tasks and the nature of communications required to reach agreement are not foreign to practitioners of the traditional approach.

The Rules of Play

Interest-based bargaining requires practitioners to discuss separate and mutual interests, to cooperate, to share information, and to avoid tests of strength. The rules of play are discussed below.

Rule: The parties promote interests and not positions.

Union and employer representatives are expected to approach bargaining prepared to discuss each other's employment-related needs and concerns rather than promote preconceived solutions to problems. For example, if the topic is subcontracting, union representatives talk about the loss of jobs due to such practices, but no remedy is proposed. By contrast, in traditional bargaining the union would probably advocate an outright ban on the practice and champion it forever or until forced to compromise. Management would discuss its interest in controlling cost.

Freed from the need to defend particular outcomes, the union and employer are able to explore a broad range of potential options to satisfy the needs and concerns expressed. In the case of subcontracting, the parties search for a "win-win" remedy, one that reduces cost so the work can be done in-house.

Rule: The parties must practice openness and not secrecy.

Where interest-based bargaining is practiced, the parties often work together to identify, collect, and organize the data needed to identify options and reach agreements. It is easier to find solutions to problems when the parties are working with a common fact base. In traditional bargaining, on the other hand, the union and the employer collect information independently and often distrust each other's reported findings. For example, management claims the union's choice of comparables for pay and fringe comparisons are biased and the union, in turn, charges the employer with inflating the cost of fringes.

The employer must also be willing to provide facts and figures in its possession relevant to the matters at hand without prompting from the union. Conceivably, such disclosures could go beyond what is required by law to include details of company finances; operating costs; competitors' products, services, and prices; management's structure and compensation, and investment plans.

Further, openness means the caucus is seldom used in interest-based bargaining. Interests, problems, and outcomes are discussed in an open and candid manner. If one party does caucus, it is obliged to reveal the purpose. Eliminating caucuses means the parties spend more time together, perhaps working to build a relationship of trust.

Rule: Everyone Participates.

There are no chief spokespersons where interest-based bargaining is practiced. Everyone in attendance participates in problem solving and decision making.

Rule: The parties must avoid contests of power.

Strikes, lockouts, and other manifestations of power have no place in interest-based bargaining. The employer and the union are expected to forgo tests of strength and adopt mutually agreed upon standards as the basis for decision making.

Rule: The parties should avoid deadlines.

As noted earlier, the contract expiration deadline in the traditional approach helps bring bargaining to a conclusion. By contrast, interest-based bargaining is free of such pressures. The participants can take as much time as needed to solve problems. Further, fatigue is not supposed to be a contributing factor in settlements in interest-based bargaining as is often the case where the traditional method is practiced. Well rested participants, it is presumed, make more thoughtful decisions.

On the other hand, in the absence of a deadline, there is nothing motivating the parties to bring bargaining to a conclusion. One report about a lengthy interest-based proceeding claimed the participants had identified and discussed 400 possible solutions to one problem. To avoid excessively long periods of bargaining, participants would be well advised to set limits on the number of topics dealt with in any one bargaining period and to establish a target date for completing the entire process.

Rule: The parties must acknowledge their commitment to interest-based bargaining.

Employers and unions who enter into interest-based bargaining for the wrong reasons are soon disappointed and quickly end the experiment. This new approach to bargaining will not necessarily keep labor cost from rising nor is it a way to manipulate the opposing party. Before jumping in, therefore, both unions and employers should learn something about the changes in behavior demanded by a bargaining method that requires cooperation, trust, and problem solving. In addition, unions should have serious internal discussions about whether interest-based bargaining will satisfy their longer term objectives.

If the employer and the union decide to try interest-based bargaining, they must agree beforehand, either orally or in writing, not only to follow the rules, but to give the method the time, effort, and personal attention required to make it work. If the process breaks down, the old adversarial relationship is likely to resume with heightened intensity.

Sequence of Bargaining Table Activities and Communications

The procedural rules establish the environment for the practice of interest-based bargaining. The process itself consists of a number of tasks, some of which occur in the beginning stages, others during the middle period, and still others near the end.

Early Meetings

Union and employer representatives may meet around the traditional oblong conference table, but with some changes. Instead of facing each other as is the case in traditional bargaining, the parties alternate seats so that a member of management is seated next to a union representative.

At the outset each party states its willingness to abide by the rules of interest-based bargaining. Agreement on time limits for various activities may be reached as well.

Next, the parties choose the subject matter for bargaining. In interest-based bargaining, the bargaining agenda itself is jointly agreed upon. Proposed topics can run the gamut from pay and fringe improvements to concerns about work rules and practices. The parties may agree to limit the number of subjects covered because of time constraints.

—*Task*—
Determine the Subject Matter for Bargaining

Brainstorming is used to solicit ideas for a bargaining agenda from union and employer representatives and decision making is by consensus (see Chapter 9). In addition, all thoughts expressed during the brainstorming session are written on flip chart paper, with the sheets then taped to the meeting room walls. Recording ideas in this manner helps to eliminate misunderstandings and gives the parties something concrete with which to work.

Union representatives must be prepared to articulate membership needs and concerns. Consequently, many preparation tasks are the same regardless of whether interest-based or traditional bargaining is practiced. For example, the views of the membership on the new contract must be obtained and the strengths and weaknesses of the existing contract assessed (see Chapter 2, Developing Bargaining Proposals).

Middle Sessions

Once agreement is reached on bargaining topics, problem solving begins. Typically, a number of teams are created, each with an equal number of union and employer representatives as members. The teams are assigned one or more topics and instructed to go their separate ways and bargain "win-win" outcomes.

—*Task*—
Achieve Win-Win Outcomes

The major technique used to reach win-win outcomes is problem solving. Problem solving works as follows: First, the interests of the parties related to the topic at hand are identified. Next, options that satisfy the needs and concerns expressed are created. Finally, standards for identifying the win-win results are created and applied. The process involved in achieving win-win outcomes is described below.

One of the few times union and management team members caucus separately is to brainstorm the needs and concerns of their respective constituencies related to the assigned topic(s). Working independently, each side records its ideas on flip chart paper. Next, the team members regroup, tape their flip chart pages to the wall and compare lists. In the ensuing discussion, the lists are compared in an attempt to identify common interests. These mutual interests are circled on each list using pens with different colored inks. Agreement is by consensus.

Next, options for satisfying the various interests expressed are created. This joint exercise involving union and employer representatives is also accomplished using brainstorming and consensus decision making. In addition, the parties may need more information than is presently at hand. Information requirements are generally the same as those in traditional bargaining. Employer financial data, wage and fringe comparisons, and old grievances and arbitrations are examples. Collecting and analyzing these data are also a joint activity.

Brainstorming and consensus decision making are employed once again as union and management representatives develop one or more standards for judging the many optional outcomes generated. For example, "mutual gain" may be the criterion chosen. Each option is then appraised according to how each party would benefit in terms of having expressed needs and concerns satisfied. The win-win outcome is the one that meets the greatest number of mutual as well as separate interests of the parties. Sometimes the individual teams are reconvened as a committee of the whole for this step.

The selection criteria chosen in interest-based bargaining are the same ones used to judge settlement terms in traditional bargaining. They include: comparison data on pay and fringes, information on the employer's ability to pay, economic data, and facts related to past grievances and arbitrations. In interest-based bargaining, however, the parties must jointly agree on the choice of standards and jointly collect all data required to apply them.

The union should keep detailed notes during this period. They may come in handy later should a disagreement arise over what the parties intended to accomplish when they chose the particular outcome(s).

Concluding Sessions

In the final week or weeks of bargaining, the "win-win" outcomes to problems chosen by the teams must be converted to contract language. Further, union and employer representatives may find that impasse on some items on the agenda is unavoidable despite the best efforts of the parties to reach agreement.

—*Task*—
Draft Contract Language

Writing contract language can be another joint union-management project. The rules for drafting contract language are the same whether bargaining is traditional or interest-based (see Chapter 11, Bargaining Contract Language).

When necessary, new provisions should be accompanied by side letters explaining how the language is intended to work in practice. Side letters can also be used where the parties do not wish to include settlement terms in the basic document.

—*Task*—
Settle Unresólved Issues

Consensus is more difficult to achieve on some agenda items than others. The most likely candidates for impasse are pay and fringe issues. Reconciling employees' interest in income growth with their employer's need to control labor cost is difficult regardless of the bargaining method employed. The failure of the interest-based approach means the parties are likely to revert to traditional bargaining activities and communications, at least with regard to the item(s) in dispute.

Training Programs and the Use of Facilitators

First-time practitioners of interest-based bargaining need training to learn the rules and tasks associated with the new approach and unlearn traditional bargaining behaviors. Joint participation by union and management representatives in the same training program produces the best results. The actual experience of training together helps the parties shed some of the mistrust and other baggage they might have accumulated after years of bargaining as adversaries. The training should include problem-solving simulations using brainstorming and consensus decision making.

Even with training, novices may require some oversight during actual bargaining to keep from slipping back into old habits. What is needed is a facilitator, a neutral party who monitors the bargaining process and intervenes only when the rules of interest-based bargaining are broken.

Providers of training programs and facilitators include university, college, and union-sponsored worker education programs and the Federal Mediation and Conciliation Service (FMCS). There are also private consultants who offer the same services.

Communicating With the Membership

Where interest-based bargaining is being tried for the first time, steps should be taken to educate members about the method, preferably well before the start of the proceedings. Once bargaining is underway, the union leadership must keep rank and file members informed on the success or failure of the experiment.

—*Task*—
Prepare the Membership for Interest-Based Bargaining

Union members familiar only with traditional bargaining are likely to greet the advent of interest-based bargaining with skepticism, particularly when told it requires cooperation and openness on the part of management. Where joint employee-management problem solving has already been tried in connection with workplace issues, the union membership may be more optimistic. In either case, some introduction to the rules and procedures of interest-based bargaining should reduce some of the members' fears. The best approach is to provide members with the same or an abbreviated version of the training given to union and company negotiators. Of course, there would be nothing like a series of improvements in pay, fringes, and working conditions, even relatively modest ones, to convince people of the value of bargaining based on interests.

—*Task*—
Keep the Membership Informed

In general, local union members are going to trust their leaders to do the right thing at the bargaining table. At the same time, they will want to be kept informed of the progress being made. This may not be easy to do. In traditional bargaining, the leadership reports on the changing bargaining positions and conduct of the employer. In interest-based bargaining, however, the parties do not defend narrow positions, rather they explore interests and options. Consequently, the leadership may want to focus on the broad range of employee needs and concerns being discussed by the joint union-management teams and either avoid the subject of potential settlement terms altogether or avoid being too specific when discussing possibilities.

Of course, the membership must still ratify the terms of any new agreement. The ratification process was described earlier in this chapter.

Problem Solving and Traditional Bargaining

Traditional bargaining also includes problem solving. Unions and employers do not necessarily ignore each other's needs and concerns because they start out taking positions on issues. Most unions try to deal with legitimate complaints raised by employers, but not by sacrificing employees' rights to fair and equitable treatment. Many creative solutions to workplace problems have resulted from traditional bargaining.

Problem solving begins much earlier with interest-based bargaining, which is an advantage. Union and company representatives have more time to discuss their separate and mutual interests, share information, and create alternative outcomes. Consequently, the range of options to choose from is likely to be broader, so the chances of achieving a settlement superior to any reached using the traditional method is greater. The relationship between the parties is also less adversarial, which improves the general atmosphere for settling the more contentious issues of pay and fringes. The jury is still out, however, as only a relatively small number of bargaining units have tried interest-based bargaining to date.

It is also possible to use the problem-solving approach within the framework of traditional bargaining. Sometimes proposed changes in benefits or work rules are too complex to handle in the short time allowed before the arrival of the contract termination deadline. Completing the details of a child care program or major adjustments to a wage-job structure are two examples. Such matters could be assigned to a joint union-management committee for resolution under the rules of interest-based bargaining and using the same problem-solving, brainstorming, and consensus decision-making techniques. If the first experiment succeeds, the parties have established a practice that can be used to deal with similar matters in the future.

Chapter 9

The Local Union Negotiator's Toolbox

The rules, tasks, and attendant communications for both traditional and interest-based (win-win) bargaining were discussed in Chapter 8. A toolbox filled with assorted techniques, devices, directions, and suggestions for carrying out the two approaches is offered in this chapter.

TOOLS FOR TRADITIONAL BARGAINING

The contents of the toolbox applicable to traditional bargaining are examined first. Leadership tools, caucusing procedures, and record keeping techniques are in use throughout the bargaining period. Threats, bluffs, and commitments along with nonverbal communications are also used. These tools are helpful during the middle and closing phases when the union tries to communicate additional information about its needs and priorities. The toolbox also contains ways and means for handling management offers and concession making, tasks that occur during the closing rounds of bargaining. Finally, tactical considerations for bargaining a first contract are discussed.

Maintaining Leadership and Control

The union must "take charge" of the bargaining process. This means speaking with one voice at the bargaining table, keeping the focus on the union's agenda, preventing the proceedings and the discussion from faltering, and being courteous while still exploiting the employer's weaknesses. The means of implementation are discussed below.

Present a United Front to the Employer

Only one member should speak on behalf of the bargaining committee at the conference table. Other committee members can participate in the discussion, but only to help clarify or defend positions articulated by the chief spokesperson.

Committee members must not interrupt each other during discussions with the employer. Speakers should be allowed to develop their points at length, particularly complicated ones. Good union arguments can be lost due to a lack of patience.

Union representatives must never argue or disagree with one another in the presence of management. The forum for airing internal dissent is the caucus (Using the Caucus is discussed below).

Keep the Parties Focused on the Union's Agenda

Management is entitled to present its demands, but the union's agenda should dominate the discussion. In one case, union negotiators were often quite bellicose when the employer tried to discuss its list of demands. They would ignore the company spokesperson and talk among themselves in loud whispers. This seemed to work because the discussion would quickly return to the union's proposals.

The bargaining committee must never imply a lack of confidence in the reasonableness or acceptability of any of its proposals. Publicly predicting rejection of certain union proposals only encourages management to do so.

Prevent the Proceedings From Stagnating

The bargaining committee should not permit a session to become bogged down on a single issue. After all sides have discussed one proposal to the point of being repetitious without reaching agreement, the union should move on to its next agenda item.

Maintain Order at the Bargaining Table

The chief union spokesperson must police the proceedings. This usually involves keeping the speakers focused on one topic at a time. It is confusing to debate the merits of two or three proposals at once and there is also the danger of some union speaker inadvertently making a statement undercutting a union argument. Finally, management should be stopped from trying to steer the discussion away from substantive matters and on to personalities and/or irrelevant subjects.

Maintain a Courteous Atmosphere

The bargaining committee must treat the employer's representatives with respect and insist on receiving the same from them. Insults from a member of management should be criticized. In addition, employer representatives must not be permitted to interrupt while a union person is speaking.

Take Advantage of the Employer's Weaknesses

Apparent divisions among company representatives should be exploited. When management conferees are offering conflicting views on an issue, the union committee should immediately redirect the discussion toward the person whose point of view is closest to its own and ignore the others. The union, however, must avoid backing the employer into a corner from which there is no honorable exit.

Using the Caucus

The union bargaining committee can caucus, or meet in private, at any time. Caucuses can be held before, during, and after bargaining sessions with the employer. When caucusing during the proceedings, union representatives typically leave the main arena for a private room nearby. When bargaining takes place on company premises, the union may caucus in the main conference room and it is the employer representatives who leave.

Any union member sitting at the bargaining table can call for a caucus. There should be a procedure for requesting a private meeting, such as whispering or handing a note to the chief spokesperson.

The Function of the Caucus

Caucuses are helpful for a variety of reasons. The following are the most common uses:

1. To review the status of the union's priority proposals.
2. To analyze and discuss the arguments, demands, and/or offers made by the employer.
3. To verify management's assertions of facts, obtain new and additional information, and/or consult with union experts such as an accountant or attorney.
4. To confront and talk out differences in viewpoints among committee members over bargaining agenda items and/or priorities in order to speak with a single voice at the bargaining table.
5. To plan specific courses of action such as making concessions or rejecting the employer's offer of settlement terms.
6. To relieve tensions after a particularly heated exchange at the bargaining table, but only when it is to the union's advantage to do so.

Conducting the Caucus

Communications in the caucus are usually very direct, quite the opposite from what occurs in the employer's presence. Points of disagreement are discussed openly.

The "question and answer" technique can be used to analyze problems such as whether to agree to a company offer. For example, the bargaining committee members might ask and answer the following question when reviewing a management offer: "What would the membership accept?"

Sometimes committee members are unable to develop a unified viewpoint without some assistance. At such times, the chief spokesperson mediates by sorting out areas of agreement and offering suggestions for compromise.

A caveat: When the union caucuses, it gives the employer tacit permission to call a recess, which can be used as a device to waste time.

Keeping Records

As noted in Chapter 3, Bargaining Proposals and Priorities, a bargaining book is used to keep track of the progress made on union and employer proposals. In addition, the secretary of the bargaining committee should take notes on what transpires during the bargaining sessions themselves.

Taking Notes

An 8 1/2 by 11 inch spiral notebook is used for note taking. Pages are numbered consecutively. The notes for each session begin with the date, starting time, and the names and titles of all persons present, including visitors and experts. Recess, caucus, and adjournment times are also recorded.

The following additional information about each bargaining session should be recorded:

- topic of bargaining proposal,
- the nature of the employer's objection(s) to a union proposal,
- change in the employer's position on previously rejected proposals, and
- interesting comments made at the conference table such as a statement or misstatement made by an employer representative.

Such documentation can also be offered as proof anytime the union files bad faith bargaining charges against an employer.

Note Taking Technique

When taking notes, it is not necessary to record every word spoken. The best technique is to summarize the main points of the discussion. For example, if health care was the topic discussed during the first hour of a session, a three or four sentence summary of the major ideas expressed by each side is sufficient. It is not even essential to use complete sentences. A secretary pressed for time need only record key phrases or terms. Later, during a caucus, the missing information can be added with the help of other committee members.

Persuading the Employer

In traditional bargaining, union negotiators try to convince the employer of the fairness and logic of the various proposed pay, fringe, and protective language improvements with arguments and supporting evidence. Developing arguments to justify the union's pay, fringe, and protective language proposals is discussed in Chapter 3, Bargaining Proposals and Priorities and Chapter 11, Bargaining Contract Language. Other tools of persuasion such as threats, bluffs, and commitments and nonverbal communications are discussed below.

Threats, Bluffs, and Commitments

Threats are assertions of intent to cause harm if certain conditions are not met. The following verbal exchange between union and company representatives contains a strike threat:

> U: "I couldn't sell your pension proposal."
> E: "Look at the entire package. We made a lot of noneconomic changes. This is serious."
> U: "If you want to avoid a strike, then put something out we can sell."

Will this threat be taken seriously? Perhaps, if the union has a reputation for acting and not bluffing. Bluffing is making a threat with no intention of carrying it out. The employer's response may also be influenced by external factors. For example, the union's strike threat is not likely to be taken seriously when the community has a high unemployment rate and potential replacement workers abound. See Chapter 13 for a discussion of strikes and strike alternatives.

Strike Vote Meeting

The union committee can make a threat more credible by making an irrevocable pledge or commitment to do what is being threatened. This is the purpose of a strike vote taken in the final week or two before the contract expiration deadline. The leadership holds a well publicized meeting to permit the rank and file to react to the employer's most recent offer of settlement terms. Rejection takes the form of a vote authorizing the bargaining committee to call a walkout if the employer's terms do not improve. The purpose of the vote is to convince management that the bargaining committee's hands are tied on the matter of taking strike action. However, there is time enough for the employer to make a new offer. In addition, the union does not have to be too specific about what constitutes acceptable terms.

The meeting must be well attended and the outcome should be close to 99 percent in favor of strike action. This means the leadership and its supporters must contact the membership well in advance of the event to sell the idea. It is important to emphasize that it is not a vote to actually strike. The actual decision to strike is made later.

A strike vote meeting should not be called if the interest or support of rank and filers is not evident. Nevertheless, it should not be too difficult to get the membership to go along because there is plenty of time remaining before a threat to strike becomes a real possibility.

Other Forms of Communications

Delivery, repetition, and body language influence how arguments, threats, bluffs, and commitments are perceived by management representatives. The significance of such signals and cues as communication forms are examined below.

Delivery

The volume and tone of voice used to convey an argument or threat adds to its overall effect. For example, the following statements given in a loud voice emphasize the strong feelings of the speaker:

"Absolutely not! We can't do it!" or "It's bad and we want it out!" There is little doubt that the proposal, whatever it is, is unacceptable.

Repetition

Repetition is a way of communicating the importance attached to some agenda items over others. The bargaining committee should discuss its top priority agenda items at length during every bargaining session. The following is one scenario of how management might react to repetition: The first few times the committee brings an item up for discussion, management's answer is a resounding "No." The committee, however, keeps returning to the topic and, after several weeks, the employer signals its recognition of the importance of the proposal with statements such as: "We are not inflexible here," or "You raise some good points," or "Your language would hurt us, but we need to work something out."

Interpreting and Using Body Language

Can the behavior of the speaker reveal something of his or her innermost thoughts? A colleague tells about a student whose facial expression throughout a week-long labor education class appeared to indicate extreme irritation with the subject matter, the teacher, or both. At the end of the week, however, the student had only praise for the course and claimed it was the best he had ever taken.

Union and employer representatives who have spent several years together bargaining and administering labor agreements are likely to know something of each other's distinctive behavioral characteristics. One negotiator, who had worked with the same member of management for many years, claimed he always knew when agreement on one or more union proposals was imminent. On such occasions the man would put both hands behind his head and lean back in his chair even as he continued to speak cautiously about the prospects for a settlement. In other words, the company representative might be talking defiance, but his body language was signaling acceptance.

Body positions of employer representatives who may be hostile to the union's position include: (1) arms crossed on chest, (2) palms down or hidden, (3) infrequent eye contact, (4) index finger pointing, and (5) remaining behind a physical barrier such as a desk or table. Conversely, examples of mannerisms of a person showing interest and a desire to cooperate include: (1) head tilting and/or body leaning forward, (2) arms open and palms exposed, (3) frequent eye contact, and (4) eliminating physical barriers.

Further, people who are speaking falsely often given themselves away through body language. This is also easier to spot when the union has.been dealing with the same employer representatives for some period of time. Some combination of the following behaviors should arouse suspicion about the veracity of the speaker: (1) slips of the tongue, (2) voice pitched higher than usual, (3) decrease in the usual frequency of hand movement, (4) increase in the usual frequency of nose touching, chin stroking, ear pulling, or other forms of hand-to-face self-contact, (5) increase in the usual frequency of such movement as shifting position in a chair, and (6) increase in the frequency of foot and leg movement. Feet and legs are the most difficult parts of the body to control.

Finally, the union bargaining committee can use body language to send messages to management. In one case where bargaining has been going on for many weeks without much apparent progress, union negotiators signaled their displeasure by slouching in their chairs and talking among themselves in loud whispers whenever company representatives either started to repeat arguments in opposition to union proposals or attempted to discuss their own demands. It was never clear, however, what impact, if any, the union's behavior had on management's actions. Most of the time was spent discussing union proposals, but this was not surprising since they had so many of them.

A caveat: Gestures and postures must not be interpreted in isolation. A mood or attitude is usually indicated by a cluster of consistent behaviors.

Responding to Employer's Offers

Possible employer's responses to union proposals include outright rejections, conditional offers, or specific offers. The union committee must listen carefully to the employer and ask questions to obtain additional information. It is also important not to permit disagreement on one item to bring the entire bargaining process to a standstill.

Outright Rejection

The union bargaining committee should never accept a "No" to one of its proposals as being final. Instead, the union spokesperson should keep asking "Why" until the employer provides some concrete reason for denial. Perhaps management is opposed to the matter on principle and there is nothing more to talk about, a genuine impasse. Conversely, the denial may symbolize an artificial deadlock related to something the union can deal with.

The bargaining committee should ask questions to determine if something less than the union's original proposal could be considered as a basis for compromise. The following exchange between company and union negotiators illustrates this point:

E: "Full dental coverage is not possible."
U: "What else is in the cards?"

Conditional Rejection

The employer may announce the possibility of agreement on one or more of the union's proposals if certain modifications are made. When responding to an offer of this type, the union committee should focus first on the area(s) of common agreement and then gradually bring the discussion around to the more controversial one(s). It is important to obtain as much information as possible about the employer's concerns where differences do exist. Union negotiators can also try to maneuver management into making a concrete proposal by requesting a clear statement of the specific change(s) desired in the original union proposal.

Specific Offers

The union bargaining committee should never reject a specific offer out of hand unless the terms are inherently destructive to the interests of employees and the union. If the offer contains something positive, but not precisely what the union wants, the chief spokesperson should respond as follows: "This merits serious consideration and we appreciate your giving the time to our proposal. We would like to study it further." A slight pause before responding gives the impression the offer is of sufficient importance to be considered.

In general, union representatives should evaluate all employer offers in terms of whether any meaningful improvements in the existing terms and conditions of employment are likely to result. For example, an offer to increase the pension benefit will not be of any value if the existing contract places a maximum limit on the employer's share of the premium contribution. Similarly, a cash bonus is not a good substitute for an across-the-board pay increase. Again, the wording "except in cases of emergency," tacked on to a clause intended to eliminate a mandatory overtime requirement can create problems because it makes the language too easy to circumvent. However, this language may be better than nothing.

The union bargaining committee can also use the information collected about company finances, pay and benefit comparisons, cost of living, productivity, and conditions in the employer's industry as standards when judging the acceptability of employer offers. For example, a bonus proposed in lieu of an across-the-board pay increase may not seem so bad when other employee groups in the industry or community have settled for the same thing. On the other hand, the bonus offer appears less attractive when the employer earned record profits or consumer prices rose sharply during the term of the existing agreement. For more discussion see Chapter 4, Presenting Financial Information in Bargaining; Chapter 5, Presenting Pay and Fringe Benefit Comparisons; Chapter 6, Presenting Economic Data in Bargaining; and Chapter 10, Costing Out Contract Proposals.

Priorities set on individual proposals can also serve as a basis for judging the adequacy of employer offers. For example, if a substantial across-the-board pay increase is a top priority item, a bonus is not a sufficient substitute, particularly if the union is prepared to strike. Similarly, if eliminating mandatory overtime is an important union priority, adding the term "emergency" to existing language is not acceptable unless it is carefully defined. See Chapter 3, Bargaining Proposals and Priorities.

Making Concessions

Agreement is possible in traditional bargaining only through compromise. The successful negotiator learns what to concede and how to make concessions. Only novices take extreme positions and refuse to budge.

Bargaining committee members must never avoid making necessary compromises out of fear of a negative membership reaction. It is just not possible to fulfill all of the needs, desires, or expectations of every union member all of the time. All the leadership must do during any period of bargaining is to satisfy enough members to get the new contract ratified.

What to Concede

The union is not obliged to make concessions on every one of its proposals. Holding firm on top priority agenda items is not considered bad-faith bargaining provided there is a demonstrated willingness to compromise on other things. The union sacrifices its low priority proposals first since most were created expressly for that purpose. Parts of many pay, fringe, and protective language proposals can also be conceded without seriously jeopardizing original objectives. In such cases, the question is one of how much to concede. Of course, all announced concessions are accompanied by a lot of fanfare and self-congratulatory statements about the "reasonableness" of the union.

How Much to Sacrifice

The union bargaining committee anticipates the kinds of concessions it might have to make at the time the original bargaining proposals are prepared (see Chapter 2, Developing Bargaining Proposals, Chapter 3, Bargaining Proposals and Priorities, and Chapter 11, Bargaining Contract Language). The problem arises when the employer demands more sacrifices than expected.

The profit, fringe comparison, and other standards used earlier to judge employer offers can also be employed to guide concession making. For example, the union could make additional cuts in a pay proposal if the employer's offer, while below the union's original request, is above the average for settlements bargained by comparable groups of employees elsewhere. Again, the union may agree to a smaller money package after receiving information about the financial difficulties of the employer, but, as a consequence, be less willing to make sacrifices on-protective language items. Protective language may also be important if a number of major grievances and/ or arbitrations occurred during the life of the terminating contract.

Some proposals become less important as progress toward reaching an overall settlement accelerates. Others diminish in value when the union leaders and members become convinced a strike would be required to get what they want. In fact, after assessing the relative bargaining strengths and weaknesses of the union and the employer, the bargaining committee may be ready to make substantial concessions (see Chapter 13, Strikes and the Strike Alternative).

When to Make Concessions

The bargaining committee should move slowly and cautiously and not concede too much too fast. After making a concession, union negotiators should wait for the employer's response as further concessions may not be necessary. It is very important not to lose patience and give in too rapidly on a small point.

Further, bargaining continues right up until the deadline hour. Consequently, some concessions should be held back for use at the very end.

Finally, the union should never make a concession in response to an employer offer left over from the previous bargaining session without first inquiring whether the employer's position has changed. Management may have conferred in the interim and decided to compromise further.

Reciprocity in Concession Making

The bargaining committee should base its own willingness to offer concessions upon the acceptance by the employer of one or more of the union's proposals. For example, the chief union spokesperson might announce a compromise position in the following manner: "The membership must have the full 4 percent wage increase, but we will give up one of the two holidays and the extra vacation we originally proposed."

In the final hour(s) before the deadline, with only the most controversial union and employer proposals still at issue, the spokespeople for each side attempt to fashion one final package. Both parties make a series of incremental concessions contained in a succession of offers, counterproposals, and counteroffers that continues until full agreement or total impasse is reached. The following illustrates the process leading to total settlement:

> E: "If you agree to the gainsharing letter, drop the $1.00 per hour rate for machine setups and the successor clause, we will roll the COLA into the base wage, increase the pension benefit 25 cents in the second and third years, and agree to retirement at age 59 after 30 years of service."

The union caucuses and returns to the bargaining table.

> U: ". . .pension benefit of 75 cents each year, retirement at age 57 after 30 years, something on wages, and something for the skilled trades."

The employer caucuses and returns to the bargaining table.

> E: ". . .pension benefit of 25, 50, and 50 cents, retirement at age 59 after 30 years, $100 cash bonus in the first year, wage increases of 0.5 percent in the second and third years, and the union proposal on 401k plan and the skill trades bonus."
>
> U: "What you have in front of you is an agreement and a recommendation (to the union membership). A pension benefit of 75 cents each year, retirement at age 57 after 30 years, $500 cash bonus, wage increases of 1 percent in the second year and 0.5 percent in the third year. We'll accept your gainsharing letter."
>
> E: ". . .pension benefit of 50 cents each year, retirement at age 57 after 30 years, $200 bonus, wage increase of 1 percent in the second and third years, and 50 cents for machine setups."
>
> U: "Make the bonus $500 and you have a handshake."
>
> E: "You have overshot our budget, we can go to $350 on the bonus."

While this exchange of offers and counteroffers is in progress, the union must keep track of its remaining priority proposals. Some can get lost in the rush to settle.

Creative Compromises

Union negotiators should be creative when trying to fashion a final settlement package to either avoid or break a deadlock. To illustrate, a local union had initially proposed a one-year agreement, a substantial wage increase, and a long list of fringe benefit improvements. The employer, in turn, offered a compensation package based on what it said it could afford. The gap between the two positions was large, but both parties were serious about reaching agreement. They tried different ways of packaging the various proposals and finally came up with the following compromise: An extra year was added to the initially proposed term of the new agreement and the starting dates of most fringe improvements were deferred to that year. The union also "gave back" several pennies of the employer's original wage offer to offset some of the cost of the new fringes. As a result of the compromise, the union got the pay increase and most of the new fringes it wanted and the employer was able to meet its objective on cost.

Side Meeting With Management

Sometimes the chief union and management negotiators arrange a private meeting near the contract expiration deadline to talk about the differences that are blocking a compromise settlement. Usually, a telephone call is sufficient to arrange such an encounter. A private meeting of this type permits a more open and frank discussion of needs and interests than is possible when all union and employer participants are present at the bargaining table.

The union representative is cautioned to inform the other members of the bargaining committee and, ideally, obtain their consent, before attending any private meeting with management. Some committee members may not like the idea of having their chief spokesperson meet privately with management and, as a consequence, might accuse him or her of "selling out."

Haggling

Haggling refers to actions by one party to hold up final agreement in an effort squeeze one last concession out of the opposing side. It is applied when one or two relatively minor points remain unresolved at the deadline after tentative agreement has been reached on the key elements of the pay and fringe package. In one case, the item holding up final agreement was the union's request for 39 weeks of sickness and accident benefit coverage, the employer was offering 26 weeks. The union committee continued to hold out for the 13 extra weeks believing the employer would not want to jeopardize a final settlement for the sake of a minor cost item. In the end, the union got six extra weeks of coverage. In this situation, as in most, fatigue brought haggling to an end.

The Tentative Agreement Rule

Agreements reached on individual pay, fringe, or protective language terms are called "tentative" until an overall settlement is reached. The chief spokesperson announces, "We tentatively agree" and follows it with a statement of the union's understanding of the agreement. The tentative designation gives the union the right to withdraw from individual agreements, even though signed or initialed, if subsequent events, such as a new demand from management, indicate the need for reconsideration.

Once tentative agreement has been proclaimed, the committee secretary immediately records the wording of the new or amended clause, the dollar or percentage amount of the pay increase, or a description of the new or revised fringe benefit in the bargaining book. Next, the appropriate union and employer representatives initial or sign the page. In the absence of a bargaining book, the details of each agreement should be typed or written on an 8 1/2 × 11 inch sheet of paper and then initialed by the parties. These sheets should be placed in a three-ringed binder for safekeeping and easy reference.

Tentative agreements are components of the overall settlement and carry the bargaining committee's recommendation for acceptance. Conversely, the leadership may not endorse an employer's announced offer, or "final" offer, of settlement terms and could actively oppose it.

Confirming the Status of Agreement

Confirming the status of agreement involves listing the agenda items tentatively settled and those still unresolved. This should be done orally at the start of every session in the concluding period of bargaining. This will help the bargaining committee keep track of proposals and eliminate ambiguities and misunderstandings.

Tactics for the First Contract

Many employers continue to fight the organizing drive even after they have lost the representation election. Their major tactic is delay. Many try to avoid coming to the bargaining table by contesting the outcome of the election before the National Labor Relations Board (NLRB) and the courts. Even when forced to bargain, employers are under no legal obligation to make concessions or reach agreements and many do not. (see Chapter 7, The Law of Contract Bargaining). By dragging out the proceedings, the employer hopes union supporters will become discouraged and abandon the union. Unfortunately, employees tend to have less staying power than employers.

The union must fight the employer's delaying tactics. First, the bargaining committee must pressure the employer to come to the bargaining table. Once there, the union can choose a fast track gambit or a total contract stratagem in an effort to obtain a first contract.

Getting the Employer to the Bargaining Table

Strike action may bring the employer to the bargaining table, but there are risks (see Chapter 13, Strikes and the Strike Alternative). As noted in Chapter 7, the Taft-Hartley Act offers an alternative tactic. Once the union has won the representation election, management is required by the Act to bargain changes in all existing mandatory terms of employment until a first contract is signed or total impasse is reached. This applies to every change the employer decides to make in work schedules, all transfers and promotions, and any disciplinary actions taken. It is up to the union to challenge every unilateral action taken by management. The objective is to convince the employer that having a contract with rules is preferable to bargaining over every problem in the workplace.

David Rosenfeld's paper on the tactics of offensive bargaining provides a sample letter for informing the employer about its obligation to bargain over every change in mandatory employment terms.[1]

---

[1] David A. Rosenfeld, *Offensive Bargaining* (Silver Spring, Md.: George Meany Center for Labor Studies, 1992) Exhibit B.

The letter also contains a warning of the union's intent to challenge every unilateral act by management with demands for back pay for employees adversely affected. Rosenfeld also recommends the letter include a statement about employees' Weingarten right[2] to be represented by the union in disciplinary proceedings and the name of the union official the employer should contact.

In addition, the union can request information from the employer relevant to bargaining. The employer could refuse but it risks sacrificing the right to bargain over future appeals for information. Rosenfeld sees demands for information as another way of harassing the employer and includes in his paper a sample 40-page letter requesting information. The document was purposely created to be overly broad, intrusive, and burdensome on the employer.[3]

Fast Track Gambit

Once the employer is at the bargaining table, the fast track gambit is designed to prevent management from dragging out the proceedings to the point where the union is threatened with a loss of employee support and its majority status. The union bargaining committee contacts the employer immediately after winning the representation election to set a date for the start of contract talks. The initial list of proposals is short. The issues are limited to the five or six major concerns and needs expressed by employees during the successful organizing drive: wages, pay structure, dignity in the workplace, fair treatment on the job, and workplace safety, among others.

In addition to limiting the number of proposals, the union announces a deadline for agreement. The chief union spokesperson might suggest the following: "Can we shoot for four weeks from today, the 31st of May for completion of these contract issues?" If little or no progress is made on the limited agenda by the deadline, the union assumes the employer is not interested in bargaining

---

[2]In NLRB v. Weingarten, Inc., 420 U.S. 251, 88 LRRM 2689 (1975), the U.S. Supreme Court ruled that an employee has a right to union representation in proceeding that might result in disciplinary action.

[3]Rosenfeld, *Offensive Bargaining*, Exhibit A.

and looks for ways to apply pressure (see Chapter 13, Strikes and the Strike Alternative).

If, on the other hand, agreement is reached on the five or six original requests, the union presents its remaining proposals for the new contract. These can be based on a survey of both members' and nonmembers' needs and concerns. Provisions from model contracts can also be used (see Chapter 2, Developing Bargaining Proposals and Chapter 3, Bargaining Proposals and Priorities).

The risk associated with this strategy is quick impasse, which frees the employer from further bargaining. The union must be careful to avoid reaching total impasse (see Chapter 12, Bargaining Impasse and Third Party Intervention).

Total Contract Stratagem

The total contract stratagem is the reverse of the fast track gambit because the union's initial proposal consists of a complete labor agreement. The prototype contract contains a recognition clause, a duration article, and everything in between. The union will need more time to prepare when bargaining a total contract. In addition, the parties bargain article by article, a potentially time-consuming prospect.

The union can still set a deadline for agreement with the total contract stratagem. However, events do not move as quickly as they do in the fast track gambit because there is an entire contract to be bargained. The number of issues involved makes it easy for an employer to drag out the proceedings. In one case, the union and the employer spent months arguing over whether the new contract should have a recognition clause.

To maintain employee solidarity during the lengthy bargaining period required by the total contract stratagem, the union should not end the organizing campaign until a first contract is signed. The organizing committee should remain in place and continue to function in the same manner as before the election. This means continuing to nurture the enthusiasm of supporters while making a special effort to recruit those people who voted against the union. Finally, management should be blamed publicly for the slow progress being made on reaching agreement on a first contract.

TOOLS FOR INTEREST-BASED BARGAINING

Two important tools for interest-based bargaining are presented below. The first is brainstorming and the second is group consensus building.

Brainstorming

In interest-based bargaining, brainstorming is used to encourage members of problem-solving teams to express their ideas without fear of ridicule and criticism. Inventiveness is encouraged and everything and anything goes, no matter how unreal, exaggerated, humorous, and controversial.

Conducting Brainstorming Sessions

A relaxed and informal environment is needed for brainstorming. Union and management representatives should sit side by side around a table or in comfortable chairs arranged in a circle.

Brainstorming works as follows: Each participant, in order, contributes an idea related to the assigned topic. People with nothing to contribute during a round merely say "pass." All ideas suggested are written by a team member (the job can be rotated) on flip chart paper for all participants to view. The session continues until participants run out of ideas or a preset time limit is reached.

Evaluation and criticism are not permitted during the brainstorming session itself. In fact, discussion of any kind, other than to clarify a thought, is not permitted. Editing is out too, but participants can piggyback on ideas already offered.

The results of brainstorming are analyzed after the session is completed. For example, the union and employer representatives might independently brainstorm their respective organization's needs and concerns relative to a contract issue and then meet jointly to discuss each other's lists and identify interests in common. Brainstorming might be used again to create options for satisfying the commonly identified needs.

Group Consensus Decision Making

The brainstorming technique produces a long list of ideas and options. In every case, choices have to be made. Decisions can be made by majority vote or through consensus. A majority is defined as 50 percent plus 1 of the votes cast. Proponents of interest-based negotiating avoid the voting technique because it implies winners and losers, a concept that is contrary to the notion of cooperation.

True consensus requires total agreement among all participants. Individual group members must feel comfortable supporting the decision of the group even though it may not be their ideal choice. No participant is expected to sacrifice principles or beliefs for the sake of total unanimity. Consensus is difficult to achieve, but it is possible where people have shared objectives and have actively engaged in the tasks leading up to decision making.

Building Consensus

Again, an environment of informality encourages participants to take part in the discussion that precedes consensus decision making. Participants should feel free to disagree, but heated arguments should be avoided because people who believe they are under attack become defensive. A neutral party can play a role here by interrupting and asking the principals to restate and clarify their respective positions.

When the time comes to determine whether a consensus exists, every participant should be required to verbally state his or her position. Discussion continues until total agreement is reached. Again, it does not have to be a participant's first choice, but everyone must be willing to support the decision made. Often, ideas generated in the brainstorming sessions have to be creatively reworked before consensus can be achieved.

Chapter 10

Costing Out
Contract Proposals

A considerable amount of time is spent in traditional bargaining trying to allocate a limited number of company dollars among a long list of union pay and fringe requests. Consequently, the local union negotiator's toolbox must also include some means for estimating the cost of union proposals and employer offers. A relatively quick but simple method for costing out the contract is presented in this chapter.

THE IMPORTANCE OF COST INFORMATION

The employer places an upper limit on spending for wage/salary and fringe improvements. The total dollar amount is usually below, often by a considerable sum, what is needed to cover all of the union's requirements. Consequently, the union bargaining committee is forced to pick and choose among individual proposals of relatively equal priority to secure the best possible combination of a pay increase and improved fringes while remaining within the monetary constraints imposed by the employer. One way of making the selection is to compare the dollar cost or value of individual fringe benefits.

161

Rank and filers also want to know what the new contract is worth in dollar terms. They may measure bargaining success by how well they did in terms of the money settlement in comparison with other groups of workers who are viewed as rivals because of similar employment characteristics.

A union bargaining committee could ask management to provide cost data on fringes. However, employers tend to be overly generous when making assumptions about the utilization of benefits. For example, when costing a jury duty proposal, an employer is likely to assume most employees will use the benefit during the year. The bargaining committee, relying more on personal experience, is unlikely to assume such a high rate of usage. Consequently, making independent calculations of fringe cost gives the union some basis for challenging employer cost figures. The probable net result is a more realistic cost estimate that works to the advantage of the union.

A caveat: The bargaining committee must not get bogged down in disputes over cost and forget to discuss the merits of the union's pay and fringe proposals.

INTEREST-BASED (WIN-WIN) BARGAINING

Cost determination is a joint union-management activity where interest-based bargaining is practiced. The parties are required to work together to discover all of the facts and costs relevant to solving a particular problem (see Chapter 8, Bargaining Activities). Even in traditional bargaining, there is room for some cooperation between the parties, and perhaps cost determination could be an area for joint activity.

BASIC TERMINOLOGY

The vocabulary of cost estimation includes terms such as direct wages/salaries, wage/salary-related fringes and nonwage/salary-related fringes, base periods and rates, and paid and productive hours.

There are also numerous ways of expressing costs. Some definitions are provided below.

Total Compensation

The individual components of compensation are examined in detail in Chapter 3, Bargaining Proposals and Priorities. However, for costing purposes, compensation consists of direct wages/salaries and fringes. In addition, there are fringes with dollar benefits directly related to changes in wages/salaries. Examples of wage/salary-related benefits include paid vacations, paid holidays, and personal leave.

There is a second category of fringes with benefit values that are not tied to the employer's pay structure. The dollar values of these benefits are determined by such factors as negotiated formulas, in the case of pensions, or the package of health care services selected by the bargaining unit. Other examples of nonwage/salary-related fringe benefits include tuition reimbursements; employer provided personal safety equipment, wearing apparel, and tools; and employee meals. Finally, some fringes can be offered either way. For example, a shift bonus is sometimes established as a percentage of a worker's wage rate and at other times as a flat cents per hour amount.

Base Period

The base period is the reference point against which changes in costs are measured. Typically, the base period is the final year of the terminating contract. Pay and fringe costs in the base year are computed first, then the cost of each component of compensation for each year of the proposed new agreement is estimated separately and compared to the base period.

Base Rate

The base rate is the wage or salary employees earn for all regularly scheduled straight-time hours. Excluded from the base rate are shift, overtime, incentive, and longevity payments. These payments are treated by employers as separate categories of expense.

Pay structures of most enterprises are composed of many base wage/salary rate brackets, classifications, or labor grades. However, the method of cost estimation described in this chapter uses one representative base wage/salary rate. The statistic used is the weighted average of all wage/salary brackets.

The weighted average is determined by multiplying the numbers of employees in each pay bracket by the applicable wage/salary rate, adding the results for each bracket together, and then dividing the final dollar figure by the total number of employees in the bargaining unit. Exhibit 10-1 shows how the weighted average is calculated.

The weighted average is only one of four possible ways of expressing an average. Others are the arithmetic average, median, and mode. The weighted average is more representative because the distribution of employees within the pay categories is taken into account. However, this fact might not stop the employer from

Exhibit 10-1. Calculating a Weighted Average

Wage Bracket	Current Base Hourly Pay	Current Number of Employees	Hourly Pay Times Number of Employees
1	$9.75	3	$29.25
2	10.00	5	50.00
3	10.25	2	20.50
4	10.50	2	21.00
5	10.75	2	21.50
6	11.25	3	33.75
7	12.00	2	24.00
	Total Employees	19	Total Pay $200.00

Weighted Average Base Wage = $200.00/19 = $10.53

using another measure because it shows a higher average wage/ salary rate and makes the company look better. The average wage/ salary is used in formulas for estimating the cost of fringes; consequently, answers vary depending on which statistic is selected.

In the case of a first contract, the weighted average may be difficult to obtain because the employer may not have a rational pay structure. For example, employees performing the same jobs are earning different rates of pay. Perhaps creating a joint union-management committee to study jobs and develop a pay schedule is one of the union's key bargaining objectives. However, for the purpose of costing out new fringes, the arithmetic average can be used. The arithmetic average is obtained by adding together all of the individual wage/salary rates and dividing by the total number of employees in the new bargaining unit.

Paid Versus Productive Hours

Wages/salaries of employees are typically paid on the basis of a work year averaging 2,080 hours. Actual hours worked are fewer because of holidays, vacations, coffee and lunch breaks, jury duty, and other leave arrangements. Employers view the time employees spend off the job as nonproductive hours and do not include them when calculating the hourly cost of a fringe benefit. The customary approach is to spread the cost of wage/salary-related fringes over the hours (months in the case of salaried employees) employees actually perform work during the year.

Paid productive hours are determined by subtracting nonproductive hours from paid hours and adding on overtime hours. For example, if 100 employees are paid for 208,000 hours in a year (2,080 × 100 = 208,000), take 26,000 hours of leave, and work 8,000 overtime hours, total productive hours for the period are 190,000 and average productive hours, 1,900 (208,000 − 26,000 = 182,000 + 8,000 = 190,000 / 100 = 1,900). The total cost of each fringe is divided by 190,000 hours to determine the cost per hour worked.

Expressing Costs

In contract bargaining, the cost of a single fringe benefit proposal or the total money package is reported in at least three different ways. Total Annual Cost (TAC) for all bargaining unit employees is one. Another is the Total Annual Cost Per Employee (TACPE). A third, and the one noted above as favored by employers, is Total Annual Cost Per Employee-Hour Worked (TACPEHW). Of course, the union committee may prefer to talk in terms of value rather than cost when referring to the results of the estimator model.

THE COST ESTIMATION METHOD

The formulas used to calculate the cost of direct wages/salaries, wage/salary-related fringes, and nonwage/salary-related fringes are presented below. The arithmetic involved is quick and simple to use and only a pencil, paper, and hand-held calculator are needed. Some practical applications are also provided.

—*Task*—
Estimate the Cost/Value of Direct Wages/Salaries

If the employer offers a 5 percent wage increase to all employees in each year of a new two-year agreement, the bargaining committee must know what this offer amounts to in dollars. The answer for year one is found by multiplying the base wage in the base period by the proposed percentage increase. If the weighted average base-period wage is $10.53 per hour, the first year increase is $0.526 per hour ($10.53 × .05 = $0.526). Rounding to mills is not uncommon when calculating costs. TAC is found by multiplying 52.6 cents times the number of bargaining unit employees times 2,080 hours. The second year wage increase is estimated using the first year hourly base rate of $11.056 ($10.53 + $0.526 = $11.056) and is 55.3 cents per hour ($11.056 × .05 = $0.553).

The total wage increase for two years is $1.079 ($0.526 + $0.553 = $1.079). Or is it? The employer would argue that the first year increase is paid again in the second year and should, therefore, be included in the two-year total. The combined hourly cost, according to the employer, is $1.605 ($0.526 × 2 years +

$0.553 = $1.605), and the average hourly cost for two years is $0.80.

Front Loading

Front loading occurs when the larger portion of the wage increase is paid during the early year(s) of a multiyear agreement. Assume the 10 percent wage increase in the previous example is distributed differently, perhaps 8 percent the first year and 2 percent the second year. The first year increase is 84.2 cents per hour, the second year is 22.7 cents. The total hourly cost per employee for two years is $1.911 ($0.842 × 2 + $0.227 = $1.911).

Notice what has happened to cost. Front loading is more expensive than a wage increase offered in two equal installments ($1.911 versus $1.605). From the employee's viewpoint, however, front loading provides more take-home pay.

End Loading

Postponing the major portion of the wage/salary increase until the later years of a multiple year contract is end loading. Suppose 80 percent of the wage adjustment in the above example is not paid until the second year of the agreement. The first and second year hourly increases are $0.211 ($10.53 × 0.02 = $0.211) and $0.859 ($10.53 + $0.211 = $10.74 × 0.08 = $0.859) respectively. The total hourly cost per employee for two years is $1.28 ($0.211 × 2 + $0.859 = $1.28). Clearly, end loading is the least expensive ($1.28 versus $1.911 and $1.605). For employees, end loading provides less take-home pay than the other options.

—Task—
Estimate Cost/Value of Wage/Salary-Related Fringes

Turning now to benefits, the following information is needed to calculate the cost of wage/salary-related fringes: the weighted average base wage/salary rate, the size of the bargaining unit, and the number of hours of benefit. Further, as noted above, compensation costs are typically expressed as Total Annual Cost (TAC), Total Annual Cost Per Employee (TACPE), and Total Annual Cost Per

Employee Hour (month for salaries) Worked (TACPEHW). Consequently, there are three formulas for estimating the cost of wage/salary-related fringes:

1. Weighted Average Base Wage / Salary Rate × Number of Employees in the Bargaining Unit × Hours of Benefit = TAC.
2. TAC / Bargaining Unit Size = TACPE.
3. TAC / (Average Productive Hours in the Year × Number of Employees in the Bargaining Unit) = TACPEHW.

Four bargaining problems are presented below to demonstrate how the formulas are applied.

Bargaining Problem 1—Comparing Fringe Costs: A Clean-up Period Versus Hospitalization

The union is proposing a 10-minute clean up period and improved hospitalization (which would raise total annual premiums by $41,675). The employer is offering one, the choice is up to the union. Which of the two benefits has the greater monetary value?

The following information applies to the 10-minute clean-up period: the base period straight-time hourly wage is $10.53, the bargaining unit consists of 100 employees, and the hours of benefit are 39.58 (1,900 hours / 8 hours = 237.5 work days × 10 minutes per day / 60 minutes = 39.58 hours). Inserting the data into the formulas generates the following results for the clean-up period:

TAC = $10.53 × 100 × 39.58 = $41,677.74.
TACPE = $41,677.74 / 100 = $416.777.
TACPEHW = $41,677.74 / (1,900 hours worked × 100 employees) = $0.219 or 22 cents.

The 10-minute clean-up period and the additional hospitalization have the same monetary value. Consequently, other factors, such as membership or leadership preferences, may be more influential in determining which of the two benefits is chosen.

Bargaining Problem 2—Saturday Overtime

The union proposes raising the premium paid for Saturday overtime work from the current one and one-half times to double the straight-time hourly pay rate. What is the cost?

If the same basic data provided in the previous problem are assumed, the only new information required is the hours of benefit. In the case of Saturday overtime, the hours of future benefit is an estimate based on an examination of old payroll records. Suppose 95 percent of the work force is expected to work an average of 1,500 hours of Saturday overtime during the first year of the new contract. Introducing the data into the formulas provides the following results:

TAC = ($10.53 × 0.5) × 1,500 hours = $7,897.50.
TACPE = $7,897.50 / 100 employees = $78.97.
TACPEHW = $7,897.50 / (1,900 × 100) = $0.0415 or 4.2 cents.

Notice in the third formula, while 95 employees benefit from the proposed increase in overtime pay, the entire bargaining unit of 100 people are charged for the benefit.

The cost of increasing Saturday overtime may seem expensive. However, overtime hours are not included as hours of benefit when calculating vacation pay or other benefit amounts; consequently, overtime work lowers the average hourly cost of all benefits to the employer. Further, management can eliminate the need for Saturday overtime by doing a better job of scheduling work during the normal workweek. Actually, ending overtime was the original goal when unions first proposed this type of premium pay.

Bargaining Problem 3—Comparing Fringe Costs: Skilled Pay Versus a New Holiday

The bargaining committee is proposing a 20 1/4 cents per hour pay adjustment for 20 skilled employees and one additional paid holiday for the entire bargaining unit. Management has offered one, the choice is up to the union. Which proposal has the greater economic value?

The TAC of the pay adjustment is $8,424.00 ($0.2025 × 20 beneficiaries × 2,080 hours = $8,424.00). The total cost for the extra holiday is the same ($10.53 × 100 employees × 8 hours = $8,424.00). Considerations other than money could influence the decision made. Politically the wisest choice is the holiday because more employees benefit. The TACPEHW for each benefit is 4.4

cents ($8,424.00 / 190,000 total productive hours = $0.044 or 4 cents).

Bargaining Problem 4—Vacation Improvement

What is the cost of a fifth week of vacation for all employees who have completed 20 years of service? The only new information needed is the number of prospective beneficiaries. This can be found by examining a list of employees and their hiring dates compiled from company payroll records or a seniority roster.

Assume 22 employees are eligible for an extra 40 vacation hours during the first year of the new agreement. The TAC is $9,266.40 ($10.53 × 22 beneficiaries × 40 hours of benefit = $9,266.40). The TACPEHW is 4.9 cents ($9,266.40 /190,000 = $0.049 or 4.9 cents). Although $10.53 can be used as the base rate, the weighted average wage for the 22 employees would have been more representative.

—Task—
Estimate Cost/Value of Nonwage/Salary-Related Fringes

As explained earlier, the cost of some fringes are independent of wage/salary rates. Two of the three formulas used to calculate fringe costs remain the same. However, the formula for Total Annual Cost (TAC) must be changed because cost is based on the benefit's price rather than the average wage/salary rate. The following is the revised equation: TAC = Benefit Price × Number of Employees. The equations for TACPE and TACPEHW are unchanged. Two examples of costing out nonwage/salary fringes are given below.

Bargaining Problem 5—A New Health Plan

The cost of the basic group health plan is typically not tied to the pay structure. Further, only the employer's share of the cost is estimated. TACs and TACPEHWs, along with the information needed for the calculations, are as follows:

Exhibit 10-2. Group Health Plan Total Annual Cost per Employee Hour Worked

Type of Plan	Number of Employees	Monthly Employer Premium	Premium Periods	TAC	TACPEHW[a]
Insurance					
Family	60	380.00	12	$273,600.00	$1.440
Single	20	170.00	12	40,800.00	0.215
HMO					
Family	15	360.00	12	64,800.00	0.341
Single	5	150.00	12	9,000.00	0.047
Totals	100			$388,200.00	$2.043

[a]Total employee hours worked in a Year = 1,900 hours × 100 employees or 190,000.
TACPE = $388,200 / 100 employees = $3,882.00.

Bargaining Problem 6—The Second-Shift Bonus

Data needed to determine the cost of a 5-cent increase in the second-shift bonus include the number of assigned employees and their hours of work in the base year. These data can also be obtained from payroll records.

Assuming 20 employees work an average of 1,900 hours per year, the total annual cost of a 5-cent increase in the shift premium is $1,900 (20 employees × 1,900 hours × $0.05 = $1,900). If the bargaining unit has 100 members, TACPE is $19.00 ($1,900 / 100 = $19.00) and TACPEHW is 1 cent ($1,900 / (100 employees × 1,900 hours) = $0.01 or 1 cent). Note once again that while the number of beneficiaries is only 20, the cost of the improvement is charged to the entire bargaining unit.

—Task—
Estimate Cost/Value of the Money Package

The cost/value of the money package is obtained by combining all of the individual pay and fringe items. For example, adding together the costs of the individual items estimated in the six preceding problems produces a money package totaling:

First Year Wage Increase	$0.526
Clean-Up Period	0.219
Saturday Overtime	0.042
Additional Holiday	0.044
Additional Week of Vacation	0.049
New Health Care	2.043
Second Shift Bonus	0.010
TOTAL	$2.933

In other words, the total annual cost of the proposed money package is $2.933 per employee hour worked.

—Task—
Estimate Rollups

Management will view the $2.933 figure as understating the true cost of the proposed money package for several reasons. First, the figure does not reflect the increased cost of current wage-related fringes that will occur when the 52.6 cents wage increase takes effect. Second, the total amount is underestimated because all new wage-related fringe improvements were costed out at the existing wage rate. Again, the proposed wage increase was not included in the formulas.

The employer will raise the total cost of the money package by adding on the indirect costs. An estimate of the increased cost of existing fringes is called the wage/salary rollup. The measure of the undervalued new wage/salary-related fringes is referred to as the package rollup.

The Wage/Salary Rollup

The wage/salary rollup estimates the increase (or decrease) in the cost of all preexisting wage/salary-related benefits when the base wage/salary rate is raised (or lowered). It is calculated for each year of the new agreement.

The wage/salary rollup is computed in two parts. First, a rollup percentage for the base period is calculated by dividing the cost of all existing wage/salary-related benefits by the current base wage/salary rate. Assume the same hourly base wage of $10.53 used in the earlier problems and a TACPEHW of existing wage/salary-related fringes of $9.00. The rollup percentage is 85 ($9.00 / $10.53 = 0.85 or 85 percent). Next, the rollup amount is determined by multiplying the proposed wage increase by the rollup percentage. The proposed wage increase is $0.526, so the wage rollup is 45 cents ($0.526 × 0.85 = $0.447 or 45 cents). The total annual money package cost increases to $3.383 per employee hour worked ($2.933 + $0.45 = $3.383).

The Package Rollup

The package rollup compensates for the incorrect base wage rate used when estimating the cost of wage/salary-related fringes. It too is calculated for each year of the new agreement.

The package rollup is also computed in two parts. First, the rollup percentage is obtained by dividing the value of the proposed new wage/salary-related fringes by the base period straight-time rate. For example, combining the TACPEHW of new wage-related fringes in the above problems equals 35 cents, the rollup percentage equals 3 ($0.35 / $10.53 = 0.033 or 3 percent). Next, the rollup amount is determined by multiplying the proposed wage increase by the rollup percentage. The package rollup is 2 cents ($0.526 × 0.33 = $0.017 or $0.02). Adding the package rollup of 2 cents to the total money package increases the amount to $ 3.403 per employee hour worked.

In conclusion, the annual cost of the wage and fringe package in the example is 47 cents more per employee hour when indirect costs are included. The union, on the other hand, may or may not be concerned about the rollup. Membership interest is in the value of the newest gains and not in the higher cost of existing benefits. However, the rollups do offer one explanation of why the employer's estimate of the money package is likely to be higher than the one made by the union.

LEGALLY MANDATED BENEFITS

The employer may try to include employee benefits required by federal and state statutes as part of the cost of total compensation.

Unemployment insurance, workers' compensation, and social security are examples of legally mandated benefits.

The union must object to any attempt by the employer to include mandated benefits with those won as a consequence of bargaining. The employer must provide these statutory benefits regardless of the presence of a labor union or collective bargaining. Combining mandated and bargained benefits only serves to artificially inflate the cost of collective bargaining.

USING A PERSONAL COMPUTER TO CALCULATE COST

Negotiators using the cost estimation method have to take a few short cuts because of the large volume of data involved. For example, a weighted average of all base wage/salary rates, rather than individual employee rates, is used to estimate wage/salary and fringe cost. Precision suffers because a person with only a pencil, paper, and calculator cannot process a lot of information. However, the opposite is true when a desktop or portable computer is available. Computers calculate the cost of pay and fringe proposals and offers with speed and accuracy.

In addition to the computer, the local union interested in developing a costing model must have a program. The program consists of the cost formulas and other operating instructions. Programs of this type can be developed using any one of a number of inexpensive, commercially available spreadsheet software packages.[1]

Once the program is written, the computer does most of the work. Descriptive information about individual fringes, such as hours of benefit and number of beneficiaries, must be typed on the spreadsheet model using the computer keyboard. Once that is accomplished, the computer quickly and automatically calculates

---

[1]Persons interested in learning more about costing contracts using a computer should write the author at the School for Workers, UW-Extension, Madison, WI 53703.

and displays the cost data on a video screen or prints a paper copy when a printer is available. As new data are entered, the computer instantaneously recalculates the cost and displays the new numbers. Most spreadsheet programs are capable of presenting data in both tabular and graphic forms.

Chapter 11

Bargaining Contract Language

Contract language, more commonly referred to as the protective language provisions of the labor agreement, are the rules of the workplace. These rules establish individual employee rights in the job, govern union security, and create procedures for contract enforcement, renewal, and termination.

The tasks of developing protective language requests are discussed in this chapter (see Chapter 3, Bargaining Proposals and Priorities for a discussion of wage/salary and fringe benefit proposals). In addition, general guidelines for writing contract language are offered along with information about the design and format of the contract booklet.

PREPARING THE BARGAINING AGENDA: PROTECTIVE LANGUAGE

Protective language problems are revealed when the bargaining committee reviews the existing contract, examines old grievance and arbitration records, and listens to the views of stewards, officers, and the general membership (see Chapter 2, Developing Bargaining Proposals). The resulting list of ideas, needs,

177

suggestions, and concerns are converted into specific proposals for the bargaining agenda. Conversion is a multitask process. It begins with a search for rule-making guidelines or principles. Next, arguments to support individual language proposals are prepared. Time is also spent anticipating employer responses as a guide to creating potential compromise solutions. The actual writing of new or revised rules comes at the end.

—*Task 1*—
Identify Basic Principles

When preparing protective language proposals, the bargaining committee is guided by organized labors' long-cherished principles of individual employee rights in the job, protection for the union and its leaders, and procedures for handling disputes and changing the labor agreement. Two examples are the right of individual employees to grieve and seniority as the basis for all personnel actions. Similar standards are found in thousands of individual labor agreements and in collections of prototype contract clauses. Most national and international unions prepare model language guides based on these security principles.

In practice, union and employer negotiators bargain first over the version of the principle(s) to incorporate in the rule. As previously noted, the actual wording of a new or revised provision is not drafted until later in the proceedings.

To illustrate, suppose the union's objective is to give stewards the right to investigate grievances during normal working hours. As a result of time spent examining provisions in other collective agreements, the bargaining committee proposes the following list of principles:

1. Stewards must be allowed time off during working hours to receive and investigate complaints and grievances.
2. Stewards must be allowed time off upon notice to their immediate supervisors.
3. The employer must pay stewards at their average hourly rates for time spent in grievance handling and arbitration.
4. A grievance committee member (the chief steward, a union officer, a health and safety committee member, or other

specified union representative) must be available to stewards upon request.

5. A grievance committee member, or other specified union representative(s), must be allowed time off during working hours for union business on notice to the immediate supervisor.

—*Task 2*—
Develop Supporting Arguments

The employer must be convinced of the value of any proposed rule change. Even the union membership may have to be persuaded to support the leadership on protective language. Consequently, the bargaining committee must be prepared to argue the merits of each proposal.

Many of the same arguments presented in Chapter 3 to support pay and fringe proposals are also used to promote rules changes. The equitable treatment and promise of mutual gain arguments are examples. Just as the union cites the findings of pay and fringe comparisons to justify economic improvements, it points to protective language commonly found in other labor agreements when arguing for similar treatment. On the other hand, with the promise of gain argument, union negotiators try to demonstrate to the employer how it will benefit along with the work force when the proposed rule is added to the labor contract. For example, the union could describe the protection as having a positive effect on employee morale.

In addition, the bargaining committee may cite the number of grievances and arbitrations lost during the term of the existing contract to argue for clearer definitions of important employee and union rights in a new agreement. Finally, the union leadership may be required to craft special arguments to win rank and file support for protective language proposals.

All of the arguments presented above can be made in support of the rule giving stewards the right to investigate grievances during working hours. The following are illustrative:

1. Grievance records show many missed filing deadlines and a sizable number of incomplete investigations because stewards have insufficient time to make inquiries.

2. Without the proper contract language, the union can only do a perfunctory job of representation, which is unacceptable.
3. Labor contracts elsewhere in the employer's industry and in the local community contain such arrangements.
4. Contracts with such provisions are common in other industries.
5. Paying stewards and other union officials for production time lost when handling complaints and grievances is one of the costs of doing business.
6. The new language will reduce the number of grievances since stewards now often file without conducting a proper investigation.
7. The union will do a better job of handling grievances.

This last argument may not convince the employer, but it should please the membership who want the grievance procedure to work better.

—*Task 3*—
Anticipate Employer Counterarguments

Management can be expected to object initially to anything and everything the union proposes despite the cogency of the arguments presented. This opposition may stem from concern about the dollar cost of administering new rules, fear of employee abuse, and dislike of having limits placed on its prerogatives to manage the work force. The employer is likely to raise these and other objections to a proposal creating new rights for stewards. The following are representative:

1. Production will be disrupted.
2. Investigations on company time will cost too much money.
3. Management will be paying the union to represent its own members.
4. The proposed new rights will be subject to abuses.
5. These rule changes will make the union more effective in handling grievances and therefore stronger.

Management is unlikely to actually verbalize this fifth point, but it may very well believe it.

—*Task 4*—
Predict Employer Counterproposals

Completing task 3 should provide bargaining committee members with clues about the kinds of restriction the employer might demand. To illustrate, the employer is likely to want the following modifications made to the union's proposal on stewards rights:

1. Cap the total number of hours stewards and other union officials can remain off their regular jobs to handle grievances.
2. Keep records of the hours stewards and other union officials spend off their regular jobs handling grievances.
3. Cap the total amount of lost time wages/salaries paid within a preset time period.
4. Set up a procedure to remedy any alleged abuses of the new rights.

—*Task 5*—
Determine Potential for Compromise

With tasks 3 and 4 completed, members of the union bargaining committee have some idea of what principles they may have to modify or sacrifice in order to reach agreement. The union in the example could be required to make the following concessions on the matter of steward's rights:

1. Agree to limit the total number of production hours used for grievance handling.
2. Agree to an upper limit on the employer's total annual lost time pay liability with the union picking up the cost after this ceiling is reached.
3. Agree to require stewards to obtain permission from their supervisors before leaving their work stations.

4. Agree to establish a recordkeeping system based either on time cards punched or on computer entries "For Union Business."
5. Agree to a forum, such as the grievance procedure, for handling alleged abuses of the new rules.

The bargaining committee has to decide whether the compromise required to satisfy management poses a problem for the bargaining unit. In other words, can the union live with less protection than the principles laid out in task 1?

—*Task 6*—
Put the New Rule Into Writing

Once agreement is reached on principles, the task of writing out the new rule(s) begins. Unions make a mistake when they relinquish the job of writing contract language to management. Authorship gives the bargaining committee an opportunity to put its understanding of the agreement on paper. Management's insistence on writing final language should be countered by a union demand to divide the work in half.

In general, contract language should be relatively easy to read, so members can readily understand their rights. The words used should be simple and straightforward. Slang expressions and legal jargon such as "the party of the first part will . . . ," must be avoided.

The bargaining committee can find useful language in the contracts of other unions. When borrowing from other labor agreements, the words, phrases, and clauses chosen must cover all of the agreed upon principles and still be understood by the employer.

Two sample texts containing the rights of stewards are presented below. The first contains all of the principles originally proposed by the bargaining committee in task 1. The clause reads as follows:

> The Employer recognizes the right of stewards and grievance committee members to receive and investigate complaints and grievances during working hours without loss in pay upon notice to the supervisor. Compensation for lost time must be at average earnings. Griev-

ance committee members may leave their jobs on Union business and must be available to stewards on request.

The second sample is a compromise version of the first because it incorporates management's likely (actual) objections as anticipated by the union in task 5. This revised provision is much lengthier and more complex. The following is the compromise text:

> The Employer recognizes the right of stewards and grievance committee members to receive and investigate complaints and grievances during working hours without loss in pay. Compensation for lost time shall be based on time cards punched 'For Union Business' and shall be at straight time average hourly earnings. Stewards shall also have the right to request and obtain the presence of grievance committee members for the purpose of consultation regarding grievances and complaints, and grievance committee members shall have the right to consult with stewards at their respective work locations for the same purpose.
>
> Before leaving the job for any of the purposes noted above, the steward or grievance committee member shall obtain permission from the immediate supervisor and such permission shall not be unreasonably delayed. If a steward or grievance committee member enters a department other than his or her own, the steward or member shall first notify the departmental supervisor of his or her presence and purpose.
>
> It is the Union's obligation to conduct its business under this section in such a manner as to avoid interference with the efficient operation of the enterprise. When, in the opinion of Management, the Union or any of its representatives are not meeting this obligation, Management shall bring the matter to the attention of the grievance committee and if the subsequent discussions do not yield a satisfactory adjustment, Management may use the Arbitration section of the contract to obtain a final determination of the dispute.

ESTABLISHING PRIORITIES

When the preparatory tasks are completed, the union is likely to have a long agenda of protective language proposals to accompany an equally lengthy list of pay and fringe requests. Consequently, it is just as important to set priorities on protective language proposals as it is on compensation items (see the discussion of priorities in Chapter 3).

THE IMPORTANCE OF LANGUAGE IN THE FIRST CONTRACT

The first contract affords a union the best opportunity to achieve an advantage in protective language. Employers are extremely reluctant to add or change rules in subsequent periods of bargaining, unless it is to their advantage. For example, many unions whose members accepted mandatory overtime rules when they were younger, found employers unwilling to alter these provisions in later years when such work became less desirable.

INTEREST-BASED (WIN-WIN) BARGAINING AND THE RULE-MAKING PROCESS

Clearly the rule-making process described above, with the exception of writing language, is consistent with traditional bargaining. Where interest-based bargaining is practiced, the company and the union are not supposed to be advocates for any particular set of principles. Rather, each party is open to the other's needs and concerns. Further, the tasks of identifying problems, collecting and analyzing the pertinent facts, and developing solutions are performed jointly by union and management representatives (see Chapter 8, Bargaining Activities).

MORE ON WRITING CONTRACT LANGUAGE

The remainder of this chapter is devoted to a discussion of the writing task itself. Some writing aids and tips are offered, a glossary of frequently used terms with their meanings is provided, and the layout and organization of contract provisions and the contract booklet are described.

Writing Aids ‹

One useful writing aid is a good dictionary of American English. Another is a thesaurus or book of synonyms. Finally, a dictionary of legal terms might also come in handy. Other reference works are catalogued in Appendix 2.

Writing Tips From Arbitrators

Arbitrators, by virtue of their pivotal position in the grievance procedure, are required to decipher the meaning of ambiguously written words, phrases, and even entire contract clauses. Over the years, arbitrators have developed a set of standards for interpreting contract language.[1] Some of these are also prescriptions for writing good contract language. The following rules for language construction are based on criteria used by arbitrators:

Rule: Contract language must clearly and explicitly express the intent of the union and the employer.

Suppose union and management agree to amend the performance appraisal program to increase employee involvement in the procedure and to require written evaluations. The following is a clear and explicit statement of principles: "Employee performance evaluations shall be reviewed with the employee before such evaluations are placed in the employee's personnel file. After such evaluations are completed in ink or typed, the employee shall sign the evaluation and be given a copy of same."

Rule: Specific wording carries greater weight than general wording.

Assume the following set of facts: An employee with 15 years of service and a superior performance record is caught by a supervisor

---

[1]For a fuller discussion of standards used in arbitration see Frank Elkouri and Edna Asper Elkouri, *How Arbitration Works*, 4th ed. (Washington, D.C.: BNA Books, 1985) with 1985–89 *Cumulative Supplement*, Marlin M. Volz and Edward P. Goggin, eds., 63–78.

leaving work with company property in her possession and is discharged for theft. The contract contains the following clauses: (1) "Discipline and discharge only for just cause," and (2) "Stealing of Company products and property shall result in discharge." Does the language of the contract help or hurt the grievant?

The "just cause" wording in the first clause does favor the grievant. The language is general and gives the arbitrator leeway to consider the discharge in light of such mitigating factors as the grievant's seniority and work record. The second clause, however, is more restrictive because it requires discharge once management provides evidence of theft. Since specific language takes precedent, the arbitrator must uphold the discharge when there is credible proof of guilt, such as a confession, or as in this case, a witness.

In general, words that minimize employer discretion should be used in situations where events are predictable. The term "seniority" is an example. Seniority has meaning in labor relations and can be measured in terms of hours, days, months, and years. Making seniority the sole criterion for all major personnel actions restricts employer freedom of action.

Alternatively, there are times when language should not be too specific. As previously noted, the phrase "just cause" is broad enough to give arbitrators great latitude when judging incidents of discipline and discharge. Putting a list of specific rules and penalties in the contract limits arbitral discretion.

Rule: The meaning of words, phrases, paragraphs, and clauses is determined in relation to the contract as a whole.

Contradictions creep into the language of the contract as provisions are added and amended over the years. In one case, a new pension right was unintentionally created because both the local management and the union failed to pay attention to the relationship between contract provisions. The first pension agreement established "normal retirement at age 65 with 15 years of credited service."

Ten years later, the following early retirement provision was added:

> An employee who shall have had his continuous service with the
> Company broken on or after July 1, by reason of a permanent shut-

down of a plant, department or subdivision thereof, or by reason of a layoff, or physical disability and who at the time of such break in continuous service shall have had 20 years of credited service and shall have attained the age of 55 years, shall be entitled to a pension upon his retirement.

After two additional years, the words, "or who resigns," were added. The amended early retirement clause now read: "An employee who shall have had his continuous service with the Company broken or who resigns on or after July 1 . . . shall be entitled to a pension upon his retirement."

Four years later, an actuary reviewing the pension plan for the union reported that the words, "or who resigns" in the early retirement provision meant normal retirement was at age 55 with 20 years of service and not, as everyone had believed, at age 65 with 15 years of service. Without knowing it, the local union had one of the most liberal retirement programs in the entire United States.

Management was in a bind. A major outlay of cash was necessary to bring the pension reserve up to the level required to fund the more generous benefit. Eventually full retirement at age 65 was restored, but not until management agreed to make several improvements in the pension plan. In this case, the union came out ahead as a result of the contradiction written into the contract, but the opposite also occurs.

Rule: Words and phrases carry their ordinary and popularly accepted dictionary definitions.

Arbitrators use the dictionary when interpreting contract provisions, so a bargaining committee should refer to one when writing contract language. To illustrate, an arbitrator was called upon to interpret the phrase "as quickly as possible" in the sentence "An employee transferred will be returned to his job as quickly as possible." The union's interpretation would have required temporary transfers to return to their regular jobs within 30 minutes once more qualified operators became available. In his decision, the arbitrator defined the word "possible" to mean "as soon as practicable" and cited Webster's *New Collegiate Dictionary* as the source.

The definition, he concluded, allowed the employer more time than the 30 minutes claimed by the union.[2]

Terms with special meanings must be clearly explained, preferably in the text of the provision itself. For example, a contract provision on "wet time" pay defined the term as "the time during which a worker is prevented from working (in a citrus fruit orchard) by excessive moisture on the trees." An arbitrator found the definition to be "clear and unambiguous" when finding for the union in a dispute involving this premium.[3] Further, trade and technical language is always interpreted in a trade or technical sense unless other definitions are provided.

Glossary of Terms Used in Writing Contract Language

Some words or phrases are better at imposing a contractual duty on an employer to either act or refrain from acting in some manner. To illustrate, suppose union and employer representatives are writing a new rule based on the principle of preserving bargaining unit work for union members. The following is the text of the first version of the proposed clause:

> Work normally performed by members of this Bargaining Unit, to the extent that it is appropriate to do so, may not be performed by supervisors.

This text gives full discretion to the employer. Replacing "appropriate" with "practical" or "practicable" makes the phrase slightly more compelling because there is room for argument over whether something is practical. The employer, however, still makes the final decision because terms such as "when practical," "when practicable," and "to the maximum extent practical" allow the employer to decide what actions are workable. Nevertheless, there is some room for discussion and argument over whether something is practical. It would be better to substitute "possible" for "practical" and

---

[2]Warner Press, Inc. and Graphics Communication Union, 89 LA 814 (1987) (Brunner, Arb.).

[3]L & O Growers Association and United Farm Workers Union of America, 82 LA 814 (1984) (Weiss, Arb.).

"practicable" although, as noted in an earlier example, some arbitrators use the terms interchangeably.

A more forceful statement of the rule is: "When possible, work normally performed . . ." The impossibility of doing something, a particularly difficult case to prove, is the only argument for inaction.

Next, an attempt to further strengthen the clause produces the following text:

> Work normally performed by members of this Bargaining Unit may not be performed by Supervisors.

The words "may" and "can" imply possibility and permission, but not a duty. Substituting the auxiliary verb "should" is not much better because it expresses a moral obligation only. Stating something "will" happen in the future does not imply a duty either. Using the verb "shall" is an improvement because it means compulsion. An even stronger obligation is implied in the word "must." Finally, eliminating the adverb "normally" enhances the text even more. The term "normally" weakens the language because it allows the employer to decide when the situation is "other than normal." A final, stronger, version of the clause reads:

> Work performed by members of this bargaining unit must not be performed by Supervisors.

PRODUCING THE CONTRACT BOOKLET

The original labor agreement signed by the representatives of the union and the employer should be stored away with other important local union records or, as is sometimes required, mailed to the national or international union. Copies of the primary document are reproduced in booklet form, usually at the employer's expense, for distribution to both bargaining unit employees and members of management. In terms of organization, the original document and the booklet are the same. The latter, however, usually contains a table of contents and/or an index to help readers quickly locate topics of interest.

Contract Design

A labor contract, in both its original and booklet forms, is arranged by article, section, and paragraph. All benefits and rights pertaining to a single subject, such as vacation hours, pay, and eligibility, are grouped together in the same article. Occasionally, unrelated topics requiring only brief explanations are grouped together in one article for convenience under the heading, "General."

Some subjects may apply to more than one article. For example, job posting may be a requirement for both promotion and job transfer. If these are separate articles, the job posting rules should be stated in both of them.

Articles, in turn, are subdivided into sections. Each section usually contains a one paragraph statement of a single benefit or rule. Paragraphs should be kept as brief as possible. Short paragraphs and short sentences are easier to read.

Exhibit 11-1. Sample Contract Provision

ARTICLE XIII
Vacations

Section 13.1. Vacation Schedule. Each employee shall receive a vacation with pay in accordance with the following schedule:

(a) All employees who at the start of the current year had more than six (6) months but less than one (1) year service shall receive a one-week vacation. . . .

(b) Vacation for all other employees shall be computed from the following table:

All employees who at the start of the vacation period of the current year had

—1 but less than 20 years of service—2 weeks vacation (80 hours)

—20 or more years of service—3 weeks vacation (120 hours).

Section 13.2. Vacation Pay. (a) For each week of vacation, an employee shall be entitled to an allowance of forty (40) hours' pay at the regular hourly rate of the employee at the time the employee leaves for vacation.

(c) An employee who terminates will be paid for earned vacation not taken.

Articles and sections must also have topical headings designed to give readers a clue about the subject being covered. In addition, articles, sections, and paragraphs should be numbered, particularly where there is more than one. This format is illustrated in Exhibit 11-1.

Reading Aids

The two most common forms of reading aids are the Table of Contents and the Subject Index. Their purpose is to make it easier for the user of a contract booklet to quickly locate the page containing the desired subject.

Table of Contents

A table of contents lists the articles and their titles in numerical order. It is placed at the front of the contract booklet and is all most people need to find a desired provision. A sample table of contents is provided in Exhibit 11-2.

Subject Index

A detailed index makes it even easier to locate information in the contract booklet. An index is created by going through the

---

Exhibit 11-2. Sample Table of Contents

TABLE OF CONTENTS

Article	Page
I. Recognition	3
II. Nondiscrimination	4
III. Union Security	6
IV. Management Clause	11
V. Representation	12
VI. No Strikes or Lockouts	15
VII. Grievance Procedure	18
VIII. Discipline and Discharge	26
IX. Seniority	27

---

contract section-by-section and identifying a descriptive word or phrase for each. The representative terms are listed alphabetically, with corresponding page numbers, at the back of the contract booklet. A sample index is presented in Exhibit 11-3.

Exhibit 11-3. Sample Index

INDEX

	Page
Arbitration	24, 25
Bulletin Board	120
Call-in Pay	28
Discharge	26
Discipline	26
Funeral Leave	35
Grievances	18–25
Nondiscrimination	4

Chapter 12

Bargaining Impasse and Third-Party Intervention

The arrival of the expiration date and hour of the current agreement is the built-in deadline in traditional bargaining. Passage of the deadline without total agreement on settlement terms causes a rupture in the process. In the extreme, total impasse, or deadlock, occurs. A new actor called a mediator, fact finder, or arbitrator, also appears on the scene either at the request of the union, employer, or public official. Representing the public interest, the role of this neutral is to work with the principal parties to avoid or end impasse. This chapter examines union options at the deadline, at impasse, and third-party intervention.

UNION OPTIONS AT THE DEADLINE

At the contract expiration deadline, the union bargaining committee must reappraise its bargaining proposals and priorities in light of the employer's announced positions on pay, fringes, and protective language. Based on this assessment, the union bargaining committee must choose a course of action for the postdeadline period. The following options are available:

1. The union agrees to the package of pay, fringe, and protective language terms contained in the employer's final offer. The potential for settlement is greatest where the union's highest priority objectives have been satisfied. Similarly, where the terms of agreement compare favorably with those being bargained elsewhere in the employer's industry or local geographical area. Alternatively, the bargaining committee might view the money offered as the maximum affordable in light of the employer's financial position. Again, the leadership may view the union as being too weak vis-à-vis the employer to mount a successful strike for more money and protective language (see Chapter 13, Strikes and the Strike Alternative). Finally, bargaining committee members often rely on their own collective intuitions to tell them when they have gotten as much as they can from the employer.

2. The union proposes extending the provisions of the terminating agreement several hours or days while the bargaining process continues. This option is usually selected when the parties are very close to total agreement. All provisions of the existing agreement remain in full force and all new improvements in pay and fringes are made retroactive to the deadline.

3. The union agrees with the employer that their differences are irreconcilable and nothing more can be gained by continuing to meet. This is total impasse. Total impasse is not the same as reaching impasse on a single issue. Single-issue impasse does not suspend the obligation to bargain on other unsettled matters.

   At total impasse, the employer is free to implement its final offer and the union can strike provided the proper Taft-Hartley Act notices have been given to the federal and state or territorial mediation services (see Chapter 1, Organizational Activities, and Chapter 13, Strikes and the Strike Alternative). The employer also has the option either to keep the business operating during a strike with replacement workers or to agree in writing to close the facility. Alternatively, at total impasse, the employer can lock out its regular employees and hire replacements.

The legal duty to bargain continues in the period after impasse. The union and the employer must return to the bargaining table when (1) a third party intervener requests a meeting, (2) the union or the employer announces a significant change in its bargaining position, (3) the business outlook of the employer changes, or (4) a strike occurs. See Chapter 7, The Law of Contract Bargaining, for a discussion of the general bargaining obligation.

4. The union rejects the employer's final offer, but continues to bargain even though management refuses to extend the existing contract. The bargaining committee avoids impasse by continuing to meet, discussing the items at issue, and making new proposals. As long as the commitment to bargain continues and union members stay on the job, all pay, fringe, and other mandatory terms of the existing agreement remain in force. The employer, however, could cancel the union shop, dues checkoff, and other permissive conditions. The grievance procedure survives if neither party makes a move to end it.

WHEN IMPASSE IS UNDESIRABLE

There may be times when the union bargaining committee seeks to postpone reaching total impasse. This may be the best course of action at times when the employer is demanding major concessions and/or the union bargaining strength is weak.

—Task—
Avoid Impasse

Union negotiators must be flexible and creative in fashioning new concessions without totally gutting the union's original proposals. Further, a considerable amount of time should be spent exploring employer positions. Company demands, no matter how outrageous or impractical, must never be rejected out of hand. Rather, the bargaining committee should discuss every detail of every proposal at length while making numerous requests for clarification and more information. In his paper on offensive bargaining, David Rosenfeld emphasizes using information requests as a way of delaying impasse. He provides a sample 40-page letter requesting information covering over four dozen topics.[1] It is purposely designed to be as broad, intrusive, and burdensome on management as possible. Bargaining over how much information the union is entitled to receive will in and of itself consume a considerable amount of time.

In addition, the bargaining committee should caucus frequently and take as much time as needed to adequately review all information obtained from management. If necessary, the union should seek the help of an attorney, actuary, or other expert. The national or international union may be able to help local affiliates obtain the services of specialists.

The employer may believe total impasse has been reached while the union may not. A disagreement over whether a genuine impasse exists is resolved by the National Labor Relations Board (NLRB). Consequently, should the employer declare impasse and refuse to continue bargaining, the union should file unfair labor practice charges (see Chapter 7, The Law of Contract Bargaining).

IMPASSE AND INTEREST-BASED (WIN-WIN) BARGAINING

Impasse is not viewed as a viable option by practitioners of interest-based bargaining. Nevertheless, some conflicts of interest, usually involving compensation, prove just as intractable when problem solving is tried. As a result, the parties often return to traditional bargaining on pay and fringe issues. However, proponents claim the successes achieved using the interest-based approach carry over and mitigate the adversarial nature of the traditional proceedings so that total impasse is avoided. See Chapter

---

[1]David A. Rosenfeld, *Offensive Bargaining* (Silver Spring, Md.: George Meany Center for Labor Studies, 1992), Exhibit A.

8, Bargaining Activities, for discussion of both interest-based and traditional bargaining.

THIRD-PARTY INTERVENTION

The purpose of third-party intervention is to avoid or end impasse. Mediation is the most frequently employed form, particularly in the private sector. Fact-finding is widely used in both the public and the private sector when disputes are judged by a governmental body to have serious public consequences. Interest arbitration is practiced almost exclusively in the local government sector and is covered in Chapter 14, Bargaining in the Public Sector.

Mediation

Mediators intercede either before or after total impasse is reached. Actually, the presence of a mediator delays impasse because it is evidence of an ongoing effort by the principal parties to reconcile their differences.

An important source of mediators is the Federal Mediation and Conciliation Service (FMCS), with 9 district and 70 field offices nationwide. In addition, all states and territories have their own mediation agencies. The union can join with the employer to request the services of a mediator from the FMCS or a state or territorial agency or it can do so on its own volition.

Sometimes mediators from the aforementioned agencies take the initiative and approach the parties with an offer to intervene. They have already been officially notified by the union (or employer) that bargaining is underway and may even be monitoring the progress of negotiations. Aware that impasse has occurred, a federal or state mediator may telephone the parties and request a meeting. It is considered bad faith bargaining (an unfair labor practice) when the union or employer refuses to comply with such a request.

Mediators have no authority to impose a settlement. Their function is to help narrow the differences between union proposals and management offers. They try to identify areas of agreement and disagreement and then nudge the parties toward a resolution with suggestions on where concessions might be made.

A mediator can sometimes help the parties overcome conflicts that have nothing to do with the substantive issues but still get in the way of agreement. Personality clashes and distrust of each other's motives are examples of misunderstandings that are often cleared up by a mediator.

—Task—
Use Mediation to Get Bargaining Back on Track

Suppose the parties have reached total impasse and either a strike is in progress or employees are working without a contract. The bargaining committee, however, is ready to resume the bargaining process, but is afraid to take the initiative for fear of losing face or appearing weak. All it has to do is telephone the nearest FMCS field office or state or territorial mediation agency and request a mediator. The mediator, in turn, contacts the employer directly and, without revealing the union's role, schedules a meeting. The employer responds to the invitation of the representative of the public interest because not doing so is considered a breach in the legal duty to bargain.

—Task—
Bargain With the Mediator

Mediators employ various tactics in their quests for settlements. For example, union and company negotiators are physically separated with the mediator serving as the communication link between them. This ability to control the flow of information permits mediators to influence the decision-making process of each party.

Mediators are interested in achieving settlements and the responsibility for the quality of the terms of any agreement reached is left to the principals. Consequently, the bargaining committee is forced to bargain with the mediator and the employer over who makes concessions and what is conceded. Many of the same techniques used in the collective bargaining process are employed when dealing with a mediator. The following are some important bargaining guidelines:

1. The union must present a united front in the presence of the mediator so there must be one main spokesperson. In addition, members of the bargaining committee should meet in private when discussing internal differences.

2. Union negotiators must never reveal their true positions and priorities to the mediator. Preserving maneuverability is important so all priorities and concession-making options should be reviewed in private before being announced to the mediator.

3. The union must be willing to compromise. However, concessions should not be made unless the employer is willing to give up something in return.

4. Union negotiators must keep priorities in mind. They should remain firm on issues where compromise is not possible.

Fact-Finding

Fact-finders are usually private citizens who are asked by public bodies to hold hearings, listen to arguments, facts, and proofs offered by unions and employers, and report their findings. Sometimes they are also authorized to propose settlement terms. Although such recommendations are not binding on the principal parties, they can and do influence public opinion.

Fact-finding offers the union an opportunity to turn public opinion against the employer. Support for the union position by the fact-finder often motivates customers, government officials, and/or the general public to pressure the employer to compromise.

—*Task*—
Prepare for Fact-Finding

Influencing public opinion is the objective, so the bargaining committee must make a strong and well-documented presentation.

All of the arguments and proofs developed to support the union's original bargaining position should be presented to the fact-finder (see Chapter 3, Bargaining Proposals and Priorities, and Chapter 11, Bargaining Contract Language). This is not the time for concession making.

Chapter 13

Strikes and the Strike Alternative

The union's major weapon at total impasse has traditionally been the strike. However, in periods marked by high unemployment, the loss of legal protections, and a hostile political environment, strikes are difficult to win. In recent years, unions have begun to experiment with new approaches to concerted action. Two major innovations are the use of "outside" or public pressure, often referred to as corporate campaigns, and "inside" pressure, called workplace actions. These new strategems can be used either as alternatives to strikes or to make work stoppages more effective.

This chapter is divided into two parts. The first discusses strikes. The second examines a no-strike option.

STRIKES

The decision to strike over pay, fringes, and other terms and conditions of employment is an important one. The risks are enormous and potentially catastrophic, since the loss of employment and even of the union itself is possible. The alternative to a strike is to accept the employer's terms or work without a contract. In the latter situation, the no-strike campaign is initiated.

The ultimate decision to strike rests with the membership of the local union and the leadership may not always be able to maintain control. Sometimes members have become so angered by management's actions and policies that there is nothing the leadership can do or say to prevent a strike. When passions are less aroused, however, the bargaining committee has considerable influence over whether a strike is called.

Before pulling employees off their jobs, bargaining committee members must carefully evaluate the potential for a successful strike. The leadership must also plan and implement the activities associated with running the strike. The decision to strike and the implementation of strike action are discussed in the first part of this chapter.

The Decision to Strike

The actual decision to strike is not made until the very last moment when an impasse appears inevitable. However, an evaluation of the union's ability to conduct a successful strike begins much earlier. The bargaining committee should start to investigate the possibilities as soon as notice of intent to renegotiate the contract is given or, in the case of a first contract, while the organizing drive is in progress.

The bargaining committee must search for telltale signs and clues about whether the union membership and the employer can endure the financial and other hardships associated with a strike. The same kind of appraisal must be made of the social and political climate existing in the local community in terms of how it is likely to affect the strike.

—*Task*—
Assess the Strengths of the Employer

The purpose of withdrawing the services of the bargaining unit is to force the employer to stop operating and, when the cost of lost business becomes high enough, to compromise. In recent years, a number of factors including automation, favorable court decisions, high unemployment, a decline in the number of high paying industrial jobs, and a loss of respect for the sanctity of the picket line have made it relatively easy for employers to continue to operate with strikebreakers. As a consequence, the strike has been used to harm the union in some instances.

The Strike as a Management Weapon

Some employers have provoked strikes in an effort to break unions. The scenario goes as follows: The employer makes demands that are inherently destructive to the bargaining unit. The union strikes and the employer hires strikebreakers as permanent replacements. After 12 months, a decertification election is held and with only the replacement workers voting, the union is out.

The bargaining committee must determine whether the employer is seeking to provoke a strike. The following are telltale signs of management's hostile intentions:

1. The employer hires an outside consultant, with an established reputation for busting unions, as its chief negotiator.
2. The employer demands a significant cut in pay and fringes and a substantial weakening of rules governing individual employee and union security without any pretense at justification.
3. The employer refuses to compromise despite concessions made by the union.
4. The employer ignores requests for information relevant to the subject matter of bargaining.
5. The employer replaces bargaining with a public relations campaign claiming financial distress, budget deficits, or the possibility of bankruptcy.

The preceding behaviors may appear to be examples of bad-faith bargaining by employers (see Chapter 7, The Law of Contract Bargaining). However, the National Labor Relations Board (NLRB) and the courts do not always sustain unfair labor practice (ULP) complaints brought by unions.

Ability of the Employer to Withstand a Strike

Even when management is not trying to cause a strike, the bargaining committee must always assess the employer's ability to endure a work stoppage should one be called. Rationally, a strike should not be undertaken unless the company is vulnerable. The following are indicators of employer weakness:

1. Demand for products or services is high as measured by such indicators as the current backlog of orders, the current rate of customer or client deliveries, and/or the level of current employment.
2. Risk of permanent loss of customers to competitors is high.
3. Risk of permanent closure of the struck facility is low because it is new, profitable, or a major investment.
4. Risk of the struck operations being shifted to facilities in other locations, including foreign countries is low.
5. Amount of short-term financial obligations owed to banks and/or other creditors is large and, as a consequence, an uninterrupted cash flow is required.
6. Substitution of nonbargaining unit personnel and other strikebreakers for the regular work force is difficult due to the skill requirements of the jobs and/or the absence of automation.
7. Strike assistance in the form of help from an employers' or merchants' association, a parent company, a mutual aid pact, or a special insurance policy is unavailable.

—*Task*—
Assess Conditions in the Community

The union's ability to conduct a successful strike is affected by the state of the local economy. For example, the unemployment rate in the community could determine the willingness of local citizens to become strikebreakers and the success strikers have in finding temporary jobs. Similarly, the cost of living in a geographical area determines how well strikers can get along without their regular paychecks.

Community leaders can also be a factor in a strike situation by being actively partisan. Influential political, business, news, and even religious groups are in a position to make life difficult for whomever they oppose. A review of how the community has reacted to past strikes should be part of any assessment of the potential for success of any future action. (See Chapter 1, Organizational Activities, for a discussion on building local community support.)

A history similar to the following would not bode well for a local union contemplating a work stoppage:

1. Employers have little difficulty finding strikebreakers in the local community.
2. The local cost of living is relatively higher than in other communities.
3. The police and the judiciary side with employers by acting quickly to arrest and convict strikers for misdemeanors committed on the picket line.
4. Local politicians support employers by actions such as ordering the police to protect strikebreakers or by issuing antiunion statements to the press.
5. The news media are biased in favor of the employers' positions in their coverage of labor disputes.
6. Merchants are unwilling to extend credit to strikers.

—*Task*—
Assess the Strengths of the Membership

Strikes impose financial hardship and psychological cost on union members. Stresses and strains may also occur within families. These pressures are likely to build as the strike lengthens. The following are positive signs of membership ability to weather a strike:

1. Members are likely to have some money saved because wage/salary rates are sufficiently high.
2. Members' work skills cannot easily be replaced.
3. Members strongly support the union's proposals and priorities.
4. Other unions in the community can be counted on to support the strike.
5. Financial and other aid is available from the national or international union and community social services.

6. Members knows what to expect because they have been through a strike before.

The leadership should use the union newsletter and other forums, such as the membership meeting, to give members advance warning about the financial hardships imposed by a strike. Employees must be encouraged to save as much money as possible on the assumption that the strike could last longer than one or two weeks. They should also be advised not to take on any new consumer debt and to make arrangements with major creditors for possible postponement of current debt repayments. Dispensing this type of information serves a double purpose. It prepares members to withstand a possible strike and also increases the credibility of strike threats made at the bargaining table.

Strike Administration

Preparations for a strike should begin no later than the first bargaining session with management. The moment the decision to walk off the job is made, the strike machinery must be ready to function. Again, evidence of early preparations also adds credibility to the union's strike threats.

The strike leadership must be in place well before the walkout occurs. Picketing is an important strike activity and all the appropriate arrangements, including printing of signs and leaflets, must be completed before the strike starts. Preparations for support committees, the involvement of other labor organizations, and a media campaign must also be made in advance. Finally, planning is required to mobilize the membership, to actually get the strike underway, and to deal with employees who cross the picket line.

—Task—
Choose the Strike Leadership

The bargaining committee could assume overall responsibility for planning and conducting the strike in addition to its duties at the bargaining table. However, both jobs involve a considerable amount of work and are time consuming. As an alternative, a separate strike committee is appointed by the bargaining committee or local union executive board from among union officers who are not directly involved in contract talks and other interested members. At least one bargaining committee member should be included on the strike committee to serve as a liaison between the two groups.

The strike committee makes all policy decisions related to strike operation. It also creates and staffs the subcommittees needed to carry out the various activities associated with running the strike. All subordinate committees report daily to the strike committee.

The chairperson of the strike committee obtains strike authorization from the national or international union president as required in almost all union constitutions. In addition, he or she handles all unusual incidents or emergencies. Ideally, the chairperson is a veteran of earlier strikes who is given enough authority to provide help and advice as circumstances require.

—Task—
Establish a Strike Headquarters

One of the first tasks of the strike committee is to choose a site for a strike headquarters. The spot selected should be located as close as possible to the employer's premises. The facility must also be spacious enough to permit members to congregate freely and, ideally, contain both sanitary and cooking facilities. Possible locations include the union hall or office, a vacant store, or a house trailer temporarily parked on nearby property.

—Task—
Prepare for Picketing

Strikers picket by marching back and forth in front of the employer's place of business carrying signs and distributing leaflets. Pickets can be stationary where conditions make it unsafe or impracticable to march. The purpose of the picket line is to keep employees off the employer's premises. Pickets also inform customers, suppliers, and the general public about the dispute and help persuade them to stop doing business with the employer for the duration of the strike.

No more than three or four pickets should be stationed at each entrance to the employer's facilities. The total number of pickets required is inversely related to the length of time people will spend on the line. For example, 36 pickets per day, 252 per week, are needed if three pickets are placed at each of two gates or entrances for four-hour shifts around the clock, seven days a week. If shifts are shortened to two hours, the requirement is doubled.

The Picket Subcommittee

The strike committee should appoint a picket subcommittee to handle the logistics of manning the picket line. The picket subcommittee recruits pickets and schedules picket line duty times and locations. The subcommittee also selects picket captains, orders signs and leaflets, and serves as the communication link between strike headquarters and the pickets on the line.

Once the strike is underway, picket subcommittee members provide pickets with hot coffee, drinking water, food, and sanitary facilities. They also arrange for special rallies, picnics, sing alongs, and other events held on the picket line.

Picket Captains

The picket subcommittee appoints picket captains and alternates. One picket captain and alternate are assigned to each picket site, on each shift. The duties of a picket captain include

- instructing pickets about their duties and behavior,
- maintaining discipline on the picket line,
- keeping records of picket line attendance, and
- keeping alert for unusual incidents.

Union activists do not necessarily make the best picket captains. Instead, it is preferable to identify and appoint the unofficial leaders of departments or work groups. Members will feel more confident if their respected and trusted co-workers are part of the strike leadership.

Picket Signs

The actual printing of signs and leaflets is done on short notice. The picket committee makes all necessary arrangements with a union print shop in advance of need. The printer is then alerted by telephone to produce the materials. The initial order of signs should be equal to one and one-half times the number of expected pickets.

Messages printed on picket signs are short, simple, and easy to read by passing motorists and pedestrians. The issues in the strike determine the choice of slogan. Examples include: "Local Union On Strike," "On Strike For Better Health Care," and "On Strike For Justice."

Leaflets

One or two key issues in the strike can be publicized in greater detail in a leaflet handed out by pickets to passersby. Bulk quantities are delivered to other unions and friends in the local community for wider distribution.

Leaflets are prepared using either a typewriter or a computer with word processing software and a printer. For best results, messages should be limited to one side of an 8 1/2 × 11 inch sheet of paper. The heading, in bold print, alerts the reader that a dispute is in progress. Some examples are: "PLEASE DON'T BUY" or "XYZ COMPANY UNFAIR." The message itself must be clear and simple. In addition, sentences and paragraphs should be short. White spaces are left between short blocks of text to avoid an overcrowded look and a sketch or cartoon is usually pasted on. The completed copy is taken to a union print shop for reproduction.

Instructions for Pickets

A list of rules of appropriate conduct for pickets, and all strikers generally, is prepared by the picket subcommittee and a copy is given to each member. The rules are reviewed again at a special meeting in order to impress upon the membership the importance of both knowing and adhering to them. The rules are restated again on the picket line by the picket subcommittee and/or the picket captains.

In general, pickets must be told to avoid getting into direct physical or verbal confrontations with nonstrikers, to keep the picket line moving, and to avoid blocking entrances to the employer's premises. Many employers monitor picket lines, often with video cameras and sound recorders, looking for evidence of this type of misconduct. Strikers should also be warned not to possess or consume illegal drugs and alcohol while on picket duty, traveling to and from the picket line, or at strike headquarters.

In addition, remarks made to a friendly appearing outsider could be distorted in ways detrimental to the union. Consequently, strikers and their family members should be cautioned not to discuss the strike with representatives of the news media, friends who are supervisors or members of management, nonbargaining unit employees, and members of the general public. Each member should be provided with the name of the designated union spokesperson and told to direct inquiries from outsiders to the person named. Strikers and their families should also be advised not to respond to communications from the employer, whether by mail, telephone, or personal contact.

Further, federal, state, and local laws affecting picket line conduct must be explained. Typically, communities prohibit littering, which includes dropping cigarette butts on the ground, parking in fire zones, and/or sleeping in parked automobiles. Laws regulating mass picketing and other picket line behavior are discussed later in this chapter.

Union members must be told to be on time for their scheduled picket shifts and to remain on the line until their replacement arrives. Individuals who are unable to serve at assigned times are required to obtain their own replacements.

Finally, pickets should be instructed to report all unusual incidents and emergencies immediately to the picket captains. Examples of uncommon occurrences should be provided. They include photographing of the picket line, attempts by the employer to contact strikers and their families, and the presence of news reporters.

—Task—
Establish Support Committees

Some strikers may experience financial difficulties, particularly if the strike lasts more than three or four weeks. Subcommittees should be established, as needed, to administer a variety of striker assistance programs. Support committee members make regular appearances at strike headquarters to meet with employees needing assistance. Typical activities of support committees include

- applying to the national or international union president for strike benefits and distributing the funds,
- finding temporary and part-time jobs for strikers,
- contacting community service organizations and agencies on behalf of members with emergency needs,
- meeting with officials of community lending institutions and local merchants to discuss mortgage payment deferments and credit extensions, and
- collecting and distributing food and clothing.

The AFL-CIO Community Services representative in the local community is also in a position to offer support. This person can be particularly helpful to strikers in need of public and community emergency financial aid programs such as food stamps and Aid to Families with Dependent Children (AFDC).

—Task—
Coordinate With Other Labor Groups

Support from other local unions and the local AFL-CIO central labor body is important to the success of any strike. The strike committee should make contact with these organizations well in advance of the strike to give their leaders time to decide on a course of action. Speakers could attend local union meetings to explain the nature of the dispute and answer questions.

Supportive unions typically offer financial aid and observe the striking union's picket line. In one instance, individual truck drivers delivering supplies refused to cross the picket line of another union in their local community. This action followed a meeting between the drivers and the strikers where the issues were explained and help was requested. As it turned out, this strike was over rather quickly.

—Task—
Plan a Media Campaign

Presumably a media relations committee is already in place and has been functioning throughout the bargaining period (see

Chapter 1, Organizational Activities). Committee members must now prepare a positive and aggressive media campaign to publicize the reasons for the strike. This implies doing more than just reacting to the employer's public relations campaign.

The complex issues of the strike must be explained to reporters. Consequently, only knowledgeable and well-rehearsed union representatives should speak in public. As previously noted, a union spokesperson must be designated and union members instructed to refer all media requests for interviews to him or her.

—*Task*—
Maintain Solidarity

Strikers have a lot of time on their hands and boredom and isolation can lead to a decline in morale. Rumors will circulate almost continuously and some could cause great harm.

It is the strike committee's job to keep members' commitment and morale high throughout the strike. All union members should be kept actively involved in the strike. Every striker should be assigned to picket line duty for short periods of two to four hours each and every day. People who are unable to picket should be assigned other duties. In addition, strikers should be assigned to support tasks based on their interests and skills. For example, writers compose leaflets and cooks prepare food.

Union members must be kept informed and in frequent contact with each other. Informational meetings should be scheduled even when there is little to report. Pep rallies and marches also tend to energize people. Pot luck meals and songfests held on the picket line can help relieve the tedium of picket duty.

Strikers need a place where they can mingle together informally. Strike headquarters is a good location provided there is sufficient space for people to comfortably sit, visit, and have a cup of coffee or a soft drink. Local union officials knowledgeable about the efforts being made to settle the strike should be available on a regular basis to answer questions and respond to rumors.

Another way to encourage communications between strikers is with telephone "trees." In this system, members are asked to telephone five or six of their union brothers and sisters on a regular basis to pass along information, squelch rumors, and just plain talk.

One more vehicle for communications is a daily newsletter. The one- or two-page publication can be used to educate members as well as provide them with a forum for participation. The contents might include short articles poking fun at the employer, news items about members, stories about life on the picket line, letters to the editor, and cartoons about the employer and the strike. The newsletter is written at night and delivered to the picket line and strike headquarters in the morning. Most national and international unions have staff people who can offer advice about newsletter preparation.

—*Task*—
Kick Off the Strike

The bargaining committee quits the bargaining table after announcing the strike. Next, committee members enter the employer's facilities and lead all employees out. Pickets are put in place as quickly as possible.

A mass meeting of all bargaining unit employees is held immediately after the breakdown in bargaining. At this meeting, the employer's final offer is compared with the union's requests and priorities. At the conclusion of this meeting, members and officers march en masse to the picket line. After picketing together for a couple of hours, the strikers who are scheduled for other picket shifts are sent home to rest.

—*Task*—
Deal With Nonstrikers, Strikebreakers, and Crossovers

The problem of nonstrikers, strikebreakers, and crossovers arises when management continues to operate the business during the strike. The union leadership must find ways to respond to employees who make the strike less effective by crossing the picket line to support management.

Nonstrikers

Nonstrikers are employees who refuse to join the strike. They may be employees who have not joined the union, although entitled to do so, or union members who are opposed to the strike.

The strike committee should identify potential nonstrikers early. Committee members and/or other union activists can then meet with targeted employees on a personal, one-on-one basis in an attempt to persuade them to change their minds. One approach is to discuss the inequities and discriminatory elements in management's bargaining position and demonstrate how the proposed improvements in pay, fringes, and protective language will directly benefit the employee. Alternatively, an effort could be made to find out what bothers the employee about the job and then point out what the union can or is doing to help alleviate the problem.

Nonstrikers should be greeted with stony silence when they cross the picket line. This is a way of informing them of their exclusion from the group. One union photographed nonstrikers crossing the picket line using a Polaroid camera and posted the pictures on a makeshift bulletin board it had set up on the picket line.

Strikebreakers

Nothing hurts the morale of strikers more than watching replacement workers cross the picket line to perform their jobs. Unfortunately, employers often find it relatively easy to recruit strikebreakers. Management doesn't even have to worry about the cost of training strikebreakers because, under current law, they can be kept on as permanent employees after the strike is settled.[1]

Strikebreakers should be greeted with shouts of "scab" and other taunts and insults as they enter and leave the employer's premises. It is permissible to shout at scabs in their automobiles. Some strikers have used the potentially dangerous tactic of walking in front of strikebreakers' cars in an attempt to force them to stop. However, scabs cannot be permanently blocked from entering the employer's premises. Throwing nails under automobiles, damaging property of strikebreakers or the employer, and massing pickets to block entry are examples of illegal acts. Strikers found guilty of such conduct can be permanently discharged.[2] Verbal threats may also be viewed as coercive and intimidating to nonstrikers and

---

[1]NLRB v. Mackay Radio & Telephone Company, 304 US 333, 2 LRRM 610 (1938).

[2]NLRB v. Fansteel Metallurgical Corp., 5 NLRB 930, 4 LRRM 515 (1939).

grounds for discharge, even when there are no accompanying gestures or physical acts.[3] State laws may be applicable as well.[4]

Crossovers

As the strike lengthens, some strikers may return to work. When this happens, rumors about a failed strike typically begin to circulate. The strike committee must act quickly to squelch the rumors and reassure the membership. The best approach is to accuse the employer of pressuring employees to return to work in an act of desperation and claim that only a very few members are responding.

Unions can establish rules that impose monetary fines on members who cross the picket line. Payment of fines is enforceable through civil court action only. A better approach is to reach potential crossovers beforehand in an effort to regain their support.

Taft-Hartley Rules

Picketing is regulated and strikers have legal rights. In the private sector, the applicable law is the Taft-Hartley Act[5] as interpreted by the National Labor Relations Board (NLRB) and the federal courts of appeals.

Picketing

Picketing, to be protected activity, must normally take place on public property. Picketing on private property, which at times can include sidewalks and parking lots, is illegal. The exception to the private property rule is where there is no other safe or practicable means of communicating with the public.

The union should always seek Taft-Hartley protection whenever the legality of a picket line location is questioned. If the employer contacts local authorities to stop picketing on what is alleged to be private property, the union should immediately file

---

[3] NLRB v. Clear Pine Mouldings, 268 NLRB 1044, 115 LRRM 1113 (1984).
[4] One example is the Wisconsin Peace Act, Wis. Stat., §§111.01–111.19.
[5] Taft-Hartley Act is the more popular title for the National Labor Management Relations Act of 1947 as amended (LMRA).

a Section 8(a)(1), employer ULP charge with the NLRB (see Chapter 7, The Law of Contract Bargaining). This action removes the matter from the jurisdiction of the local police and courts. They will be unable to stop the picketing until after the NLRB proceedings have concluded, which can take some time.

Picketing must also be nonviolent. The point at which peaceful persuasion becomes intimidating and threatening is not clearly defined. The NLRB and the courts decide such questions on a case-by-case basis. In general, the union should avoid having excessive numbers of pickets marching in front of entrances to the employer's facilities or in any way block people from going in or out.

Strikers have a right to persuade customers, suppliers, and employees of other companies not to cross the picket line. Nevertheless, excessive shouting and waving of picket signs at persons crossing the line should be avoided, particularly when the employer is recording the action on video tape.

Rights of Strikers

Although strikers do not lose their status as employees under the Taft-Hartley Act, there are risks. Employees who strike as a result of a dispute over pay, fringes, or other conditions of employment are classified under the law as economic strikers. Employers have the right to replace economic strikers with temporary and permanent workers. Temporary replacements must themselves be replaced by returning strikers as soon as the union makes an unconditional offer to return to work.

The employer is not obliged to discharge permanent replacement employees at the end of an economic strike unless an alternative arrangement is made in a separate strike settlement agreement. Names of strikers not immediately recalled must be placed on a preferential hiring list, but management is only required to rehire strikers when vacancies occur for which they are qualified.

A strike begun over economic objectives becomes an unfair labor practice strike when the employer engages in illegal conduct. The NLRB must determine whether the employer provoked or prolonged the original strike by violating Sections 8(a) and (d) of the Act (see Chapter 7, The Law of Contract Bargaining). In the absence of any misconduct, ULP strikers must be reinstated in their former jobs when an offer to return to work is made even if the employer has to terminate replacement workers.

Alternatively, strikes may initially be called to protest what union leaders perceive are employer ULPs rather than in support of economic positions. This is risky, however. The NLRB may subsequently view the conduct of the employer as nothing more than perfectly legal, hard-nosed, or tough, bargaining. In that event, the strike is illegal and the participants can be discharged with no further opportunities for rehire.

Acts of civil disobedience such as tying up the employer's phone lines at critical times, blocking delivery trucks, and staging sit-ins can be effective, as the actions of the Pittston Coal Company strikers in 1989 demonstrated,[6] but there are risks as well. These job actions along with intermittent strikes, partial in-plant/office strikes, slowdowns, and secondary boycotts are not protected activities under the Taft-Hartley Act. Penalties include injunctions, fines, and permanent discharge of convicted employees.

Employer Lockouts

Not all employers wait for the union to decide whether to strike or work without a contract. Some take the initiative and lockout, or close their doors to, union members. Replacement workers are often hired and the business continues to operate.

In the case of a lockout, replacement workers are considered temporary. Former employees must be reinstated to their jobs once the lockout has ended.

During a lockout, the union can establish a picket line. In addition, state law must be examined to determine whether employees are eligible to collect unemployment benefits. Finally, the parties can continue or resume the bargaining process while the lockout is in progress, just as during a strike.

---

[6]"As Bitter Coal Strike Ends, Ripples From the Dispute Are Widely Felt," *New York Times*, Dec. 23, 1989. The union amassed over $60 million dollars in fines as a result of members' acts of violence, civil disobedience, and destruction of company property.

Strikes and Picketing at Health Care Institutions

The union must notify the employer and the Federal Mediation and Conciliation Service (FMCS) in writing of an impending strike at least ten days before taking any action. The notice must state the starting date and time of the strike and picketing.

The strike notification is in addition to the 60- and 90-day notice requirements discussed earlier (see Chapter 1, Organizational Activities). In the case of a first contract, the 10-day announcement cannot be given until the period of the 30-day notice to the FMCS has elapsed.

Upon receipt of notice of an impending strike, the FMCS can establish a fact-finding board to investigate the issues and make a written report. Once the fact-finders begin their work, there is a 30-day cooling off period during which strike action and picketing are illegal.

The Strike Settlement Agreement

A separate written agreement is required to restore strikers to their jobs and rights as employees. Strike settlement terms are permissive, not mandatory bargaining subjects. In other words, they cannot be the basis for prolonging the strike if tentative agreement has been reached on pay, fringes, and the other compulsory terms of employment. Consequently, the union's proposed strike settlement terms should be included in a counteroffer dealing with one or two mandatory bargaining subjects.

—*Task*—
Bargain a Strike Settlement Agreement

The bargaining committee must keep a file containing notes on all potential back to work problems including pending lawsuits and charges filed with the NLRB. These should be resolved before the strike officially ends. After the return to normal, the employer is less interested in dealing with disputes left over from a presumably settled strike.

A number of principles or standards for strike settlement terms have been developed by labor unions over many years. Among these are the following:

1. No disciplinary action against strikers;
2. No disciplinary action against strikers charged and/or arrested for strike-related incidents;
3. Guaranteed right of strikers to return to their former jobs, shifts, departments, and equipment and the discharge of all temporary and permanent replacement workers;
4. No break in seniority and eligibility requirements for vacations, sick leave, pensions, or any other benefits;
5. Procedure for rescheduling vacations canceled during the strike;
6. Timetable for calling strikers back to work; and
7. Arbitration of all disputes involving returning strikers.

For its part, management is likely to demand protection from union retaliation for nonstrikers and crossovers.

The terms of the strike settlement agreement are ratified by the membership. The bargaining committee must carefully explain the contents of the document before the vote.

ELEMENTS OF A NO-STRIKE ALTERNATIVE

When a decision is made not to strike at total impasse, bargaining unit employees remain on the job and work under terms and conditions unilaterally set by the employer (see Chapter 12, Bargaining Impasse and Third Party Intervention). The challenge facing the union is to force management to resume bargaining by making continued disagreement costly. Clearly, this is a tall order for a local union too weak to use the strike weapon. Nevertheless, the union can bring pressure to bear on the employer even when its members are forced to remain at their jobs.

Corporate campaigns and workplace actions are at the heart of the no-strike strategy. A corporate campaign is designed to use public opinion and policy to pressure the employer. Workplace actions, by contrast, consist of demonstrations of union solidarity and acts that reduce efficiency and increase the employer's operating costs. Before the corporate and workplace campaigns can begin, however, a foundation for the no-strike approach must be put in place.

Laying the Groundwork

The preconditions for a no-strike strategy and strike action are not dissimilar. First, the entire membership must be mobilized and involved. Second, the employer's vulnerabilities must be discovered.

—*Task*—
Organize the Membership

Maximum membership participation is required to develop and execute the no-strike strategy. One local union transformed its six-person bargaining committee into a 30-member Solidarity Committee in the weeks prior to the contract's expiration. Each committee member took an item from management's final offer and, as one participant described it, "distilled it into the essence of its ugliness" and then made it into a slogan. The results were communicated to every union member on a personal, one-on-one basis. This educational process was credited with turning most members into enthusiastic participants in the corporate and workplace actions that followed.

In general, a steering committee is created to recruit as many local union members as possible to perform the hard work of keeping the pressure on the employer for what conceivably could be a long period of time. Recruits are needed to lead small group discussions about the issues in the dispute, the reasons for working without a contract, and the components of the no-strike alternative. Others can compose and hand out leaflets, prepare and circulate petitions, print signs, research the employer, operate phone banks, talk to community groups, contact other labor organizations, write to elected government officials, attend meetings of company stockholders, and wear special hats, buttons, and other symbols of unity when requested. All members participate in rallies and marches.

A general request for volunteers is not likely to produce enough recruits to help carry out a no-strike strategy. A more personal approach is often necessary. This means the local leadership meets with members individually or in small groups to explain what the union is up against and how the members can help.

The local union should call upon the national or international union or an intermediate body for assistance. Headquarters staffs are sources of research assistance, legal advice, and help in planning strategy. They may also have a supply of printed materials and radio and television advertisements available for local use. In addition, service representatives in the field can help implement tactics. Finally, the national or international leadership is often able to exert greater pressure on targets such as the employer's bankers, investors, and creditors.

—*Task*—
Research the Employer

No-strike campaigns require more information about the employer than is customarily gathered by unions engaged in contract bargaining. The employer's manufacturing operation or service delivery system must be carefully studied to identify those points where it is vulnerable to internal pressures. For example, there may be key groups of employees whose absence for a day or more, due to sudden illness such as the "white" or "blue" flu, would severely curtail the operation of the enterprise. Members know about the weaknesses in the system and their ideas should be sought through surveys and at small group meetings.

A group of four or five members who like to read, are not afraid to ask questions, and are not easily discouraged, should be recruited to investigate the employer. This might include interviewing the company's important customers, suppliers, large shareholders, lenders, and creditors to determine whether these groups might be induced to put pressure on the employer to settle the labor dispute. For example, would a consumer boycott accomplish anything? Further, newspaper clippings in the "vertical file" at the local public library might yield useful material, including personal information about the owners of the business, outside directors, and/or managers. Local radio and television stations maintain similar files.

Federal, state, and local government records might be sources of useful information. Perhaps the employer is receiving special tax breaks, training subsidies, or other public loans or grants. If so, the union's political connections might be used to help block these benefits. The employer could also be out of compliance with some state laws and/or local ordinances. The union can use this information in a bid to garner support from advocacy groups in the larger community.

Information is also available about labor relations consultants used by employers. These consultants are required to file LM-20 and LM-21 forms with the U.S. Department of Labor, Office of Labor Management Standards (OLMS). These forms are available at OLMS field offices located around the country. Check the local telephone directory under "Government" or write U.S. Department of Labor/OLMS, Room N5613, 200 Constitution Avenue, N.W., Washington, DC 20210.

Components of a No-Strike Strategy

With the research completed and the membership mobilized, the union is ready to implement the corporate campaign and workplace actions. The corporate campaign brings the outside community into the dispute with the employer. Workplace actions, on the other hand, involve the work force in solidarity demonstrations and efforts to harass the employer.

—*Task*—
Implement the Corporate Campaign

Corporate campaign tactics are part of the no-strike strategy, but they can also be effective when implemented in conjunction with a strike. The union might first threaten to make its dispute with the employer public and then follow up with a few well-timed actions. The following are examples of corporate campaign tactics:

1. Customers are asked to boycott the goods or services of the employer. The Taft-Hartley Act permits advertising of

labor disputes by leafleting customers as they enter a business which is selling the product or service of the intransigent employer. The signs carried and leaflets distributed must clearly identify the target of the picketing. Conversely, informational leafleting combined with picketing or marching is illegal. To avoid possible legal complications, the union should discuss the specifics of its boycott with a competent attorney before taking action.

2. Public opinion is mobilized by publicizing the labor dispute in the local community. Union members go house-to-house and business-to-business to describe the nature of the dispute with the employer. In one case, a union gained both sympathy and financial support from the local community, including businesses, by publicly portraying the owners of the company as out-of-state giants who were abusing long time community residents, namely, the employees, by refusing to bargain over a new labor contract.

3. Pressure is applied to members of the employer's outside board of directors. These directors may also serve on other corporate boards or are executives of other companies. Where this is the case, union supporters write letters to these corporations threatening a consumer boycott, a campaign of negative publicity, or some other action if the named board member or executive is not forced to resign. Informational leafleting at the headquarters of these corporations is another possibility.

4. Protest demonstrations are organized in the community to win favorable attention from the local news media. Employees and their families, retirees, members of other unions, and local area supporters are recruited to participate in public meetings, marches, and rallies in the local community. The issues with potential for generating the most sympathy are emphasized.

5. Corporate executives are confronted at stockholders' meetings. Entry to annual meetings of shareholders is possible when the union either owns stock outright or has access to shares held by pension funds or individuals. Union representatives attending the meeting can use it as a forum for speaking publicly about the labor dispute. In addition,

union-directed shares can be voted against management or used to nominate friendly candidates to the board of directors.

6. Government regulatory agencies are alerted to law violations. Every instance of employer noncompliance with laws regulating business behavior is reported to the appropriate federal, state, or local regulatory agency. Types of violations to look for include wage and hour, health and safety, race and sex discrimination, environmental, and local zoning.

7. An attempt is made to embarrass the employer's financial and corporate allies. Informational leafleting is conducted at the headquarters of companies underwriting debt or otherwise allied with the targeted employer in an attempt to inform the public about their association with a "bad corporate citizen." It is hoped that local supporters and other unions will withdraw funds that are on deposit with the lending institutions and boycott the products or services of the other companies.

8. Friends in the community are mobilized to help exert pressure on the employer. The makeup of the work force and the nature of the jobs performed usually determine which groups are potential union allies. For example, unions with large numbers of women and minority members have a natural constituency in women's and civil rights organizations. Teachers and nurses, on the other hand, can connect with education and health advocacy groups. Other potentially useful coalition partners, depending upon the circumstances, include religious, small business, farm, consumer, senior citizen, student, and citizen watchdog groups.

One union was able to form an alliance with environmental activists in the community who were opposed to the employer's waste dumping policies. The two groups issued joint press releases criticizing the employer for damage done to the environment. In this way, the union kept the question of the employer's standing as a good corporate citizen before the public.

Coalition building usually requires a long-term commitment. The union is expected to help promote the issues of the groups with which it has become allied. See Chapter 1, Organizational

Activities, for more discussion of community involvement and coalition building.

—Task—
Implement Workplace Actions

There are two main types of workplace actions: demonstrating union solidarity and, at the same time, imposing sanctions on the employer. A discussion of each type follows.

Demonstrating Union Solidarity

The employer must be reminded of continued employee support for the union. The following are examples of tactics designed to exhibit both membership resolve and unity:

1. Daily meetings and rallies are held. One participant spoke of his experiences at a prework, curb-side rally as follows: "Our leaders gave us a few words of encouragement and then we marched into the plant singing Solidarity Forever." He also described hearing a large group of men and women singing together as "awesome."

2. Symbols of union solidarity are worn at work on a daily, or periodic, basis. These include tee shirts, caps, armbands, stickers, and buttons printed with the union logo or a slogan. Union members can show off their creativity with their designs and slogans.

3. A special newsletter is published to inform and educate members. News about the activities underway to bring management back to the bargaining table and articles explaining the employment rights of employees working without a contract should be included. Humorous cartoons and stories are useful additions, particularly when they are at management's expense.

4. Employees refuse to participate in employer-sponsored activities. Company holiday parties, awards programs, retirement dinners, and similar social events are boycotted. Management's attempts to hold captive audience meetings to explain company policies are turned into protest rallies.

Imposing Sanctions

The actions described in this section are designed to slow down production and raise costs and remind the employer of the advantages of having a contract. If the union has done its homework and identified the weak points in the employer's production or service delivery system, it will know the appropriate actions to take.

There are plenty of opportunities for imagination and creativity in the development of lawful workplace tactics. Questions of the legality of particular courses of action should be taken up with competent legal counsel. In addition, some thought should be given to the implementation of tactics. Periods of harassment should be interspersed with days when employees work in a normal manner so management can see the difference. The following are examples of coercive tactics:

1. Union members perform only the tasks required in their job description, no extra effort is expended. For example, a group of nurses refused to answer telephones, move beds, or perform other work outside of their job classification. Voluntary overtime was also turned down.

2. Union members do only what their supervisors order, no more and no less. Management has to supply ideas and take charge of problems.

3. Union members refuse to use personal tools or equipment. All such items are left at home. The employer is required to supply whatever is needed to get the job done.

4. All union members participate in handling grievances. Every incident in the workplace is grieved and every employee in the affected department, office or work area stops work and marches to the offices of management to present the grievance. Every grievance filed results in a loss of production and is an opportunity to remind the employer of the advantages of having a jointly determined grievance procedure.

   Mass grievance filings are a protected activity under the Taft-Hartley Act. Employees can continue to file grievances even when the formal grievance procedure has terminated with the contract. Management can unilaterally implement a grievance procedure, but it cannot set limits on the number of union representatives at each step of the grievance procedure nor specify which union members can represent the union. Finally, it is important that employees act collectively, not individually.

A caveat: Management may harass employee activists using disciplinary action up to and including discharge. As previously noted, all disciplinary acts must be grieved. The union should also establish a special fund to provide financial assistance to discharged members.

Part III

Special Bargaining Situations

Chapter 14

Bargaining in the Government Sector

Contract bargaining is not universally practiced in the public sector. Strong opposition by public officials is one reason. Giving government employees private sector bargaining rights, many have argued, would hinder elected leaders in their duty to protect the public interest and, by extension, the democratic processes. In truth, government employers are no different than private sector employers in their aversion to sharing power with their employees.

Even where bargaining in the public sector is patterned on the traditional private sector model, important differences exist. Labor law and politics play a greater role in public sector bargaining. Further, profit and the profit motive, the source and justification for improving pay and fringes in the private sector, are absent. In the public sector, budgets and the ability to tax are the controlling factors.

This chapter examines the unique features of traditional contract bargaining as practiced in government employer-employee relations at the municipal, county, and school board levels. Included are discussions of the roles of law and politics, guidelines for handling special bargaining problems, tools for analyzing budgets, and techniques for comparing pay and fringes among public employers. Preparation for interest arbitration is the concluding topic.

Topics covered in the other chapters are also relevant to public sector bargaining. These include bargaining preparations (see Chapters 2, Developing Bargaining Proposals, and 3, Bargaining Proposals and Priorities), cost of living and other economic barometers (see Chapter 6, Presenting Economic Data in Bargaining), bargaining activities, both traditional and interest-based (win-win) bargaining (see Chapters 8, Bargaining Activities, and 9, The Local Union Negotiator's Toolbox), costing the compensation package (see Chapter 10, Costing Out Contract Proposals), and bargaining contract language (see Chapter 11, Bargaining Contract Language).

THE RIGHT TO BARGAIN COLLECTIVELY

There is no single comprehensive law governing bargaining in the federal, state, and local government sectors. Federal law only covers federal employees. Public policy is exceedingly diverse at the state level. Some states ban contract bargaining outright while others have legalized the practice for certain groups of employees such as teachers, police, and fire fighters. A few jurisdictions have adopted alternative forms of employee participation called "meet and confer." Finally, a number of states have more inclusive laws giving all state and local government employees a limited right to bargain. There are also some local government jurisdictions with ordinances affecting employee bargaining.

Collective "Begging"

Some states deny bargaining rights to most or all groups of public employees. The sole recourse these employees have to affect their terms of employment is to lobby elected officials in competition with all other special interest groups. Some union officials call this activity collective begging in order to emphasize the absence of employee bargaining rights.

Meet and Confer

Laws in some states provide for meet and confer conferences between union and public employer representatives. At these meetings the parties discuss compensation and other conditions of employment. There is no duty to bargain in good faith or procedure for resolving impasses.

Agreements reached during meet and confer are written as memoranda of understanding and are signed by the parties. Such documents, however, are often nonbinding on employers. Employers are free to abrogate an agreement at any time and unilaterally change the terms of employment.

Collective Bargaining

Some state statutes create bargaining requirements similar to those found in private sector labor law.[1] They establish prohibited, unfair labor practices; direct the parties to meet at reasonable times, make offers and counteroffers, supply information, and make good faith efforts to reconcile differences; create procedures for resolving impasses; and mandate written agreements. However, all these laws either prohibit or severely curtail strikes, limit the subject matter covered, and provoke weak penalties for employers who fail in their duty to bargain. In addition to the federal and state statutes, city and county governments may have ordinances dealing with contract bargaining within their jurisdictions.

—Task—
Know the Law

Current public policy on collective bargaining in state and local government employee-employer relations is contained in state statutes, judicial rulings, and attorney generals' opinions. Copies of state statutes are obtainable from legislative branches of state governments; some states have legislative reference bureaus to provide this service. Court cases and attorney generals' decisions are available from the appropriate court clerks and public officials. City or county clerks' offices are repositories for copies of local ordinances. Finally, state labor departments or equivalent agencies

---

[1] Reference here is to the Taft-Hartley Act, otherwise known as the Labor Management Relations Act of 1947 as Amended (LMRA).

are also potential sources of information about public sector bargaining policy.

Where contract bargaining is lawful, the union should know the rules covering prohibited practices, mandatory bargaining subjects, the nature of the duty to bargain, procedures for ending impasses or deadlocks, and the extent to which agreements are binding on the employer.

LEGISLATIVE AND POLITICAL SUPPORT FOR BARGAINING

Legislative activities and contract bargaining are inextricably linked in the public sector. For example, monies budgeted for employee compensation must be ratified by a legislative body such as a city or county council, school board, or state legislature. Even the subject matter of bargaining is often constrained by legislation. Retirement and all terms and conditions covered by civil service rules and merit systems are nonbargainable subjects in many jurisdictions. Other legislative acts such as privatizing a public institution, a county hospital or mental health facility for example, dramatically alter the existing bargaining relationship.

Politics enter the picture because the public administrators and legislators, who are in effect the employers for the purposes of bargaining, are elected officials. They create and approve budgets, their representatives bargain with the union, and they ratify bargaining agreements for the affected governmental jurisdiction.

—Task—
Lobby on Behalf of Bargaining Objectives

Every local union should have a legislative action committee. Committee members are the spokespeople for the union's position on the budget, the labor agreement, and other legislative issues of concern. They attend budget hearings and legislative forums dealing with labor agreements and other employment-related issues, meet face to face with elected representatives, write letters, or bring public officials to local union membership meetings. To fulfill this role, committee members have to identify important budget and other legislative measures affecting the terms and conditions of employment, keep track of them as they progress through the legislative process, and articulate the reasons why the union supports particular outcomes and opposes others.

—*Task*—
Politick on Behalf of Bargaining Objectives

Lobbying and bargaining efforts are likely to be more successful if the union has played a role in electing the public officials involved. Participation in the political process makes it possible for unions to reward political friends and punish opponents.

The local union's political action steering committee, perhaps combined with the legislative committee, interviews candidates for local political office, makes informal endorsements, and dispenses financial contributions.

The legislative and political committee is also responsible for recruiting other union activists to operate phone banks, plant yard signs, stuff envelopes, knock on doors, and perform the other nuts and bolts work of supporting political candidates. The local union newsletter is used to urge support for friendly politicians and encourage members to vote.

PREPARING FOR BARGAINING

In general, preparations are the same whether bargaining occurs in the public or private sectors. Tasks include organizing the bargaining committee, surveying membership interests, reviewing the contract, collecting relevant information, preparing proposals, and setting priorities (these topics are covered in Chapters 1, 2, and 3).

Some unique characteristics of public employment affect the way certain tasks are performed. Three activities in particular re-

quire some additional comment: organizing the bargaining committee, researching the employer, and preparing bargaining proposals.

—Task—
Organize the Bargaining Committee

The membership of many local public sector unions is both
large and geographically dispersed. In addition, the range of occupations covered is often broad. For example, all nonprofessional
employees in a city- or county-operated hospital, including cooks,
porters, orderlies, laboratory technicians, and practical nurses, may
be combined in a single bargaining unit. Clearly, members in such
diverse occupations have different needs and some may even be
in conflict. Consequently, even more care must be taken to ensure
all major geographical locations and occupational groups are represented on the bargaining committee whether elected or appointed.
Members who believe their particular concerns are not being adequately represented are less likely to support the bargaining committee.

—Task—
Research: Who Speaks for the Employer?

Lines of authority are often blurred in government with its
systems of checks and balances. It is not unusual for elected officials
to revise or veto decisions made by administrators. For example,
the city's labor relations representative may bargain a labor agreement with the local union only to have it overturned by the city
council for any number of reasons. The author is aware of at least
one occasion where a contract bargained by the mayor's office was
vetoed by the city council because the two political entities were
feuding.

Unions may experience delays in the bargaining process due
to the complexities of governmental decision making. Nevertheless,
efforts should be made to determine who has the ultimate authority
to commit the employer. The union may be able to expedite the
bargaining process by lobbying those public officials with decision-

making authority. Sources of information about formal authority relationships among appointed administrative and elected governmental officials include official handbooks, resolutions of legislative bodies, executive orders, and administrative procedure memoranda. It is also useful to talk directly with public officials because the people with real power are often not easily identified by reading a handbook or some other document.

—*Task*—
Develop Bargaining Proposals

There are fewer mandatory bargaining subjects in government than in the private sector. As previously noted, legislative acts, civil service rules, and merit systems eliminate some terms and conditions of employment from consideration in bargaining.

Conversely, some public sector unions have successfully expanded the scope of bargaining at the expense of what has traditionally been viewed as management's rights or prerogatives. For example, some units of social workers bargain the size of their case loads. Similarly, teachers in some school districts have a voice in determining class size, number of required class preparations, and the faculty-to-pupil ratio. The ability of union negotiators to successfully breach the limits of management's rights at the bargaining table appears to be greater in the public sector.

PRESENTING BUDGET INFORMATION

Preparation activities include collecting information about the local government employer, particularly budget and financial data, and surveying wages/salaries and fringe benefits of comparable groups of public employees. Budgets and the comparables are used to justify proposals for improvements in compensation. Activities associated with collecting, analyzing, and presenting budget and financial data are examined below. Pay and benefit comparison tasks are covered later in this chapter.

Developing the Budget Argument

A budget is a financial plan containing estimates of revenues, expenditures, and surpluses (or shortfalls) for one or more years into the future. Governments prepare budgets prior to collecting revenues or spending money.

A budget determines the amount of new money available for collective bargaining. A union has an easier time justifying proposals for pay and fringe improvements when revenues are projected to increase. The opposite is true when declining tax revenues force cuts in expenditures.

Budgets are also political documents created by administrators and elected public officials and based on the authors' perceptions of the needs and concerns of residents in the community. The union's best opportunity to influence budget makers is at the time they are preparing the plan. After the budget is adopted, the union may not be able to do much to influence the allocation of monies unless contingency funds have been set aside.

The Budget Cycle

Most local governments and school boards prepare a general fund, or operating budget, and special use or dedicated fund budget for such things as improving streets, sewers, the airport, and classroom buildings. Budgets for the upcoming fiscal year are prepared in the current operating year. The preparation cycle begins at the agency, department, or program level, moves through the administrative branch (e.g., mayor, city manager, county executive, or school board president) and ends in the legislative branch (e.g., city council or county or school board). The following sequence of preparation, consideration, and adoption activities is part of the typical general fund or operating budget cycle. Individual locales can and do vary from this general sequence of events.

1. Seven to eight months in advance of the budget adoption deadline, the comptroller or budget authority releases projections of revenues and expenditures for the approaching fiscal year. These estimates serve as guidelines for the budget preparers.

2. Five to six months before the end of the process, agency and departmental staffs formulate their budget requests. These proposals, in turn, are submitted to the chief administrator or executive.
3. With four months remaining, the chief executive completes the proposed budget plus an accompanying budget message. Both documents are delivered to the legislative branch.
4. Three months before adoption, the budget documents are circulated to the appropriate legislative committees. Debate on the budget begins.
5. With one to two months remaining, the general public, which includes union members and their leaders, is invited to testify for or against the proposed budget at one or more public meetings. Notices of hearing date(s), often accompanied by a summary budget, are generally published in all local newspapers of record well in advance of the scheduled event(s).
6. More weeks of debate by members of the legislative body follow, eventually leading to final adoption. Tax bills are mailed to citizens and taxpayers at the beginning of the new fiscal year.

—Task—
Participate in the Budget-Making Process

Union activists must lobby the budget preparers at every phase of the budget cycle. Making the union's position known to an agency, department, or program staff at the time budget requests are being prepared is the place to start. At the same time, budget briefings with the top executive are requested as a means of exchanging views with this key administrative official.

Opportunities to influence the allocation of budget dollars remain even after the proposed budget has left the executive for the legislative branch. Members of the legislative committees reviewing the budget are contacted and made aware of the union's preferences. In addition, union officers attend the public hearing(s) to testify in favor of and in opposition to various budget items.

Finally, union leaders lobby sympathetic legislators to amend the budget in the union's favor.

Sources of Information for the Budget Review

Union representatives participating in the budget process must know how to read and interpret the budget document. The first step is to obtain a copy of the employer's proposed general fund, or operating, budget for the new fiscal year as soon as it becomes available. Copies of the operating budget for the current period and one or two preceding fiscal years should also be on hand. Yearly changes in revenue and expenditure projections can be revealing. Copies of special or dedicated fund budgets are needed if the union intends to review these proposals as well.

In addition to the budget, the union will need data on real or actual revenues, expenditures, and surpluses. This information is used to check on the accuracy of the budget estimates made in prior periods. Actual data appear in financial reports which are published on a quarterly, semiannual, or annual basis. A minimum of 6 months of real data for the current fiscal year and 12 months from the previous fiscal year should be obtained. If less than 6 months of current year data are available, comparisons should be limited to the previous year's actual data. Real data are also needed for comparison purposes when dedicated or special fund budgets are reviewed.

An audit report by an independent auditor should be part of each annual financial statement. If not, the union should ask for a copy. The function of the audit is to verify that the financial statement presents an accurate representation of the underlying accounting records.

—Task—
Collect Information for the Budget Review

General operating and other types of budgets and the periodic statements of actual revenues, expenditures, and surpluses are information in the public domain and available for citizen and tax-payer scrutiny upon request. The likely repository for these items is an office or department such as comptroller, city/county clerk, chief administrator, finance, or budget.

Government officials who unduly delay or refuse outright to provide the union with budget documents are usually violating either a collective bargaining law or a freedom of information statute or both. The union may be required to pay for copies of some materials, but the amount collected cannot be unreasonable (usually interpreted as anything above actual cost). All instances of noncompliance should be reported to either the district attorney at the local level or the attorney general at the state level.

Look around for other potentially useful sources of information. Some state and local governments forecast local revenue and expenditure trends. In addition, "watchdog" studies prepared by business, taxpayer, and public interest organizations, such as the League of Women Voters, can provide the union with ready-made analyses of local budget and tax issues.

Budget Nuts and Bolts

What does annualizing data mean? What are trends? What are the differences between program and line item budgets, operating and capital expenditures, and contingency, surplus, and reserve accounts? The following is an explanation of a number of terms and techniques associated with budgets and the budget review process:

1. The accuracy of annual budget projections is tested by comparing them with the actual revenues and expenditures for the same period. Sometimes a full year's worth of actual data are not available. Annualizing involves estimating full year equivalents of revenues and expenditures when only partial year data are available. For example, suppose the public employer has earned $320,000 in total interest on investments during the first six months of the current fiscal year. This amount cannot be compared with the budget projection because the latter is for 12 months. As a consequence, the interest receipts must be annualized. Annualizing is accomplished by dividing $320,000 by the number of months it represents (6) and multiplying the results by 12. The estimate of $640,000 for the year is

compared with the amount originally budgeted for the same period.

A revenue or expenditure item should not be annualized unless there is a minimum of six months data available. In addition, local income or property tax revenues should not be annualized because they are collected only once or twice during the year.

2. The direction of increases or decreases in budget projections or actual data over a period of years is called the trend. Suppose property tax collections have increased by roughly 1 or 2 percent annually over the past five years. While the size of the increase has varied from year to year, the trend has been upward for the entire five-year period. If improvements in employee compensation are tied to property tax increases, the union will want to explore whether this growth in tax revenues can be expected to continue. This would involve looking at such factors as tax levy limits and taxpayer unrest.

3. Program and line item budgets refer to different methods of budgeting. A program budget shows revenues and expenditures by activity, such as training and education, and general administration. By contrast, the line item budget identifies revenues by source, such as taxes and users' fees, and expenditures by type, such as payroll, material, and supplies. Both budgeting methods are often followed in the same document.

4. Operating and capital expenditures categorize purchases on the basis of durability. Operating items such as office supplies are purchased with current year's revenues and used during the same fiscal year. Capital items, on the other hand, include desks, chairs, and motor vehicles, which serve for many years. Long life items should not be charged to current fiscal year expenditures. Further, monies for capital expenditures are frequently held in reserve accounts.

5. Contingencies, surpluses, and reserves define categories of employer savings. Contingency funds are monies set aside to meet unanticipated expenses. For example, the employer might budget money for wage/salary increases and

then set aside extra dollars in a reserve account to be used if contract bargaining produces a larger money settlement than originally anticipated.

Surpluses occur when budgeted or actual revenues exceed budgeted or actual expenditures. Surpluses may also be earmarked for special uses, such as acquiring art works for display in local public buildings. Funds earmarked for special purposes are held as reserves until they are expended.

—Task—
Conduct the Budget Review

The reviewer should examine the total budget picture first and then focus on each component separately. A general impression of the financial condition of the city or county government or school district can be formed by giving the entire budget document a quick inspection. Is the city operating with a surplus, a deficit, or breaking even? What are the spending priorities? Perhaps the city is planning to close a fire station and open a new golf course. This would be important news for a fire fighters' union.

Next, the revenue side of the budget, the source of funds for higher pay and fringes, is examined in more detail. The reviewer begins by identifying the sources of funds: taxes, revenue sharing, grants-in-aid, user fees, and interest on investments. Does the budget estimate for each revenue source appear reasonable? Budget projections should also be compared with actual monies collected in the current and earlier fiscal years. Perhaps revenue collections are consistently higher than the projections. Public employers have a tendency to understate income because it is good public relations when unexpected surpluses appear at the end of the fiscal year.

Trends in revenues are indicators of the employer's longer term ability to improve employee compensation. Consequently, it is important to know whether the local employer's tax base is growing, shrinking, or remaining constant. The level of revenue sharing, grants-in-aid, user fees, and interest on investments could also be changing and should be investigated. Revenue growth is also influenced by the government's ability to collect delinquent taxes and the frequency with which it grants unreasonable tax holidays or lower property assessments, or abatements, to favored taxpayers. Anticipated changes in revenue sources and policies should be reflected in budget estimates.

Finally, budgeted revenues can be compared with changes in the rate of inflation. Are government revenues keeping pace or falling behind the prices paid for products and services?

Moving to the expenditure side, the reviewer should identify where the money is being spent, for example: public safety, community development, public works, payroll, general government administration, debt service, and capital equipment and facilities. Are the spending estimates higher or lower than actual expenditures in the current or previous years? Some employers have a tendency to overestimate spending.

The budget estimate for each type of expenditure is also evaluated for reasonableness. In addition, some expenditure areas may be getting larger increases than others. The employer should be asked to justify all differences in treatment.

The employer's payroll cost should be given special scrutiny because the actual expenditure is often less than the amount budgeted. This occurs when vacant jobs are left unfilled and retiring workers are replaced with new hires earning less money.

Indebtedness and the employer's bond rating should be examined. A public employer near the top of the legal tax levy limit, with lots of indebtedness and a poor bond rating, is likely to resist union efforts to increase pay and benefits.

The consulting category is often used as a hiding place for projected surpluses or unspent money. In addition, the first indication that the employer is considering subcontracting or privatization is an expense item for a consulting contract to study its feasibility. Monies budgeted for consulting should always be questioned.

Finally the size of projected surpluses, contingencies, and reserves should also be checked. How do the estimates compare with actual experience in the current and past fiscal years? Uses of surpluses should be investigated. There may be funds hidden in contingency and other reserve accounts that could be diverted to finance improvements in employee pay and fringe benefits.

—*Task*—
Present the Budget Review

The following example is limited to the spending side of a general fund budget. Exhibit 14-1 shows the union's work sheet containing budgeted expenditures for the City of Brandy Bay for the current fiscal year, amounts actually spent during the previous 12 months, and the differences between the two. The differences are given in both dollar and percentage terms to aid analysis.

A work sheet, similar to the one in Exhibit 14-1, can be prepared for the bargaining committee's own use or for presentation to the union membership or the employer. Whatever the application, the work sheet must be accompanied by either a written or oral explanation of what the data mean. In the example, projected spending for the year 1993 is up 4.1 percent. Data showing actual expenditures for years prior to 1992 are needed to determine

---

Exhibit 14-1. Sample Budget Review Work Sheet
City of Brandy Bay 19XZ Budget Summary
Actual 1992 and Budgeted 1993 Spending

Expenditure Classification	1993 Budget	1992 Actual	Difference ($)	(%)
Public Safety	$31,283,620	$30,399,546	$ 884,074	2.9%
Police	17,390,410	16,892,119	498,291	2.9%
Fire	13,893,210	13,507,427	385,783	2.9%
Community Development	2,915,460	2,477,398	438,062	17.7%
Public Works/ Transportation	21,739,340	20,729,544	1,009,796	4.8%
Health & Human Services	7,915,370	7,823,016	92,354	1.2%
Administration	9,910,200	9,640,826	269,374	2.8%
Debt Service	8,808,628	8,105,140	703,488	8.7%
Capital Budget	2,890,000	3,000,000	(110,000)	3.8%)
Miscellaneous	1,631,920	1,523,863	108,057	7.1%
Total General Fund	$87,094,538	$83,699,333	$3,395,205	4.1%

---

whether this increase represents the continuation of a trend. Next, the budgeted increase can be compared with the inflation rate to determine whether it represents new spending or just maintains the existing level (see Chapter 6, Presenting Economic Data in Bargaining, for a discussion about measuring changes in the cost of living).

Further, the new budget projects growth in all expenditure categories except capital. The smallest increases, however, are in programs where unionized employment is probably greatest: police (2.9%), fire (2.9%), health and human services (1.2%), and administration (2.8%). Consequently, prospects for more than very modest pay and benefit increases look bleak.

The miscellaneous category needs further investigation since a hefty 7.1 percent increase is forecast. Comparisons with earlier years are needed. The city's comptroller should also be questioned about the composition of the miscellaneous category. For example, the employer may be setting aside sizable amounts of money for executive travel, membership dues in professional organizations, and journal subscriptions at the same time as it is claiming that there are no funds available to improve wages/salaries and fringes. Surpluses and contingency funds found buried in the miscellaneous account are other potential sources of funding for higher employee compensation.

Finally, the budget shows debt service growing substantially over the preceding year. Again, comparisons with past years are needed. The comptroller should also be questioned about the circumstances leading to a higher debt service.

PRESENTING INFORMATION ON COMPARABLES

The budget argument is defensive in nature. It is most serviceable where the public employer is claiming a shortage of funds. On the other hand, the bargaining unit does not automatically receive pay increases and fringe improvements even when the employer has the ability to fund them. The union is still required to justify its money proposals. This is accomplished with pay and fringe comparisons.

Developing the Comparables Argument

The comparables argument uses a standard of fairness to justify improvements in wages/salaries and fringes. Earnings data are collected to demonstrate how bargaining unit members have fallen below the compensation levels achieved by other employee groups with employment characteristics in common.

The credibility of the argument is affected by the target groups selected for comparison purposes. The union must find the best and most direct "apples to apples" comparisons possible. In the public sector, there are external and internal sources of comparables.

—Task—
Select External Comparables

City, county, or school employees seeking matching groups of employees for wage/salary and fringe comparisons can find them in other cities, counties, and school districts. To be valid, the government jurisdictions targeted must have features in common. The most frequently selected characteristics are population size, geographical proximity, per capita income, labor market characteristics, economic base, tax rate, assessed property evaluation, and pay scale. The more qualities in common, the better the fit.

School districts in the same athletic conference are often used as comparables. They are usually composed of institutions with similar student enrollments, investments in facilities and equipment, numbers of faculty members, and community resources.

Employer characteristics must match, but so must the content of the jobs involved. Suppose two related counties have social service departments staffed with professional social workers. One county has two job classes labeled social worker while the other has three. Clearly, relying on job titles is not sufficient; descriptions of all five social work jobs have to be examined to determine whether their contents are sufficiently similar for pay comparison purposes.

Additional complications arise where methods of pay differ. For example, pay rates may not be immediately compared if social workers are paid by the hour in one jurisdiction and by the month in another. Hourly earnings must be converted to their monthly equivalents or vice versa. The hourly to monthly conversion is accomplished by multiplying the hourly rate by the number of hours worked in a month. For example, assuming a work year of 2,080 hours and a work month of 173.3 hours, an hourly wage rate of $15 is equivalent to a monthly salary of $2,599.50. Conversely, monthly earnings are changed to hourly earnings by dividing the salary by the number of hours worked in a month.

Further, some jobs have minimum and maximum pay rates. In such cases, comparisons have to take into consideration the number of steps between the minimum and the maximum and the length of time it takes to move between the two rates.

Occasionally, private employers can be targeted for comparison purposes. Skilled trades are examples of jobs with similar content whether performed in the public or private sectors.

—Task—
Make Internal Comparisons

Maintaining relative differences in earnings between occupational groups, both union or nonunion, working for the same public employer is another part of the fairness argument. Consequently, groups of employees working for the same public employer can target each other for wage/salary and fringe comparison purposes. For example, white collar courthouse employees are entitled to the same percentage wage increase received by white collar health center employees employed in the same county.

Pay and benefits have historically moved together for some occupations. For example, in many jurisdictions there is a tradition of "parity," or something close to it, between salaries and benefits of police officers and fire fighters. Such long-term relationships, particularly those established through the process of collective bargaining, should be preserved.

Some occupations are easier to compare because they have counterparts in most functional areas of government. For example, clerk typists are found in most agencies and departments and most are performing the same sorts of tasks. To be on the safe side, however, job descriptions should be compared.

—Task—
Determine the Mix of External and Internal Factors

The union should use whatever mix of internal and external comparables is necessary to support its case. For example, the blue collar public works department employees decide to break new ground and request a dental plan. The union must target external comparables with dental plans, including those that may not be the best choices for other comparisons, such as wages. Internal comparisons may not be available because the benefit is so rare.

Management can be expected to challenge the validity of the union's choice of comparables. Some will be dismissed as attempts to compare "apples with oranges" and others will be downgraded as "handpicked" samples. Union negotiators must be prepared to explain why they chose one set of comparables over another.

—Task—
Attack the Employer's Choice of Comparables

Bargaining representatives of a city or county may also use pay and fringe survey data to support their offer of pay and benefits. The union can apply the same criteria used to select its comparables to attack the ones used by the employer. For example, an external comparable chosen by the employer because of population match could be challenged on the grounds that it is located too far away geographically.

—Task—
Collect Data on Comparables

Information about employment terms and employers is much easier to obtain in the public than in the private sector. Most states and localities have freedom of information and open meeting laws. The following are sources of data:

1. Government jurisdictions themselves can provide information on wages/salaries, fringes, and all other terms and conditions of employment. The appropriate agency to con-

tact is either a city or county clerk's office or a personnel or human resource department.

2. Every state publishes a "Blue Book" containing census, economic, government, and geographic data. Revised periodically, Blue Books can be purchased from a state's department of administration or are available for viewing in the reference section of most public libraries. Sometimes copies can be obtained gratis from state legislators.

   The contents of labor agreements requiring ratification by public employers, often in the form of statutes or ordinances, appear in the proceedings or minutes of the legislative bodies involved, such as city councils, county boards, or school districts. Statutes and ordinances are also public records.

3. Union contracts contain information about current wages/salaries and benefits. These are readily available by contacting officers of the local union(s) of interest.

4. Research staffs of national unions or intermediate bodies, such as councils or districts, collect wage/salary, fringe, and other types of employment data. The appropriate union official should be contacted for assistance.

5. Local unions can conduct their own pay and benefit surveys. See Chapter 5, Presenting Pay and Fringe Benefit Comparisons, for examples of survey methods.

6. The weekly *Government Employee Relations Report* contains the latest federal, state, and local government statistics on earnings, hours of work, and employment. Developments in public sector contract bargaining are also reported. This service is available from The Bureau of National Affairs, Inc., 9435 Key West Avenue, Rockville, MD 20850, (800) 372-1033. This publication may also be found in some university or college libraries.

—*Task*—
Present the Comparables

The following example illustrates a format for presenting the findings of pay comparisons. Assume the union representing the

Brandy Bay department of social service employees is seeking salary increases of 7.75 percent for social workers and 8.25 percent for nonsocial workers. The County of Brandy Bay, the employer, is offering 7 percent and 8 percent respectively.

A chart describing characteristics of the external comparables selected is shown in Exhibit 14-2. Eleven counties meet the criteria of common borders or similarities in taxable value, population size, and land area. The state's Blue Book is the source of this information.

Next, a table containing salary data is presented in Exhibit 14-3. Current year, 1992, salaries and proposed 1993 increases for Brandy Bay's social service employees are compared with the settlements bargained for the year 1993 in the 11 counties selected as comparables. Salary is the issue in this example, although sometimes total compensation is used. All counties granted percentage pay increases.

Should the union use the table in Exhibit 14-3 in its entirety? Salary increases vary among counties and some fit the Brandy Bay

---

Exhibit 14-2. Characteristics of the External Comparables
Brandy Bay and 11 Counties, 1993[a]

Common Borders	Common Taxable Value, Population Size, and Land Area
Dodge	BRANDY BAY
Manitowoc	Calumet
Outagamie	Dodge
Sheboygan	Eau Claire
Winnebago	La Crosse
BRANDY BAY	Manitowoc
	Marathon
	Outagamie
	Ozaukee
	Sheboygan
	Washington
	Winnebago

---

[a]County data source: State Blue Book.

Exhibit 14-3. Salary Comparisons

1. Salary Rate for 1992, Brandy Bay County[a]

Social Workers ($ per Month)	Proposed Increase (%)	Nonsocial Workers ($ per Month)	Proposed Increase (%)
$1,581	7.75%	$1,000	8.25%

Source: The 1992 Agreement
[a]Based on a 37 1/2-hour work week.

2. Salary Increases for 1993, 11 Comparable Counties[b]

County	Social Workers ($ per Month)	Increase (%)	Nonsocial Workers ($ per Month)	Increase (%)
Calumet	$1,735	8% on 1/1 2 on 7/1	$ 987	8% on 1/1 2 on 7/1
Dodge	1,688	5.22	1,191	8.2
Eau Claire	1,742	8.5	977	8.5
La Crosse	1,583	9.0	912	9.0
Manitowoc	1,774	8.25	1,093	7.75
Marathon	1,846	6 on 1/1 2 on 5/1	1,135	6 on 1/1 2 on 5/1
Outagamie	1,714	7.0	1,066	7.0
Ozaukee	2,018	7.5	1,323	7.5
Sheboygan	1,890	9 on 4/1 3 on 7.1	1,246	8.0
Washington	1,628	8.5 on 1/1 2 on 12/31	912	8.5 on 1/1 2 on 12/31
Winnebago	1,661	7.0	1,072	7.0

Source: County personnel departments.
[b]Based on a 40-hour work week.

salary proposal better than others. The union's position is made more credible, however, if it does not limit the choices to only the most favorable comparisons. Finally, the question of whether the duties are the same for social service jobs among the 12 counties must still be answered.

BARGAINING IMPASSE AND
THIRD-PARTY INTERVENTION

Strikes are generally forbidden in the public sector and even where permitted their use is severely restricted. The absence of a strike deadline removes the employer's incentive to settle because there are no penalties, monetary or otherwise, for disagreeing. As a consequence, bargaining frequently drags on for an inordinately long time. Frustrated employees sometimes resort to strike substitutes such as "sick-outs" and "work to rules."

Third-Party Intervention

Most state and local bargaining statutes and ordinances provide mechanisms for resolving impasses. The most common are mediation and fact-finding. In both procedures, a neutral third party, called a mediator or fact-finder as the case may be, collects facts and makes recommendations but lacks the authority to impose a settlement on the contending parties (see Chapter 12, Bargaining Impasse and Third-Party Intervention). As a consequence, impasses frequently continue unabated.

Interest Arbitration

An alternative method for ending impasses in public sector bargaining is interest arbitration. A neutral, called an arbitrator, listens to the facts and renders a decision that is binding on the parties. Interest and grievance arbitration should not be confused. The former has to do with impasses over the terms and conditions of employment while grievance arbitration deals with disputes involving interpretations of employee and union rights in an existing labor agreement.

Wisconsin's law covering municipal government employment relations provides for a combination of mediation and compulsory interest arbitration.[2] The first attempt at intervention is made by

---

[2]Municipal Employment Relations Act of 1978 as Amended, Wis. Stat. §111:70(4)(cm) and Rules of Employment Relations Commission, Wis. Admin. Code, §ERB 31.

the state's mediation agency after determining that impasse has been reached. Should efforts at mediation fail, the parties submit their "last best (final) offers" to a mutually agreed upon arbitrator for a final and binding decision.[3]

The last best (final) offer variation on conventional arbitration is an attempt to encourage Wisconsin unions and local government employers to bargain with each other. If bargaining along with mediation fails, the parties prepare a package of final positions on issues, typically pay and fringe items, and submit them to the arbitrator. The arbitrator can only pick the final package offer of one side or the other so the principals have an incentive to try and narrow their differences prior to arbitration.[4]

Wisconsin law specifies the criteria arbitrators must consider when evaluating final offers.[5] These include (1) the public employer's ability to meet the cost of any settlement; (2) external and internal comparisons of wages, hours, and conditions of employment; (3) changes in consumer prices; and (4) the total package of benefits received. In practice, arbitrators emphasize the comparables.[6]

---

[3]Other states with statutes offering a combination of mediation or fact finding and mandatory interest arbitration for at least some group, or groups, of government employees include: Alaska, Connecticut, Hawaii, Illinois, Iowa, Maine, Massachusetts, Michigan, Minnesota, Montana, Nebraska, Nevada, New Jersey, New York, Ohio, Oklahoma, Oregon, Pennsylvania, Rhode Island, Vermont, Washington, and Wyoming. B. V. H. Schneider, "Public Sector Labor Legislation—An Evolutionary Analysis," *Public-Sector Bargaining, 2nd. ed.*, B. Aaron, J. M. Najita, and J. L. Stern, eds. Industrial Relations Research Association Series, (Washington D.C.: BNA Books, 1988), at 205. Interest arbitration is also in force for local government employees in the District of Columbia. Labor Relations Program, D.C. Comprehensive Merit Personnel Act of 1978, DC Law 2-139, §1-618.2.

[4]Statutes of 15 other states provide for a last best offer variation of interest arbitration. Breakdown by type is 4 with last best offer package, 8 with last best offer issue by issue, and 3 that offer a choice. *Id.* at 206. The District of Columbia statute also provides for last best offer, package or issue by issue, arbitration. *Id.*

[5]Municipal Employment Relations Act of 1978 as Amended, Wis. Stat. §117.70(4)(cm)7. For a general discussion of standards used by arbitrators, see F. Elkouri and E. Elkouri, *How Arbitration Works, 4th ed.* (Washington, D.C.: BNA Books, 1985), Chapter 18, "Standards Used by Arbitrators of Interest Disputes" 803-51, and *1985–87 Supplement to How Arbitration Works*, M. Volz and E. Goggin, eds. (Washington, D.C.: BNA Books, 1988) 177–83.

[6]Use of the comparables standard has helped public school teachers increase their average annual pay at a rate that has consistently exceeded the rise in the cost of living. As a result, some public officials, complaining that salaries are

Preparing for Interest Arbitration

Preparation activities include selecting the arbitrator and developing the case. Developing the case involves formulating arguments and proofs in support of the union's position on the disputed employment terms. In addition, opening and closing statements, witness testimony, and exhibits must be created. As previously noted, in some jurisdictions there is the additional task of preparing a last best offer.

—Task—
Choose the Arbitrator

Unions should follow the same process for selecting an arbitrator whether the pending case involves interests or rights. This means the past decisions of potential candidates must be examined. Arbitrator's decisions in interest cases are often published.[7] Public employee unions also share information about individual arbitrators.

—Task—
Develop Arguments, Facts, and Proofs

The union must develop arguments supported by facts and proofs for each issue. For example, the union might argue that a proposed pay increase is affordable and needed. The facts would include the results of the budget review, data showing the results of wage and fringe comparisons, and data on the changes in the consumer price index.

The sources of the facts are the proofs. Budget documents, labor agreements, and published wage surveys are examples of proofs. Some sources, such as newspaper articles, are considered hearsay or circumstantial because the writer is unknown, his or her credibility is uncertain, and the sources of information are

---

outpacing the ability of taxpayers to pay them, have proposed changing the current law to tie pay increases to the rate of inflation.

[7]In Wisconsin, for example, arbitrators' decisions in interest cases are published on a regular basis by a professional association of school administrators.

unclear. Conversely, the U.S. Department of Labor's Consumer Price Index and official documents of governmental bodies are deemed credible without further examination because of their impeccable reputations.

Witnesses can be proof that something has happened if they have directly experienced the event. Suppose the issue is whether a new job transfer policy is needed. At the arbitration hearing, the union uses four employee witnesses who testify that management had never refused requests for transfers in past years, but had done so in their cases without provocation. The testimony of the four employees constitutes the arguments, facts, and proof regarding the denied requests for job transfers.

—Task—
Present Testimony of Witnesses and Exhibits

The union presents its arguments, facts, and proofs to the arbitrator in several ways. One way, as described in the previous example, is to have witnesses give oral testimony. Representatives of the employer have an opportunity to attack the credibility and relevance of witness testimony in cross-examination.

Exhibits are another means of presenting evidence. Exhibits include charts, graphs, photographs, newspaper articles, tape recordings, and physical objects of all sorts. The table in Exhibit 14-3 showing salary comparisons for social workers and nonsocial workers in Brandy Bay and 11 other counties is an example of a display of evidence that could be used in arbitration. Pictorial representations make it easier for arbitrators to comprehend the union's arguments and facts.

Union officials who prepare exhibits must appear as witnesses at the hearing. Their presence is required to explain how the exhibit was prepared, what it shows, and how it supports the union's argument(s). The employer is given an opportunity to impugn the exhibits and the union witnesses through cross-examination.

Neatness counts in the preparation of exhibits. Exhibits should also be organized in order of presentation and placed in a three-ringed binder. Four copies of the notebook are prepared, one for the arbitrator, another for the employer, a third for the union spokesperson, and a fourth for use by union witnesses.

—Task—
Give Opening and Closing Statements

The union's opening statement is used to lay the groundwork for the union's case. It should chronicle the bargaining process that led to arbitration, particularly if the experience has been unsatisfactory. A preview of the union's arguments and proofs is also presented. For example, the union spokesperson might say something like the following: "Ms. Arbitrator, we will show that the union's 7.5 percent offer for social workers moves the Brandy Bay county salary levels closer to the mainstream of pay in comparable counties."

The closing statement gives the union another chance to summarize its arguments, facts, and proofs. It is also an opportunity to remind the arbitrator of the weaknesses in the employer's position.

Opening and closing statements are presented orally. The parties may also choose to prepare written opening and closing briefs. Briefs offer the union an opportunity to explain its position in a more concise manner. References to awards in other arbitration cases, which are difficult to do in a verbal presentation, can also be included in the closing brief.

A closing brief is not prepared until after the hearing is over. Further, the arbitrator does not render a decision until closing briefs have been received from all parties. As a result, the final outcome may not be known for months.

—Task—
Formulate a Last Best Offer

The size of the gap between final offers at impasse becomes important where a last best offer is required. Arbitrators as a rule do not pick extreme positions when choosing between two best offers; consequently, being "reasonable" is the union's best tactic during the period of bargaining prior to impasse. For example, if the issue is the money package, the union's last offer should not differ from the employer's by more than a few pennies. The alternative is to hold out for more and risk being forced to accept a totally unsatisfactory employer offer. The union leadership must balance the cost to the employer against the real needs of the membership.

A different approach is required where the arbitrator is free to modify the positions of the parties. Suppose the arbitrator is known to split the differences between money offers. Now the union's best bargaining strategy prior to arbitration is to make the gap between its own and the employer's position as wide as possible. A 35 cents spread will yield a richer settlement than one for 25 cents.

Chapter 15

Employee–Management Cooperation

Many employers are finding conditions in product and service markets becoming more competitive and less profitable than in the past. To help counter this trend, they are demanding that employees assume more responsibility for increasing productivity, containing labor cost, maintaining quality, and making the enterprise more responsive to changing customer needs. Employers call this new relationship employee-management cooperation. In practice, cooperation forces employees to adopt new work arrangements, accept new forms of compensation, and relax traditional work rules and practices. In return, employees have a limited opportunity to participate in management decisions and functions.

Various aspects of labor-management cooperation are examined in this chapter. The new employment terms and conditions being initiated by employers are described first along with a number of alternative union response strategies. Next, there is a discussion of how employees and unions are affected by these new employment policies and programs and suggestions for contractual safeguards are offered. The chapter concludes with advice on bargaining preparations and sample contract language dealing with employee-management cooperation.

VISIONS OF A NEW EMPLOYMENT RELATIONSHIP

Employers have introduced a variety of employment-related programs and policies under the umbrella term of labor-management cooperation. Examples include employee participation programs, group bonus plans, new methods of manufacturing and service delivery, pay linked to knowledge, and new work rules and practices. Specific proposals are discussed in detail below.

Employee Participation Programs

Worker participation programs have assumed a number of forms. In every case, however, employees become members of management created committees or teams. The purpose of most of these groups is to tap the creativity and knowledge of employee members to help solve work-related problems; most often related to productivity, product and customer service quality, or supplier relations. Committees and teams are also set up to help implement work and workplace reorganization programs and to perform specific job assignments.

The question of whether employee participation groups are legal per se under federal labor law remained unanswered at the time this handbook was written. However, some forms of joint employee–employer participation programs do violate both the intent and letter of federal labor law. In two cases, one in a union setting, the employer created joint committees but retained veto power over the selection of employee members. In addition, the committees bargained with management (i.e., made proposals and counterproposals) over mandatory subjects of bargaining, such as pay rates, attendance policy, no-smoking policy, and safety, that affected noncommittee employees. The National Labor Relations Board (NLRB) found these employers to be in violation of Section 8(a)(2) of the Taft-Hartley Act, which bans serious employer domination of and interference with employee organizations. The employers involved were ordered to disband the committees.[1]

---

[1] *See* Teamsters v. Electromation Inc., 309 NLRB 163, 142 LRRM 1001 (1992), and Chemical Workers Assoc. v. DuPont, 311 NLRB 88, 143 LRRM 1121 (1993).

As part of its decision in these cases, the NLRB issued some guidelines for the operation of joint employee–management participation committees and teams. Groups set up to brainstorm problems, develop ideas, give suggestions, or share information are lawful. Further, management can work with these committees or teams so long as management does not usurp the rights of employees to designate their own representatives, tacitly accord them the status of bargaining agent, or play a dominate role in their operation, such as voting on the group's proposals.[2]

Employee participation programs exist under a variety of names and perform an assortment of different functions. The following are descriptions of the most common forms:

1. Quality Control (QC) Circles and Quality of Work Life (QWL) committees, composed of employees and their supervisors, are organized in every work site and department in the factory or office. These groups generally meet on a regular basis, often weekly, during normal working hours, to discuss ways to improve workplace efficiency and product or service quality. Team members usually have no authority to act on their recommendations.

   Membership in QC and QWL groups is generally voluntary. Participants often receive two or three days of training from a private consultant on team building and the concepts of quality management.

2. Employee Involvement (EI) teams, also composed of employees and their supervisors, are usually formed to handle specific problems in the immediate workplace. An EI team organized in the finishing department of one paper mill investigated the reasons why their operating costs were higher than the competition. Team members studied such factors as direct and indirect labor requirements, workers' compensation costs, the flow of work, the management of waste, and scheduling procedures. They made a number of cost saving recommendations, many of which were adopted.

3. Steering committees composed of middle and top level managers and local union officials are formed to identify

---

[2]Chemical Workers Assoc. v. DuPont, 311 NLRB 88, 143 LRRM 1121 (1993).

and solve problems in much the same manner as an EI team. Alternatively, a steering committee may be used to coordinate the activities of the QC, QWL, or EI teams, or to administer a group bonus plan or a major reorganization of the workplace.

4. Work teams are created and assigned a series of jobs related to the production of a product or service or component thereof. Team members are often required to perform all tasks and rotate from job to job. Sometimes work teams are self-managed; that is, members have the authority to establish their own manning schedules, determine overtime, and arrange vacation rosters, duties traditionally performed by supervisors.

Group Bonus Plans

The most common forms of group bonuses are profit sharing, employee stock option plans (ESOPs), and productivity gainsharing plans. These are group incentives because all employees benefit, but only if there is a gain in total company profit or productivity. The objective is to motivate employees to cooperate with each other and with management to make the enterprise more competitive. A steering committee or EI team may be formed to help administer the plan and to search for ways to increase the bonus payout. For example, the committee may look for ways to eliminate unscheduled machine and equipment down times or office snafus in an effort to raise productivity.

Major Work and Employment Reorganization

Some employers have radically transformed the workplace and the employment relationship in an effort to improve both productivity and reduce labor cost. They have reorganized the flow of work, restructured jobs, introduced new methods of pay determination, assigned new responsibilities to employees, and modified customary work rules and practices. To illustrate, descriptions of workplace and employment changes introduced by two midwestern employers, one a paper making and converting mill and the other an insurance carrier, are presented below:

1. *Functional departments were eliminated.* At the paper mill, all manufacturing and maintenance functions related to the production of a single product, such as facial or toilet tissue, were combined into a single department. The total number of departments was reduced from 35 to 12.

   The insurance company combined three former functional departments (health, life insurance, and support services) into a single customer service unit. The employees in the new department were divided into five work groups, each serving sales agents in a specific geographical area. The time involved in processing insurance claims reportedly fell by 75 percent as a consequence of the conversion.

2. *Employees were assigned to teams rather than to specific jobs.* At the paper mill, teams were created to operate papermaking and paper-converting machines and to perform maintenance work. For example, a paper-making machine team consisted of the five original operators (all previously had been in different job classes) plus two formerly full time maintenance employees, and a learner/relief person.

   The insurance employer formed teams of between 20 and 30 employees. Each team was assigned a total of 167 processing, underwriting, and customer service tasks.

3. *Multitasking replaced job specialization.* The five operators on the new paper-making machine team were expected to learn each other's jobs plus some basic maintenance skills. The two maintenance workers assigned to the team had to master several new crafts and learn enough about paper machine operations to function as relief operators. In addition, all team members had to demonstrate "leadership" skills. Leadership skills were defined as the ability to investigate and report to teammates on topics such as how to perform work more efficiently, how to enhance product quality, how to improve customer service, and how to promote safety.

   Multitasking was also a feature of the new employment

system installed by the insurance company. For example, claims processing clerks were also expected to learn insurance underwriting.

4. *Employee wage rates were based on numbers of job skills mastered rather than on the job held.* The paper mill scrapped its wage classification plan with 137 pay brackets for one consisting of eight pay levels encompassing 21 skill blocks in the paper-making department and 15 skill blocks in departments that converted paper into finished products. Each employee had to master all of the operating, maintenance, and leadership skill block requirements in the assigned pay level. Progression through the new pay structure would depend on whether the employee acquired the skills associated with the next highest pay level. A similar pay-for-knowledge plan was also adopted by the insurance company.

5. *Limited team self-management was introduced.* Team members at the paper mill were required to meet before the start of the shift, off the clock, to plan their day. They had the authority to schedule job rotations, assign overtime, and handle other administrative tasks previously performed by supervisors. Reportedly, the jobs of over 200 supervisors were eventually eliminated.

   The insurance carrier also authorized team members to schedule their own work hours in a flextime program, allocate tasks among themselves, and schedule job rotations. The number of supervisory positions were reduced by 55 as a consequence of giving team members more autonomy.

6. *New work rules were established.* The paper mill management added a list of what they referred to as "Good Citizenship Standards" to the existing body of work rules. In general, good citizenship meant having good attendance, being concerned for efficiency and product quality, and maintaining good relations with fellow team members.

   Violations of these good citizenship rules meant disciplinary action. In one case, an employee was penalized for excessive absenteeism under the "just cause" standard in the collective bargaining agreement and was also denied a training opportunity because of his "poor citizenship" on attendance. An arbitrator did not consider this dual punishment to be double jeopardy.

New Production Processes

Not all instances of work restructuring are as comprehensive as in the two cases just presented. For example, some manufacturers, who previously relied exclusively on mass production techniques such as the assembly line, are experimenting with the more flexible cell type of work organization. A cell is formed by grouping all of the machines, fixtures, and equipment needed to fabricate, assemble, inspect, and package a component or completed product on the factory floor. Cells turning out components can feed other cells that assemble them into finished products. Employment in cells can vary; one operator cells are not uncommon.

The switch to cell manufacturing usually leads to changes in traditional work practices. Cell operators are often required to learn all of the jobs assigned to the cell. The number of skills mastered determines an employee's rate of pay. Workers may have primary job assignments but they are also expected to assist other operators in the cell when time and conditions permit. Sometimes cell members rotate primary jobs.

Passage of a skills test rather than seniority is more likely to determine which employees are eligible to transfer to the better paying jobs in cells. Once in cells, workers may be required to demonstrate proficiency in other jobs by taking and passing tests.

Cell operators are often required to participate in problem focused (employee involvement) teams or committees. Such groups usually deal with issues related to the more efficient operation of the cell. For example, the team may investigate ways to improve the quality of the work they do, reduce scrap, reduce the handling of materials, or overcome defects that have led customers to return products.

New Work Rules and Practices

Some employers exercise their contractual right to manage and unilaterally change or eliminate long-standing rules and practices not codified in the labor agreement. The objective is to increase efficiency and to reduce cost. Some examples of unilateral actions by management are: (1) jobs with substantial amounts of employee down or idle time are eliminated or combined; (2) new duties, such as quality control, or duties previously performed by supervisors, are added to existing jobs, usually without provision for corresponding increases in pay; and (3) vacant jobs are left unfilled with remaining employees being forced to take up the slack. The practice of leaving jobs vacant usually means employees are forced to work many more hours of overtime. In addition, when overtime is insufficient to meet the work load, supervisory or nonunion part time or temporary employees are used to perform bargaining unit jobs.

Extended Contract Terms

Employers favor longer term contracts because labor costs are set for that period of time. Six-year terms are becoming common, and nine-year agreements are also being considered. Many of these longer term contracts have periodic reopeners on pay and other issues. Disputes arising when a contract is reopened are settled through binding arbitration in some cases.

A variation on the extended labor agreement is the living contract. A labor agreement is called "living" when it can be amended at the will of the signatories. The living agreement is more a statement of guiding principles for a nonadversarial, problem-solving relationship than a body of hard and fast rules. The following "rules of team play" are stated in one living contract: "Participants have a responsibility to give opinions, listen to each other, and live with jointly made decisions even when they are not their first choices."

Living agreements contain grievance procedures, but they too are vehicles for problem solving. Grievances can include a broad range of subjects such as fixing production bottlenecks and bungled overtime schedules and dealing with the employment insecurities of employees. The duration of living agreements is typically five or six years. For more on problem solving, see the discussion of interest-based (win-win) bargaining in Chapters 8 and 9.

CHOOSING A BARGAINING STRATEGY

The union can respond to the employer's initiatives on employee-management cooperation in one of three ways: resistance, selective reaction, or acceptance with conditions. The union leadership must carefully consider the pros and cons of each of the options and advise the rank and file, the ultimate decision makers, accordingly.

Resistance

The union leadership may view employee-employer cooperation as exploitative of workers and want nothing to do with QC, QWL and EI groups, group bonuses, multiskilling, pay for knowledge, or any other scheme. To enforce this position, the union must have a provision in the labor contract, or a letter of understanding from the employer, prohibiting the introduction of aforementioned employment policies and programs unless agreed to in writing by the union.

The union may lack sufficient bargaining strength to make rejection a realistic option. Prior to the paper mill restructuring described previously, management announced a willingness to bargain over the details of implementation, such as procedures for converting to a skill-based pay plan, but not the policy itself. The message was unmistakable, accept management's terms or strike. At the time, union members were afraid to say "no" because they knew the outcome of an earlier strike involving the same restructuring plan at another of the employer's plants. The strikers had been permanently replaced and the new policy implemented with a new work force. Paper mill workers feared the same treatment if they struck.

Outright rejection of management's call for cooperation can be difficult for reasons other than the lack of union bargaining power. Many employees may like the idea of self-direction, pay based on skills mastered, and participation in management, particularly where the employer encourages and respects their views. Further, employers often appeal directly to the job security interests of workers. It is hard for the union leadership to say "no" when management threatens layoffs or a permanent shutdown.

Selective Reaction

An alternative bargaining strategy is to accept management's efforts to introduce new workplace policies provided the existing labor agreement is not violated. The leadership of one union tried unsuccessfully in arbitration to stop management from assigning employees extra tasks, previously performed by supervisors, without providing additional pay. They became concerned once again when the employer formed work teams in several departments in what were described as "pilot" projects. Next, maintenance workers protested when junior members of their department were required to learn additional crafts (called multicrafting). At this point, union officials queried top company executives about their longer term intentions. Management gave the impression of having no plans beyond an interest in experimenting with new production methods and the union leadership dropped the matter.

This reactive strategy is often adopted by default, particularly where, as in the example, workplace change occurs gradually and affects only a few employees. The union, however, is always on the defensive and usually counterpunching ineffectively. A much more difficult alternative, perhaps bordering on the impossible, is to persuade management to plan for future production and technological needs with the union's help. Involvement in the planning process puts the union leadership in a position where it can promote the interests of the membership in matters such as skill development, training opportunities, and employment security. On the other hand, the union risks being blamed should program failures occur, particularly if some union members are hurt in the process.

Acceptance With Conditions

The union accepts the need for some form of employee-employer cooperation, but is prepared to bargain aggressively over the implementation of all changes in the way work is organized, performed, and compensated. Cooperation also means the union will have an opportunity to propose rules to protect employees and the union against the worst features of any new program or policy.

DEVELOPING A UNION BARGAINING AGENDA ON COOPERATION

Having adopted a strategy of cooperation and activism, the union's task is to identify problems in management's proposals and generate solutions to protect employee and union interests. The leadership is responsible for preparing counterproposals, but should do so only after consulting with the membership, representatives of the national or international union, and members of other local unions who have experienced similar cooperative ventures.

The terms and conditions of employment change as a result of the new workplace and employment programs and policies introduced by the employer. For example, employees may be required to perform more than one job or learn more than one skill. They may also be required to assume more responsibility for improving enterprise productivity and profits.

The old rights and rules may not offer employees enough security in what is a new employment relationship. For example, training opportunities must be guaranteed where a skill-based pay plan is implemented. Again, employees who are responsible for improving employer productivity and profit should be entitled to share in the gains made. Further, the potential for declining employment and income levels increases as work force efficiency is enhanced. Solutions to these and other potential employment problems are discussed below.

Rules for Employee Participation Programs

As previously noted, under current federal law joint employee–management teams or committees, even with union involvement, cannot bargain or deal with mandatory subjects of bargaining. The exception might be a group, such as a joint union–management steering committee, where the participants include the elected representatives of employees with authority to bargain. On the other hand, the law does not forbid employers from communicating directly with their employees to address problems related to such matters as productivity, cost, and quality. When programs featuring QCs, QWL committees, EI teams, steering committees, and semi-autonomous work teams are demanded by the employer, the union should insist on having a role in developing the rules that will govern the modus operandi of any such groups. There are two categories of rules to consider: structural and administrative.

Structure has to do with questions of group numbers, composition, and continuity. How many committees or teams will there be? Will the groups be permanent or ad hoc? Will there be a steering committee? How many members on a committee or team? Who will they be? How will they be chosen? Group membership should be open to all employees on a voluntary basis.

Administrative rules must also be clearly established. For example, what will the scope of committee or team involvement be? Employees should be able to discuss a broad range of topics covering not only labor costs and productivity, but issues that have heretofore been considered the exclusive preserve of employers, such as the purchase and placement of new machines and equipment, and management policies and practices that contribute to waste, inefficiency, and customer dissatisfaction. Further, there is nothing to prevent group recommendations from being acted on by the appropriate representatives of the union and the employer at the bargaining table.

The authority of employee members must be clearly established when self-directed work teams are proposed. Management may talk of giving employees more autonomy in the workplace, but often clings to its old prerogatives in the absence of a specific requirement. In the paper mill example cited earlier, work team members were initially told they could schedule their own overtime as needed. One employee who did so over the objection of his department supervisor was cited for insubordination. A grievance was filed and the arbitrator found in favor of the employee based on a review of the employer's own written statements about the autonomy granted to employees when the new work system was created.

Administrative rules for employee participation committees and teams should also cover:

- how officers are chosen;
- terms of office;
- location of meetings;
- rules for meetings;
- record keeping at meetings;
- availability of staff;
- payment of expenses incurred;
- type of training provided;
- use of an outside consultant; and
- methods for evaluating team activities.

Employment Guarantee

The potential for job loss is high when an employer adopts teamwork, multitasking, and other programs designed to improve productivity and profitability. Management may refuse to guarantee individual jobs, but it should be willing to maintain the existing level of employment. Attrition alone may be an adequate buffer against permanent layoffs. If not, the employer must be obliged to find other ways to stabilize the work force including nontraditional means such as:

- converting nonbargaining unit jobs to hourly rated positions;
- keeping work in-house rather than subcontracting;
- transferring employees to other employer-owned facilities;
- keeping newly created jobs or skills in the bargaining unit;
- increasing the length and frequency of vacation or personal leave time;
- shortening workdays and workweeks;
- work sharing; and
- offering incentives for early retirement.

Income Guarantee

Employees should not suffer income losses because of changes made in the way work is performed and compensated. In the paper mill case, employees retained their old wage rates while training to acquire the skills needed to qualify for a higher rate under the new skill-based pay plan. Both the old and new hourly wage rate schedules appeared in the labor contract.

Security for Individual Employees

Employers should be prevented from weakening existing employee rights when introducing new workplace programs. The seniority rule is often one target. For example, management establishes criteria other than length of service for transferring in and out of manufacturing cells, work teams, or departments; rotating team members among tasks; qualifying employees for training under pay for knowledge; and selecting participants for QCs, QWL committees, and EI teams. In response, the union should continue to champion the principle of seniority as the overriding criterion for all personnel actions.

The union must also continue to protect the rights of employees who find it difficult to function as members of teams or cannot perform more than one task where multitasking is required. The option to quit a QC, QWL committee, or EI team, or to remain in one's old job in lieu of joining a work team without loss of pay or other penalties, is paramount. Senior employees, in particular, must be recognized for their years of service to the employer and not be forced to start new careers. One paper mill employee with 25 years in the skilled trades, when informed he would have to learn to operate a machine, reportedly commented: "I don't feel it's right that I have to be a helper once again after being a journeyman for so many years."

The employment security of disabled employees and those with health problems who cannot adjust to the requirements of a fast paced and modern workplace must also be protected. The Americans with Disabilities Act of 1990 requires the employer to make reasonable accommodations to the known physical or mental limitations of an otherwise qualified individual with a disability, unless such accommodation would impose undue hardships on the operation of the business. In addition, having provisions for disability and early retirement benefit supplements in the labor agreement provides a safety net for times when economical arrangements in the workplace cannot be made.

All matters of discipline and discharge must remain subject to the contractually established grievance procedure. The same applies to disputes involving work practices and employee rights. Management may seek to avoid the regular grievance procedure when disputes arise involving some of the new terms of employment such as a group bonus or team transfers. If so, the union should avoid any compromise that does not permit the appeal of a management decision to final and binding arbitration.

Quality of Work Life

Implementation of employee-management cooperation can be stressful for employees: a changing workplace, the faster pace of work inherent in teamwork and multitasking, the need to acquire new skills, and the pressure to be a "team player." The union should investigate the feasibility of setting up a joint union-employer stress reduction program.

Other ways to improve the quality of life in a stressful work environment include for example, increasing the frequency and length of break periods; shortening the number of hours worked in a day, week, or year; paying more attention to safety and health; and maintaining reasonable performance standards. Part of any gain achieved through higher productivity or profits could be used to pay for many of these improvements.

Information Sharing

When employees are asked to share their insights about jobs and the workplace for the good of the enterprise, the employer should be willing to keep employees and the union fully informed on matters where it, management, has special knowledge. This includes financial, operating, investment, and planning data beyond what is required by the Taft-Hartley Act.[3]

---

[3]The employer's bargaining obligation includes supplying the union with information in its possession that is relevant for bargaining. Also see Chapter 2, Developing Bargaining Proposals, and Chapter 7, The Law of Contract Bargaining.

Opportunities for Training and Education

Employees who can advance their careers and incomes only by mastering new job skills must be guaranteed ample opportunities for training and education. Features of a good training and education program include:

- literacy and mathematical training as well as technical education;
- qualification based on seniority;
- provision for ample learning time;
- no discrimination based on age or difficulty in learning;
- an active role for the union; and
- employer pays full cost.

Training is also necessary for union officials with access to company information and employees who are members of problem-solving teams. For example, recipients of company financial statements must be taught how to read them. Similarly, members of EI teams or steering committees should have the opportunity to learn the techniques of problem solving and group decision making. A good employer-sponsored program of training and education must also address these needs.

Use of Consultants

Management may propose hiring an outside consultant to help design and implement group bonus, employee participation, and pay for knowledge programs. Consultants, sometimes called facilitators, are also used when a union and an employer recognize that they must cooperate to solve workplace problems, such as high operating costs and low productivity, but are unsure how to proceed. Facilitators offer training in group problem solving and can help the parties through the steps of developing a plan.

If the decision is made to hire a consultant, the union should be an active participant in the selection process. This means interviewing prospective candidates and asking them for union references. The national or international union or the AFL-CIO organizing department should be contacted for information about the people being considered.

Consultants can exert considerable influence upon the groups they train or policies and programs they help design or implement. As a consequence, when choosing a consultant, the union should look for an individual who is both technically competent and sensitive to the needs and interests of both employees and management. A good candidate, from the union's perspective, is one who talks as much about individual employee and union security needs as he or she does about improved productivity and product or service quality. Union leaders must be able to trust the consultant.

New Technology

Additional employment issues arise when computers and automation are introduced as part of a new work system. The union should pay particular attention to workplace health and safety, electronic monitoring of employees, and the loss of skilled jobs.

Computers and automated machine tools are usually designed with the employer's needs in mind. The result is often stress, strain, and injury for the operator. New machinery and equipment should be designed using ergonomic principles. In fact, employees who will use the new machinery and equipment should participate in its design.

Employers are also able to monitor the work and personal habits of employees who operate computers and computer-driven machinery and equipment. This is already a serious problem for telephone operators, data entry workers, and clerical employees. A blanket restriction against electronic prying is desirable. If unobtainable, the union should seek a ban on secret monitoring for purposes of evaluating people for promotion, setting performance quotas, or taking disciplinary action.

Computerization and automation also result in the breakdown of job content and skills. However, machine tools and computer software can also be designed to enhance the existing skills of the work force. It is important, therefore, that employees be consulted when new technologies are being developed. In addition, employees have a stake in keeping their skill level high because it is the only way to keep the wage/salary level high.

Union Security

Union security is challenged when employee-employer cooperation is introduced into the workplace. The employer, after all, is promoting cooperation with employees and not necessarily with the union. In fact, the formation of QCs, QWL committees, and EI teams opens up new channels of communication between employees and the employer that are independent of union control. Consequently, stewards and other union supporters should actively participate on teams and committees as a way of reminding management of the union's continued presence in the factory, office, etc. Union activists on teams and committees should also work to change employer-driven agendas to include subjects that are of concern to workers.

In general, the union must police all agreements reached with the employer implementing new workplace and employment programs and policies. The union should also have the option to nullify any agreement it believes weakens the basic collective agreement and the grievance procedure. If absolute veto power is not obtainable, the union must retain the right to grieve perceived abuses all the way through arbitration.

A union shop, agency shop, or fair share provision in the labor agreement helps keep the union viable as an organization. Union leaders should insist on union security and dues checkoff in return for supporting employee-management cooperation.

Distribution of Gains

Bargaining unit employees must share in the profit or productivity gains achieved as a result of their participation in QC, QWL, or EI teams, multitasking, cell manufacturing, new technologies, and all other new employment schemes demanded by the employer. Higher wages and salaries is one possibility, but management is likely to object because the cost of some fringes would also increase. Instead, the employer may offer a profit or productivity gainsharing plan that ties rewards more directly to improvements made in either profits or operating efficiency.[4] The bargainable issues associated with profit and productivity gainsharing plans include: the formula for determining the size of the gain or bonus pool; the base and benefit periods used to calculate the gain; the formula for dividing the bonus pool among employees and the employer; the procedure for distributing the bonus among employees; and the rules governing accountability, access to information, and the resolution of disputes.

Gains in profit and productivity can also be used to expand employment opportunities or return subcontracted work to the bargaining unit. Alternatively, they could be used to upgrade the skills of employees. This is important, because the bargaining unit must learn new skills to qualify for future jobs. If the work force is not properly trained, new work opportunities will be lost to outside contractors or nonbargaining unit people.

PREPARING FOR BARGAINING

Employee participation, a group bonus plan, teamwork, multi-skilling, pay for knowledge, and the other programs and policies associated with employee-management cooperation are complex and require careful study. Union negotiators must make sure they understand the employer's proposal(s) in detail plus any additional information supplied by a hired consultant. This is necessary not only for bargaining purposes, but to enable the leadership to explain the new policies and programs to the membership.

The national or international union is a source of information about employee-employer cooperation in its various manifestations. Local union officials should also visit other work sites for direct consultation with union members who have firsthand knowledge of how programs and policies, similar to the ones proposed by the

---

[4]Information on gainsharing from a management perspective can be obtained from B. Graham-Moore and T. L. Ross, *Gainsharing: Plans for Improving Performance* (Washington, D.C.: BNA Books, 1990).

employer, work in practice. The employer should help arrange these visits and pay lost time and travel expenses.

Union leaders and activists interested in learning more about employee-management cooperation should check the class offerings at their nearest university, college, or union-sponsored labor education program. Courses dealing with subjects such as productivity, new forms of compensation, the "team concept," and the new manufacturing environment would be most beneficial.

FORMALIZING THE AGREEMENT
ON COOPERATION

Agreements reached on new employment terms and conditions should always be put in writing. Employers may prefer verbal understandings because they can be quickly and easily modified or canceled. Informal arrangement must be based on trust. Written agreements, on the other hand, are binding on the signatories and enforceable in the law courts.

Documents containing the terms and conditions for cooperative ventures are called "enabling," "cooperation," or "implementation" agreements. Content can vary, but most are not very comprehensive and omit many important safeguards for employees and the union. Clearly, some unions and employers are choosing not to formalize all aspects of their new working relationships despite the potential risks. The contents of two enabling agreements are described below.

The Paper Mill Implementation Agreement

In the paper mill case described earlier, the union and the employer signed a memorandum of understanding containing some of the terms and conditions under which the parties would convert to the new work and pay systems. A steering committee was created "with representation from the union" to advise the plant manager on the "timing and specific steps" for the transition to teamwork and pay for knowledge. There was also a pledge "to attempt to resolve disputes by mutual agreement."

The implementation accord also committed management to provide training on an equitable basis to all team members contingent on "business needs." In addition, employees were guaranteed their existing level of income provided they made "satisfactory progress" in acquiring the skills needed to qualify for the new skill-based pay plan. Finally, the parties pledged to work together to accomplish the transition as rapidly as feasible with business needs and the preparations necessary for success.

Procedures for converting to the new work system and establishing the skill-based wage structure were not included in the memorandum of understanding. However, the new wage structure based on eight skill levels was incorporated into the basic agreement and appeared along with the old wage-job classification system.

An Enabling Agreement for Union–Management Participation

A sample enabling agreement containing terms and conditions for the operation of a joint union-management problem-solving committee is presented below. Its provisions create goals and objectives, commit the parties to cooperate, establish decision-making authority, provide training for committee members, offer a procedure for hiring and firing a consultant, and provide for information sharing and accountability. In its brevity, this document is also typical of written agreements covering union and employee participatory arrangements. The text of the agreement follows:

> The Union and the Employer enter into this Agreement in order to work jointly for the continuous improvement of working conditions and plant efficiency.
>
> 1. The parties will work to improve the relationship between the Employer and the Union and to explore and develop work effectiveness.
>
> 2. In working together, the parties will seek to achieve measurable improvement in: quality and productivity, employment and pay security for all employees, employee job skills and knowledge, and union and employer leadership and organization.
>
> 3. A steering committee will be formed. This committee will consist of equal numbers of delegates from the Union and the Employer

with each party selecting its own representatives. Each party will be entitled to eight (8) representatives, for a total of sixteen (16) regular committee members. Each side will also be entitled to four (4) alternatives. The steering committee will be the only committee authorized to deal with changes that affect the aforementioned scope of activities.

4. Resolutions reached by the steering committee will be binding on the parties. The exception is specific changes in contract language agreed to by the steering committee; these must be ratified first by the Union membership using the Union's ratification procedure.

5. To help the steering committee function properly, the parties will choose a consultant whose role will be to facilitate a cooperative approach to labor-management relations. Either party may discharge the consultant at will and without agreement from the other party. The parties agree, however, to immediately find and hire another consultant if this should occur. The committee will use the services of a consultant unless the parties agree that they are no longer beneficial. The Employer will pay all expenses associated with the services of the consultant.

6. The parties agree to participate in training, led by the consultant, in problem solving, conflict resolution techniques, joint consensus building, and other related skills necessary to develop cooperative labor-management relations. Site visits will be used as a learning tool.

7. Joint consensus decision making will be the only basis for making decisions by this committee. For the purposes of this Agreement, joint consensus decision making is defined as agreement by all committee members to the decision.

8. There will be an open sharing of information in order to facilitate the work and efforts of this committee to achieve the agreed upon goals and objectives. The parties agree, upon request, to respect the other party's wish for confidentiality of shared information.

9. This committee will develop a method by which it will measure and monitor the effects of its decisions.

Indemnity Clauses

Union-management participation contains potential risks for the union. Employees and customers damaged monetarily or in other ways as a result of new workplaces employment policies and programs implemented by management, with the cooperation and participation of the union, could file lawsuits seeking restitution. The union, therefore, should include an indemnity clause in the enabling agreement that would free it from liability in such cases. A qualified attorney can draft the appropriate language.

Appendix 1

Bargaining Tasks Checklist

Checklists of bargaining tasks associated with each phase of the contract bargaining process are listed below. Some tasks will be performed simultaneously. Others may not be used in the order given. Still others may not be applicable to every bargaining situation.

ORGANIZATIONAL

____ Form the Bargaining Committee
____ Alert Other Labor Groups in the Community
____ Develop Contacts With Groups in the Larger Community
____ Conduct a Media Campaign
____ Obtain Membership Approval to Renegotiate Contract
____ Prepare and Deliver Legal Notices
____ Notify Employer of Intent to Bargain First Contract
____ Arrange a Time and Place for the First Bargaining Session
____ Arrange Compensation for Bargaining Committee Members
____ Coordinate With Other Levels of the Union Organization

PREPARING BARGAINING PROPOSALS

_____ Determine Membership Interests
     _____ 1. Membership Meeting
     _____ 2. Bargaining Questionnaire
     _____ 3. One-on-One Interviews
_____ Review the Contract
     _____ 1. Grievance and Arbitration Records
     _____ 2. Contract Language and Other Problem Areas
     _____ 3. Affects of Changing Employer Policies
_____ Collect Information for Bargaining
_____ Anticipate the Employer's Position
     _____ 1. Wages/Salaries and Fringes
     _____ 2. Contractual Rules
_____ Draft Compensation Proposals
     _____ 1. Select Pay and Fringe Benefit Proposals
     _____ 2. Develop Supporting Arguments
     _____ 3. Anticipate Employer's Counterarguments
     _____ 4. Anticipate Potential Compromise Position(s)
_____ Establish Priorities
_____ Prepare Copy of Proposals for Employer
_____ Prepare a Bargaining Book

PRESENTING FINANCIAL INFORMATION

_____ Collect Financial Information
_____ Evaluate the Financial Performance of the Employer
_____ Chart Financial Information
     _____ 1. Trends
     _____ 2. Financial Ratios

PRESENTING PAY AND FRINGE INFORMATION

_____ Identify Potential Targets for Comparisons
_____ Choose Comparable Employments

____ Collect Data for Comparison Purposes
____ Chart the Comparables

PRESENTING ECONOMIC INFORMATION

____ Collect Economic Data on the Employer's Industry/Trade
____ Chart Industry/Trade Data
____ Collect Data on the Cost of Living
____ Chart Data on the Cost of Living
____ Bargain a Cost of Living Adjustment Clause
____ Collect Data on Productivity
____ Chart Data on Productivity

THE TRADITIONAL BARGAINING PROCESS

____ The Early Sessions
        ____ 1. Argue the Union's Case
        ____ 2. Clarify the Union's Position
____ The Middle Sessions
        ____ 3. Investigate the Potential for Compromise
____ The Closing Sessions
        ____ 4. Reach Tentative Agreements
        ____ 5. Keep Track of Original Proposals
____ Keep the Membership Informed
____ Respond to Employer Publicity During Bargaining

RATIFICATION OF SETTLEMENT TERMS

____ Proofread Agreement(s)
____ Ratify Agreement(s)

INTEREST-BASED (WIN-WIN) BARGAINING PROCESS

_____ Determine the Subject Matter for Bargaining
_____ Achieve Win-Win Outcomes
_____ Draft Contract Language
_____ Settle Unresolved Issues
_____ Prepare the Membership for Interest-Based Bargaining

COSTING THE CONTRACT

_____ Estimate Cost/Value of Direct Wages/Salaries
_____ Estimate Cost/Value of Wage/Salary Related Fringes
_____ Estimate Cost/Value of Nonwage/Salary Related Fringes
_____ Estimate Cost/Value of Money Package
_____ Estimate Rollups

BARGAINING CONTRACT LANGUAGE

_____ Identify Basic Principles
_____ Develop Supporting Arguments
_____ Anticipate Employer's Counterarguments
_____ Predict Employer's Counterproposals
_____ Determine the Potential for Compromise
_____ Write the New Rule(s)

BARGAINING AT THE DEADLINE

_____ Avoid Impasse
_____ Third Party Intervention
        _____ 1. Use Mediation to Get Bargaining Back on Track
        _____ 2. Bargain With the Mediator
        _____ 3. Prepare for Fact-Finding

STRIKES

_____ Assess the Strengths of the Employer
_____ Assess Conditions in the Community
_____ Assess the Strengths of the Membership
_____ Prepare for the Strike
    _____ 1. Choose the Strike Leadership
    _____ 2. Establish a Strike Headquarters
    _____ 3. Prepare for Picketing
    _____ 4. Establish Support Committees
    _____ 5. Coordinate With Other Unions
    _____ 6. Plan a Media Campaign
    _____ 7. Maintain Membership Solidarity
    _____ 8. Kickoff the Strike
    _____ 9. Deal With Nonstrikers, Strikebreakers, and Crossovers
    _____ 10. Negotiate the Strike Settlement Agreement

ELEMENTS OF A NO-STRIKE ALTERNATIVE

_____ Organize the Membership
_____ Research the Employer
_____ Implement the Corporate Campaign
_____ Implement Workplace Actions

PUBLIC SECTOR BARGAINING

_____ Know the Law
_____ Lobby On Behalf of Bargaining Objectives
_____ Politick on Behalf of Bargaining Objectives
_____ Special Preparations for Bargaining
    _____ 1. Organize the Bargaining Committee
    _____ 2. Research: Who Speaks for the Employer?
    _____ 3. Develop Bargaining Proposals

___ Participate in the Budget-Making Process
___ Present Budget Information
    ___ 1. Collect Information for the Budget Review
    ___ 2. Perform Budget Review
    ___ 3. Present the Budget Review Findings
___ Present Information on Comparables
    ___ 1. Select External Comparables
    ___ 2. Select Internal Comparisons
    ___ 3. Determine Mix of External and Internal Comparisons
    ___ 4. Attack the Employer's Choice of Comparables
    ___ 5. Collect Data on Comparables
    ___ 6. Chart the Data on Comparables

PREPARING FOR INTEREST ARBITRATION

___ Choose the Arbitrator
___ Develop Arguments, Facts, and Proofs
___ Develop Testimony for Witnesses and Exhibits
___ Develop Opening and Closing Statements and Briefs
___ Develop a Last Best (Final) Offer

Appendix 2

The Local Union Negotiator's Bookshelf

Members of the local union bargaining committee will find these guides, handbooks, and other resources helpful when confronted with some of the more technical aspects of bargaining. The majority of these materials are moderately priced.

Barrett, Dr. Jerome T. *P.A.S.T. Is The Future: A Model for Interest-Based Collective Bargaining That Works*, 3rd ed., 1992. A training manual for practitioners of win-win bargaining. Available from Barrett and Sons Publishing Co., 301 Pine Street, Falls Church, VA 22046, (703) 241-3854.

Basic Patterns in Union Contracts, 13th ed., 1992. Offers a subject-by-subject breakdown of major provisions contained in 400 representative contracts. Available from BNA Books, P.O. Box 6036, Rockville, MD 20850-9914 (1-800) 372-1033.

Brigham, Nancy, Maria Catalfio, and Dick Cluster. *How to Do Leaflets, Newsletters & Newspapers*. Valuable tips on every aspect of publishing. Available from PEP Publishers, P.O. Box 24888, Detroit, MI 48224.

Characteristics of Major Private Sector Collective Bargaining Agreements, May 1989. *Characteristics of Major Public Sector*

Collective Bargaining Agreements, July 1990. Detailed analysis of major collective bargaining agreements. Available from Library and Information Service, Industrial Relations Center, Cleveland State University, 2121 Euclid Avenue, Cleveland, OH 44115.

Cohen, Herb. *You Can Negotiate Anything*, 1980. A primer on the art of bargaining. Published by Bantam Books, New York. Paperback editions can be found in used book stores.

Contract Campaign Manual, 1988. Covers all aspects of the bargaining process. Available from Service Employees' International Union, 1313 L Street, N.W., Washington, DC 20005, (202) 898-3200.

Cooke, William N. *Labor-Management Cooperation: New Partnership or Going In Circles*, 1990. An examination of the potential benefits and costs of labor-management cooperation and the factors that influence them. Available from W. E. Upjohn Institute, 300 S. Westnedge Avenue, Kalamazoo, MI 49007, (616) 343-5541.

Developing New Tactics: Winning With Coordinated Corporate Campaigns, 1985. *The Inside Game: Winning With Workplace Strategies*, 1986. Primers on running corporate campaigns and workplace actions. Available from AFL-CIO Industrial Union Department, 815 16th Street, N.W., Washington, DC 20006, (202) 842-7800.

Garner, Bryan A. *A Dictionary of Modern Legal Usage*, 1987. Oxford University Press, 200 Madison Ave., New York, NY 10011.

Healthcare Benefits Bargaining Manual, 1988. Contains information, strategies, and contract language. Available from Service Employees' International Union, 1313 L Street N.W., Washington, DC 20005, (202) 898-3200.

Law, Gordon T., Jr., and Michael E. Reilly. *A Guide to Information on a Closely Held Corporation*, 1986. Tells how to research a corporation that is not normally required to release its financial and operating data to the public. Available from Institute For Industry Studies, NYSSILR, Cornell University, 120 Delaware Avenue, Suite 202, Buffalo, NY 14202, (716) 852-4191.

McDonald, Jeffrey A., and Anne Bingham. *Pension Handbook for Union Negotiators,* 1986. For single-employer pension plans, the guide tells how to plan strategies, figure costs, and benefits. Includes mortality tables, Labor Department forms, and sample contract language. Available from BNA Books, P.O. Box 6036, Rockville, MD 20850-9914, (1-800) 372-1033.

Panel Answer Book Series: Pensions, 1992 ed. Everything the union needs to know about pensions in a question and answer format. Available from Aspen Publishers Inc., P.O. Box 990, Frederick, MD 21701, (1-800) 638-8437.

Participating in Management, 1989. Discusses the dangers and opportunities for unions when employees participate in management. Available from Midwest Center for Labor Research, 3411 W. Diversey, #14, Chicago, IL 60647, (312) 278-5418.

Schlossberg, Steven I., and Judith A. Scott. *Organizing and the Law,* 4th ed., 1991. Explains recent litigation and NLRB decisions and gives step-by-step advice for avoiding potential problems and recognizing opportunities in today's work environment. Available from BNA Books, P.O. Box 6036, Rockville, MD 20850-9914, (1-800) 372-1033.

"Still Singing Solidarity Forever!" An Audiocassette of songs for the picket line (or the corporate campaign or workplace action) written and performed by striking members of United Paperworkers International Union Local 20, Kaukauna, Wisconsin. Lyrics are included. Available from UPIU Local 20, P.O. Box 195, Kaukauna, WI 54130, (414) 766-0655. The Labor Heritage Foundation is a source of cassettes, CDs, and books of labor songs. A free catalogue is available from LHF, 815 16th Street, N.W., Rm. 301, Washington, D.C. 20006, (301) 434-6404, Ext. 461.

Talking Union One on One: Conducting Surveys to Guide Collective Bargaining and Internal Organizing Activities. Explains how to do a collective bargaining survey in the context of a one-on-one canvassing effort. Available from the AFL-CIO Education Department, 815 16th Street, N.W., Washington, D.C. 20006, (202) 637-5141.

Taylor, Suzanne Saunders. *Negotiating Health Insurance in the Workplace: A Basic Guide*, 1992. A guide for pricing and buying insurance, determining bargaining priorities, and negotiating a cost-effective contract. Chapters 5 and 6 are particularly useful for bargaining. Negotiators bargaining a first contract should also read Chapter 3. Available from BNA Books, P.O. Box 6036, Rockville, MD 20850-9914, (1-800) 372-1033.

What's New in Collective Bargaining. A biweekly newsletter containing the latest bargaining issues plus facts and figures on wage and salary patterns, fringes, productivity and costs, and other economic indicators. Available by annual subscription from the Bureau of National Affairs, Inc., 9435 Key West Avenue, Rockville MD 20850, (1-800) 372-1033.

Glossary

AFL-CIO Central Labor Council Chartered local affiliate of the AFL-CIO. Membership is composed of local unions located in the geographical area that choose to affiliate.

AFL-CIO Community Services Maintains a representative in the local community to assist in the delivery of services of voluntary and public agencies to union members and their families.

balance sheet A financial report showing values for assets, liabilities, and the owner's stake in the business at a particular point in time.

bargaining The process of modifying diverse positions.

bargaining agenda A list of the union's pay, fringe, and protective language proposals. A written copy of the agenda is given to the employer at the outset of bargaining.

bargaining book A binder containing a copy of the bargaining agenda, employer handouts, copies of tentative agreements, and other records.

bargaining committee Takes the lead in preparing for contract bargaining and represents the local union at the bargaining table with the employer.

bargaining proposal   A single request for a pay increase, a new or revised fringe benefit, or a new or amended protective language provision.

bargaining table   Table where company and union representatives sit when bargaining. Typically oblong in shape so the two sides can sit facing each other.

bargaining unit   Describes the employees, union, and employer in a given bargaining relationship. It is determined by the National Labor Relations Board (NLRB) prior to the representation election.

basic agreement   *See* labor contract.

benefits or supplemental benefits   *See* fringes.

brainstorming   A technique used to encourage people to express their ideas without fear of ridicule and criticism. Used with problem-solving groups.

budget   A financial plan containing estimates of revenues, expenditures, and surpluses (or shortfalls) for one or more years into the future. An important tool in public sector bargaining.

caucus   A private meeting of union or employer representatives that interrupts the main bargaining session. Called by either party for purposes of resolving internal disagreements, planning strategy, and other purposes.

chief spokesperson   The one member of the bargaining committee designated to speak for the union at the bargaining table. Other committee members participate in the discussion, but only to help clarify or defend positions articulated by the chief spokesperson. Used in traditional bargaining where maintaining a united front to the employer is important.

comparables   Groups of employees with employment characteristics in common. Used when making pay and fringe comparisons.

compensation Wage/salary, premiums, and fringes.

compromise or concession making Sacrificing all or part of one or more original bargaining proposals in order to achieve agreement. At the heart of traditional bargaining.

consensus decision making A procedure for group decision making. No decision is final until every group member either supports it or is neutral.

conference table *See* bargaining table.

contract booklet Copies of the original labor contract reproduced in booklet form for distribution to both bargaining unit employees and members of management.

contract language/contract rules *See* protective language.

corporate campaign The union uses public opinion and policy to pressure the employer during a dispute over the terms and conditions of employment. An important component of a no-strike strategy.

cost of living Prices of a market basket of consumer products and services over time. Measured monthly by the Bureau of Labor Statistics.

crossovers Strikers who return to work while the strike is still in progress.

deadline The expiration date and hour of the terminating labor contract. The point at which impasse and a strike or lockout is possible in traditional bargaining.

duty to bargain The obligation to bargain in good faith is a requirement of federal labor law. Additional interpretations are included in cases decided by the National Labor Relations Board (NLRB) and the federal appeals courts.

earnings Wage/salary plus fringes.

economic strike   Employees withhold their services from the employer in a dispute over pay and the other terms and conditions of employment. This type of strike is different from one called to protest unfair labor practices by the employer.

employee participation   Programs giving employees some small role in the management of the workplace. Some employees are part of semiautonomous work groups that plan their own daily activities. Others join quality circles or involvement teams to investigate and recommend ways to improve productivity, lower labor cost, and improve product and service quality.

employer   The party with whom the local union bargains.

final offer   The employer's last offer before the arrival of the deadline. The union leadership may not endorse the offer and could actively oppose it.

financial data   Revenues, expenditures, profits, losses, assets, liabilities, net worth, and other statistics reported on income statements and balance sheets.

first-time contract   The final payoff from a successful organizing campaign. The campaign should continue until a contract is won.

FMCS (Federal Mediation and Conciliation Service)   Federal agency supplying mediators in private employment to help resolve bargaining impasses and end strikes. This agency must be notified 30 days (60 days for health care institutions) in advance of the deadline that bargaining is in progress.

fringes   Benefits other than direct wages/salaries and premium pay. Includes holidays, vacations, sick leave, work breaks, wash-up time, jury duty, military service, personal days, family leave, medical, retirement, and supplemental unemployment benefits.

gainsharing Group bonus plans tied to improvements made in profits and/or productivity.

grievance arbitration A process whereby an impartial third party issues binding decisions in disputes involving employee and union rights. Usually, the final step of the grievance procedure.

grievance procedure Rules for enforcing the labor agreement. These rules are part of the contract itself.

impasse A deadlock in bargaining. Total impasse occurs when the union and employer agree that their differences are irreconcilable and nothing can be gained by continuing to meet. At total impasse the union has a right to strike. Conversely, deadlocks on single issues do not suspend the obligation to bargain on other unsettled matters.

income statement A financial report summarizing revenues earned from sales of products or services, expenses incurred in acquiring these revenues, and the resulting profit or loss during a specified period of time.

interest arbitration A process whereby an impartial third party issues binding decisions to resolve bargaining impasses over the terms and conditions of employment. Used in government-sector bargaining at the local level.

interest-based bargaining An approach to bargaining that features group problem solving, open communications, cooperation, and the mutual interest of the union and the employer.

intermediate bodies Administrative units between the national/international union and the local affiliates. Frequently referred to as councils, districts, and conferences. They service and coordinate the local unions on behalf of the parent organization.

labor agreement *See* labor contract.

labor contract A written document containing provisions on pay, fringes, hours, and the other terms and conditions of employment, the status of the union, and the procedure for settling disputes arising during the contract term.

labor-management cooperation   Employment terms and conditions designed to make employees more responsible for productivity growth, labor cost containment, and product and service quality. Examples of new programs include pay for knowledge, employee participation, teamwork, multitasking, employee participation, and group incentives.

local union   The bargaining representative of local employees.

local union bylaws   A set of rules adopted by the local union for governing its own affairs including contract bargaining.

lockout   The employer bars regular employees from entering its facilities. The employer must reinstate all previous employees once the lockout has ended.

lost time   Refers to the regular wages/salaries lost by bargaining committee members or other union functionaries when bargaining sessions or other union business takes place during regular working hours.

management   *See* employer.

management rights clause   Enumerates general rights granted to management in the labor contract. Other sections of the contract modify these rights.

media relations subcommittee   Handles relations with the news media. Responsible for preparing news releases and holding press conferences both before and during the period of bargaining.

money package   Found by combining the monetary values of all of the individual wage/salary increases and fringe benefit improvements. The term is used in connection with the union's proposals, the employer's offer, or the total agreement.

national/international union   The parent organization of most local unions. Affiliated local unions must be in compliance with all laws and policies established by the national/international constitution, executive board, and president. Some local unions are independent organizations and a few are affiliated directly with the AFL-CIO.

national/international union constitution   A document containing the fundamental laws governing the national union and all its intermediate and local bodies.

National Labor Relations Act   Also referred to as the Wagner Act. Passed in 1935 to provide collective bargaining rights for workers in private employment.

negotiation/negotiating   *See* bargaining.

NLRB (National Labor Relations Board)   A five-member board appointed by the President that administers, interprets, and enforces the Taft-Hartley Act.

no-strike alternative   Corporate campaign and workplace actions are used in place of a strike to pressure the employer to return to the bargaining table. Employees remain on the job following impasse and continue to work under the terms and conditions set by management.

nonstrikers   Union members or nonunion members who refuse to join the strike.

notice requirements   The party seeking to reopen (renegotiate) or terminate a labor agreement as required by federal labor law to give the other party 60-days notice and the FMCS and the state or territorial mediation service 30-days notice. The notices are 90 and 60 days respectively in the health care industry.

one-on-one interviews   Union members are contacted individually or in small groups by the union leadership. An effective method for ensuring member participation in the bargaining process.

pay   Direct wages/salaries and premiums.

pay for knowledge   A pay structure that ties wages/salaries to numbers of work skills mastered by employees. Replaces the traditional wage/salary job structure where wages/salaries are related to the contents of the job performed.

permanent replacements   Strikebreakers who are not terminated by the employer after a strike has ended.

picketing   Strikers march back and forth in front of the employer's place of business carrying signs and distributing leaflets. The purpose is to inform the general public that a labor dispute is in progress and to keep union members off the employer's premises.

productivity   Refers to the amount of labor required to produce a quantity of product or provide a specific service. It is a measure of work force efficiency.

prohibited practices   *See* unfair labor practice.

protective language   Refers to contractual rules that establish employment rights for employees and security for the union. Also includes procedural rules for handling grievances and administering the labor contract.

representation election   A vote conducted by the National Labor Relations Board (NLRB) to determine if employees of a particular employer want to be represented by a specified labor union. When the winning union is certified as the bargaining agent, the employer has a duty to bargain over a first contract.

side/supplemental agreement   A separate agreement devoted to a special topic such as health care, retirement, and gainsharing.

strikebreakers   Workers hired to replace strikers. They can be hired on a temporary or permanent basis. Frequently referred to as "scabs."

subcontracting   A term used to describe an employer practice of contracting with an outside enterprise to perform work traditionally done by bargaining unit employees. Sometimes referred to as outsourcing and, in the public sector, privatization.

supplemental benefits   *See* fringes.

Taft-Hartley Act   The more popular title given to the Labor Management Relations Act (LMRA). The 1947 amendments to the National Labor Relations Act, the major federal law covering private sector collective bargaining. Section 8 has particular relevance for contract bargaining.

temporary replacements   Strikebreakers who must be replaced by strikers once the strike has ended.

tentative agreement   Agreement reached on a single pay, fringe, or protective language item that is not binding until an overall settlement is reached.

third-party intervention   A neutral enters the bargaining process for the purpose of avoiding or ending an impasse. The most common forms of intervention are mediation and fact-finding. Interest arbitration is practiced at the local government level.

traditional bargaining   An approach to bargaining that features exchanges of proposals, arguments, and offers; deadlines, tests of strength, and compromise settlements.

unfair labor practice (ULP)   Actions of unions and employers that violate a federal or state labor law. Referred to as prohibited practices in the public sector.

union committee   *See* bargaining committee.

win-win bargaining   *See* interest-based bargaining.

workplace actions   The work force is mobilized to demonstrate in support of the union and to harass the employer by raising operating costs. An important component of a no-strike strategy.

workplace rules and practices   *See* protective language.

Index

301

About the Author

Maurice Better is Associate Professor of Labor Education at the University of Wisconsin. Since 1978 he has worked with the School for Workers at the University of Wisconsin–Continuing Education Extension where he teaches and coordinates classes, institutes, and workshops with unions in the state of Wisconsin.

The author has a B.S. degree from the University of California at Los Angeles and a Ph.D. in Labor Economics from the University of Wisconsin–Madison. His Ph.D. dissertation deals with the practice of contract bargaining by local unions.

Maurice was treasurer of the only local of labor educators in the Paperworkers' Union while teaching classes for union leaders at the University of Alabama at Birmingham. He is currently a member of the American Federation of Teachers.

Maurice and his wife Sybil reside in Madison, Wisconsin.